THE ROAD TO KOHIMA

Charles Chasie is a Kohima-based author and independent researcher. A former editor and journalist in Nagaland, he is a past winner of the prestigious Assam Media Trust Award. For more than three decades he has contributed to various journals and publications, both in India and abroad. Previous books include *The Naga Imbroglio, A Personal Perspective* and *The State Strikes Back: India and the Naga Insurgency* (with Sanjoy Hazarika), for East-West Center, Washington.

Harry Fecitt MBE TD is a former British Army infantry officer. In his retirement he has taken a keen interest in the less-well-known incidents in British military history, researching and writing for several military journals. His aim is to emphasize the forgotten contributions and sacrifices made by the soldiers of former British Imperial territories who volunteered to serve the British Crown. He is the author of *Sideshows of the Indian Army in World War I* and *Distant Battlefields: The Indian Army in the Second World War.*

THE ROAD TO
KOHIMA

THE NAGA EXPERIENCE IN THE
SECOND WORLD WAR

Second edition

Charles Chasie and Harry Fecitt MBE TD

infiniteideas

First published in 2019
This edition published 2020 by
Infinite Ideas Limited
www.infideas.com

A CIP catalogue record for this book is available from the British Library
ISBN 978–1–910902–51–6

Front cover photo © Imperial War Museum (IND 3709)

Printed in Great Britain

CONTENTS

FOREWORD

This is an exciting and timely book. Exciting because accounts of war from the perspective of peoples innocently caught up in battle are rare, and timely because the men and women whose memories make up this account are rapidly diminishing. It is for this reason that the Kohima Educational Trust and its Nagaland partner, the Kohima Educational Society, are to be congratulated for this significant undertaking.

The joint authors – Charles Chasie and Harry Fecitt – have undertaken a notable piece of scholarship, following on work by Naga historians such as Easterine Kire in *Mari* (Harper Collins India, 2010), in bringing the voices of the hitherto unheard to our attention. The great battles that raged across the Naga Hills between the British and Japanese in 1944 were uninvited by the local Nagas, who suffered tremendously in the great storm of war that descended so suddenly on their peaceful lives in April 1944. The war demanded much of them, and many suffered greatly as a consequence. Even though it wasn't their war, the Naga role against the Japanese occupation of these hills and in the climactic fighting between the Allies and the Japanese was significant in many diverse ways, as this book makes clear. The role of individual Naga men, women and children, and the Naga tribes collectively, is an essential component of the overall story of what the world knows as the Battle of Kohima. Thanks to this book, we have a new and fascinating insight into what Nagas at the time really thought about the turmoil swirling around them, and how they made sense of the war.

— Dr Robert Lyman FRHistS

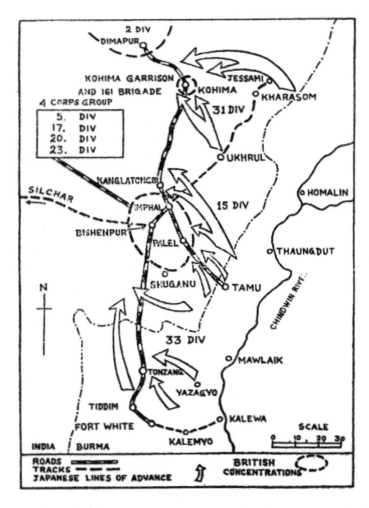

Japanese routes to Kohima (Operation U-Go)
Map courtesy Peter Steyn MC, Captain, The History of the Assam
Regiment *(Orient Longmans, India, 1959).*

INTRODUCTION

In the Naga experience, the Second World War has always been called the Japanese invasion by people who lived through it. In Tenyidie, it is *Japan kepar tei* or *Japan Rüwho*. The nature of the war as it affected the Naga Hills was different from anywhere else – that is what we were told in the post-war years.

Growing up in the 1960s, we played soldiers in my grandfather's garden in Mission Compound where the wartime trenches had been left as they were. My brother managed to fill up a tin trunk with bullets collected from the garden.

In 1977, nine children were playing with an undetonated mortar shell in Kohima village when it exploded and killed eight of the youngsters.

In the 60s, many households used British ammunition boxes as baking ovens. My mother and her friends baked the most wonderful cakes in the rectangular boxes for birthdays, Christmases and any festive occasion. By the 70s, electric ovens had replaced the ammunition boxes and no one seems to have thought they should have kept the ammo boxes for museum purposes.

In the Naga Hills, the war has stayed with us many years after it was over. No Naga family is without its personal wartime story to tell.

It is so heartening to see that a comprehensive account of the war has finally been written that highlights Naga participation, and its particular importance. It may be superfluous to mention that the Battle of Imphal/Kohima, long referred to as 'the forgotten war' and its fighters 'the forgotten heroes', was, in 2013, voted

'Britain's greatest Battle', winning over the celebrated battles of D-Day and Waterloo. The undeniable significance of the Battle of Kohima has been asserted by this recognition even if it comes a bit late.

Certainly, books have been written before about the Battle of Kohima and most of them were very well written. But all the books, with the exception of *Mari* in 2010, were written by non-Nagas and largely focused on the military aspects of a hard-won battle. *The Road to Kohima* has the added benefit of being an insider story as the authors have spent a great deal of time in collecting personal accounts from Naga war veterans. This is a labour of love. Without the stories that the insiders have to offer, the story of the Battle of Kohima would not be complete. Many of those storytellers have passed on without ever seeing this book in print. But it still has a purpose to serve. The year 2019 is the 75th jubilee of the Second World War, and the time is most appropriate to let younger Nagas hear this story. This book brings the war to a proper closure in our hills by allowing the Naga voices to be included, an element that had been missing in war narratives on the Battle of Kohima.

Robert Lyman's book *Japan's Last Bid for Victory* (2011) was probably the first book to feature some Naga memories of the war. *The Road to Kohima* has now made sure that the stories of the unsung heroes of the Battle of Kohima, the Naga soldiers who fought alongside the Allied forces, are finally heard. The civilian Nagas fought as 'scouts and spies, guiding the British and gathering intelligence for them; they became stretcher-bearers, trench diggers, etc. Slowly, as the Japanese behaviour became more and more intolerable, even this civilian segment of Nagas would become warlike, leading the Japanese into ambushes, giving them wrong directions, and even killing them. In the process, some lost their lives.'

It was an alliance that might not have happened because incidents had occurred directly before the invasion that caused great distrust of the British government among the Nagas.

The 161st Brigade under Brigadier Warren had been moved

to Dimapur, and the Nagas interpreted it as the British leaving them to their fate at the hands of the Japanese. They considered themselves abandoned and there were many Nagas who did not want to support the British government against the Japanese. The authors record that it was the action of one individual, Charles Pawsey, that turned the tide in favour of the British again when he adamantly declared he would never abandon his Nagas. The Deputy Commissioner refused to retreat from Kohima even when asked to 'for security reasons', and he remained at his post throughout the war. Pawsey's decision not to abandon Kohima was an example which helped the vast majority of Nagas determine which side to choose.

Several writers have mentioned the invaluable support from the Nagas in winning the war.

General W. J. Slim, Commander of the 14th Army, is the most eloquent: 'Their active help to us was beyond value or praise.'

The first part of the book authored by Charles Chasie goes into a detailed account of the cultural background of the Nagas. It helps the reader to understand how a people that had stubbornly fought British entry into their hills a hundred years ago was now assisting them to win the war. The author gives us a close look at the Naga sense of honour that went into operation even towards former enemies. This cultural factor became a deciding factor in the war leading to their participation, which was vital in shaping the final outcome.

As Chasie writes, 'The book is about how the Naga people saw the Second World War, how they faced it, participated in it, how they were affected and the kind of changes the war brought into their lives and society.' The course of Naga life underwent a sea-change after the war, not just in terms of the political turmoil of later years, but their contact with the modern world which ensured that a return to the Naga village-world as they knew it before the war would not be possible.

The aftermath of the First World War introduced money into Naga economy in a significant way. The 2,000 plus Naga Labour Corps who went to serve in France and Mesopotamia received their pay after the war, and it changed the mentality of the Nagas. When the Second World War began, many Nagas voluntarily joined the army and many worked as labourers on the road in Tiddim knowing they would earn good money. After the war, the money economy replaced the agricultural economy for good.

According to Chasie, the book addresses a Naga audience 'as part of their history'. The Naga part in the Second World War is certainly a tremendous part of our history and *The Road to Kohima* ensures that it will now be remembered as such. This book is the effort of 'collective memories and personal memories'.

Co-author Major Harry Fecitt, who has written the second section, provides the military perspective of the battle, unravelling the many twists and turns the battle took to end in a major defeat of the theretofore invulnerable Japanese army. Fecitt's account begins from Burma with its description of the Indian population in Burma, who were the first refugees to cross over into India via the Naga Hills. He ends the narrative by following the Allied forces back into Burma in their attempt to completely rout out the invaders.

The sight of refugees from Burma trailing down the Imphal–Kohima Road was the first sign of war for many Nagas. It convinced them that the rumours of the Japanese invasion were now a reality. Already in 1942, Ursula Graham Bower had been made a Captain heading a 'V' Force Watch and Ward centre at her base in Laisong. The V force scouts were armed with old muzzle loading guns to perform their task of scouting the country, reporting crashed aircraft, reporting on enemy movement, and bringing all non-authorized travellers to Laisong at Graham's headquarters. The scouts were appointed from all the villages along the range.

Fecitt's account states that while General Mutaguchi was launching 'his 33rd Division against the British 17th Indian Light Division at Tiddim, General Sato was advancing on Kohima in order to isolate Manipur, and then attack the British supply bases in the Brahmaputra valley. The invasion of the Princely State of Manipur and the Naga Hills was called Operation U-Go. The aim of this invasion was the capture of Imphal, the capital of Manipur, and the occupation of Kohima to the north, which would block the route that the Allies would have to take to recapture Manipur.'

As General Sato's division crossed the Chindwin in mid-March, they were delayed at Sangshak by a fierce resistance put up by the 50th Indian Parachute Brigade, which considerably slowed the 31st Division's advance on Kohima. Stories of valour like these were the backdrop for the final victory of the allied forces against the invaders.

Fecitt recounts the harsh ground realities in which the war was won: Brigades and divisions crossed dense jungles and steep mountainous terrain between Burma and the Naga areas, supplied and resupplied by airdrops in order to relieve and defend Kohima. In all this, the British army received the support of the Nagas, who 'carried food and casualties ... sheltered wounded and lost soldiers and bailed-out airmen, recovered supplies ... constructed landing strips', and enlisted as sepoys to fight alongside the British. Fecitt writes that the Naga Levies were raised and authorized 'to support the British and Indian formations fighting in the defence of Kohima including 23 Long Range Penetration Brigade.' The Naga Levies received three Military Crosses, one Indian Distinguished Service Medal, and eight Military medals in their active service of a few months.

Fecitt adds that books on the war have not adequately mentioned the considerable contribution of Indian troops to the Kohima fighting. Many Indian troops fought at Kohima including a battalion from the Nepalese army. It was an Assam Rifles patrol that encountered Japanese soldiers at Aradura and killed fifteen of them. It was the Assam Regiment that occupied Jail Hill, GPT ridge and IGH spur. The Punjab Regiment relieved the Assam Regiment on the last day of the siege of Kohima. The 'Battle of the Tennis Court' was a vehemently fought battle in the most horrific conditions, as the living fought on from the trenches they had to share with dead companions.

Many of those who fought at Kohima were awarded military decorations. The desperate nature of the battles brought out selfless courage in many men; at least two men were awarded the

Victoria Cross and one officer was honoured with a plaque back in his native Glasgow.

One cannot help remarking on the marvellous sweep of the book as it introduces pre-war British–Naga relations in the light of fiercely independent Naga cultures, and goes on to explain, dissect and record the events of the Second World War in the Naga Hills, bringing to light the key role of the Nagas and the cultural considerations that propelled it, while also linking the historic event with the Naga present of unsolved political conflict with India and the sense of great betrayal by the very people whose war they helped to win. It introduces the takeover of the Naga Hills by India, which resulted in military atrocities and numerous killings of civilians and the emergence of individualism, corruption and self-seeking among latter-day Nagas.

The most important aspect is that the book puts names to the Naga veterans and heroes whose efforts have been forgotten for so many decades. It also traces the journeys of the Naga veterans and the courses of their lives after the war. A large number of them died in the war or shortly after. Many tragic stories have been uncovered of soldiers returning home from Burma after years of service, but not receiving their dues and left to fend for themselves on the hasty departure of the British government from India. They suffered, they were 'disoriented, confused and felt useless as civilians'. Many of them lost their precious medals and citations in the upheaval of the Indo–Naga war that followed shortly after the Second World War. For the former soldiers, the loss of army papers and documents was a big blow. They had sacrificed their prime years to fight for the British Government but felt they had not received anything in return, having lost their pay and pension. They felt 'totally forgotten'. Neither were there records on their service available in the UK nor in India. To make matters worse, they became caught up in the Naga nationalist struggle whether they wanted to be part of it or not. Former soldiers like Havildar Zhavise Vihienuo, among others, was 'imprisoned for 16 months by Indian authorities without any charge against him and no reason given to him although he asked the reason for his imprisonment.'

The veterans were viewed with suspicion by the Indian Government because of their military experience and they were, thereby, unjustly treated. Their 'already difficult lives were further torn and most of them did not survive the crosshairs of this new conflict, as both sides considered those who did not join them to be enemies. Some died at the hands of the Indian Army.'

Of those who died in the Japanese invasion, Saliezhü (Linyü) Angami of Kohima Village is 'the only Naga soldier whose plaque is available at the Kohima War Cemetery, although at least fifteen other Assam Regiment sepoys of his battalion were killed at the siege of Kohima. The other sepoys killed during the siege are commemorated on Panel 53 of the Rangoon Memorial which is located inside the Taukkyan War Cemetery north of Yangon, Myanmar.' There will be inconsistency in some of the names as British records/awards sometimes differ from local usage.

Yet for all that they have suffered, the authors record that there was no bitterness or expression of regret on the part of the veterans about the past. The surviving veterans were all 'very gracious in their bearing and attitude.'

By way of conclusion, the Second World War had its positive side in that it put Kohima and the Naga Hills on the world map. *The Road to Kohima* will ensure that it stays there.

The counterparts of the Naga veterans were the British veterans who had also suffered being forgotten by their government. Called 'The Forgotten Army', the British war veterans organized themselves in order to do something of note for their former comrades-in-arms at the Kohima Battle. As the veterans planned the 60th Anniversary Remembrance event in the UK, they wondered how they might create a lasting tribute and memorial to those who fought in this battle. Led by Gordon Graham, a small group of them proceeded to lay down the plans for what became The Kohima Educational Trust. The Trust was established in 2005 as a charitable educational trust to repay 'a debt of honour' to the Nagas. It is dedicated to assisting with 'the education of Nagas including the descendants of their Naga allies in the Battle of Kohima'.

— *Easterine Kire*

ABOUT THE BOOK

The idea of recording the Naga experiences of the Second World War began in an unusual way. In April 2014, the Kohima Educational Society (KES) had taken a leading role in commemorating the 70th anniversary of the Battle of Kohima. Several groups turned up for the occasion. One of these was led by Bob Cook, Curator of the Kohima Museum in York, UK. In his team was Amanda Shapland, daughter of Brigadier Shapland (later Major-General), one of the three original Brigadiers in the Battle of Kohima. As the team was being taken around, she asked a lot of questions and when she realized there were very few Naga veterans left, she suggested to her tour guide, Linus, that perhaps the stories of the Naga veterans ought to be recorded before all the veterans passed on. The discussion was taken up in the Kohima Educational Society (KES, Nagaland) and the Kohima Educational Trust (KET, UK). After considerable discussion, it was agreed that recording the Naga experiences of the Second World War would be important particularly because the Naga narrative of the war was yet to come out. This was a broadening of the idea suggested by Amanda Shapland for veterans' stories.

After much discussion, KET-KES decided to bring out a book and a documentary film recording Naga experiences of the war. While this discussion was going on, Major Harry Fecitt MBE, TD, wrote to Charles Chasie asking if he would be interested to participate in a project of documenting the roles played by the Nagas in the Second World War, and offered to write a military account of such a project. A military text written by a distinguished retired army officer like Major Fecitt to undergird such a book sounded perfect. So his kind offer was accepted and the collaborative work on the project was started. Major Harry Fecitt's introductory words to the Nagas on the military account he has written appear below:

> Greetings to all Naga tribespeople wherever you are in the world:
>
> What I have written for you are ten individual chapters, each representing a part of what Nagas experienced during the war. Many different types of foreign men and military units marched through the Naga Hills and by treating each experience separately I have been able to go into the details of who those men were and why they were in Nagaland, and what they achieved or did not achieve. This means that there is a small amount of repetition in the chapters, but I hope that you will excuse that.
>
> The chapters have been deliberately kept short so that they remain focused and I hope interesting. A couple of chapters contain military terminology, but hopefully in or near your villages will be military or ex-military men who can explain the military words if that is needed.
>
> It is my hope that a copy of this book will be accessible for every school and community centre in Nagaland, so that the memory of what the Naga people endured during World War II and of what Naga heroes and heroines accomplished will never be forgotten.
>
> Researching and writing this book has been a privilege for me and you the readers can justifiably feel extremely proud of how the Naga people faced up to the challenges of full-scale modern warfare, and of how tribal cohesion was maintained throughout, despite all the vicissitudes of those times (Fecitt).

This project has taken the study team particularly of Charles Chasie and Linus Chasie, who was part of the discussion that helped launch the idea to all parts of Nagaland. We interviewed surviving Naga veterans of the war and members of their families.

The interviews started with a private list from informal enquiries from friends plus a list kindly provided by the Rajya Sainik Board in Kohima. The lists had a multiplier effect: one veteran or family of veteran information led us to other veterans and their families. Even in villages and areas where there were no veterans, interviews could be conducted with Naga elders who had witnessed the war personally or were participants in one way or another. Some of the Naga elders interviewed had helped the Japanese during the war, which provided a broader spectrum of the roles played by the Nagas.

A great regret was that many of the veterans and elders interviewed were already old and many were infirm. Most were hard of hearing or their memories had dimmed. In the case of one veteran, even communication was no longer possible, although the family members very kindly carried him to the kitchen, where interviewers and interviewee looked at each other mostly in silence. In some cases, veterans lying in their beds would look at us with vacant and unseeing eyes, but when they comprehended our mission, their eyes would light up, their faces would break into smiles and they would start talking about whatever they remembered of their war experiences. It did not matter any longer whether they were answering our questions. We just let them do the talking, glad that we were able to bring happiness into their lives for a few minutes.

In most cases, it was family members of the veterans whom we interviewed, as the veterans had passed on. But the meetings with the family members were always invaluable. Sadly, some veterans who had passed on did not have any direct descendants left.

One of the things our team of interviewers did was to recover, when available, and carry with us the citations of those who had won gallantry awards during the war, so that the documents could be given to the family members. In some cases the family members had no idea of the gallantry awards received. Others who knew, or even had the medals at one time, had lost them. In one case, where a Military Cross was won, on getting the citation, the son exclaimed, 'You have brought a dead man to life again!'

Two things made us sad. Many Naga families did not even have a photograph of their fathers or grandfathers who fought in the war. The few photographs we saw were of young handsome men in the prime of their youth. The second was the realization that in many cases there had been a breakdown in family communication. Children had no idea of what their fathers or grandfathers did and, in some cases, learnt with us as we interviewed the veterans. This breakdown in communication had to be understood in the context of the Indo–Naga conflict which ensued not long after the Second World War, a conflict which is yet to be finally resolved.

This book is the first comprehensive Naga narrative on the subject, covering the full spectrum of Naga experiences of the Second World War and the Battle of Kohima. This account does not cover the Imphal battle although Kohima and Imphal are usually twinned. If parts of present states of Manipur and Assam have been covered in the narrative, it is because they were routes to the Battle of Kohima or were integral to it.

The Second World War, and even the Battle of Kohima which affected the Nagas so profoundly, had never been considered as a Naga fight by the Naga people. They did not think of it as a part of their history. The obvious example of this Naga perspective can be found in the 2004 Government of Nagaland publication, 'Heralding Hope', which was brought out to commemorate 125 years of the founding of Kohima and endorsed the view of the Second World War as 'A war that was not ours'.

But as time passed, and as new generations with different perspectives arrived on the scene, more and more people are realizing how much the Second World War had affected the Naga people and profoundly changed their society. The recognition that Nagas have been getting because of the Battle of Kohima may also be changing old attitudes. And increasing war tourism today is strengthening the new perspective besides bringing income to many. The fact that young Nagas are now choosing the Battle of Kohima as their preferred subject for research and PhD studies may be a portent of the changing Naga perspective.

In any case, the Battle of Kohima has become firmly imbedded in Naga history. We hope this book will help to shed a little more light on how profoundly Naga society has been affected by this war. Even more, we hope this work will help unravel a little more why Naga society seems to continually stand at a crossroad.

THE BOOK IN A NUTSHELL

1. This is a book about how the Naga people saw the Second World War, how they faced it, participated in it, and how they were affected by it, including the societal changes the war brought into their lives.
2. The book is addressed primarily to a Naga audience as part of their history. It contains official records of their involvement in the Second World War as well as personal memories of the war recounted by revered elders.
3. It tells of the factors that led to the vast majority of Nagas supporting the British, although as a people they remained neutral. The Naga people did not particularly like the British Army, but by the time the war ended they found they had become comrades with the British Army and Government.
4. The book has a futuristic outlook in that the British–Naga collaboration between the Kohima Educational Trust (KET in the UK) and the Kohima Educational Society (KES in Nagaland) that produced it may be said to represent a new kind of transcontinental bridge between the two peoples, a bridge forged in the fires of the Battle of Kohima but one that transcends it and brings people of all nations together to work for peace in a new era.
5. The authors hope the book may inspire younger Nagas to study the Battle of Kohima as part of the history of their people.
6. Some books have unintended consequences. Writing this book has made us wonder about how many of the experiences of people like the Nagas, who were caught up in a war that they did not consider their own, have gone untold. It would be an added bonus if this book were followed by accounts from other minority groups and peoples everywhere who have been trampled over by wars and conflicts of others, and then forgotten.

ACKNOWLEDGEMENTS

To Amanda Shapland and Linus Chasie for providing the initial impetus to write this book.

To Dr Khrienuo Ltu and Khyulano Ezung for research assistance.

To the Kohima Educational Trust/Kohima Educational Society for sponsoring this work.

To Sylvia May, Robert Lyman and others in KET, for support at all stages.

To Laragh Neelin, niece of E. T. D. Lambert, temporary Deputy Commissioner of Naga Hills and Chief Civilian Liaison Officer during the war, who actually played a significant, if silent, role during the war; and Bob Cook, Curator of the Kohima Museum in York, UK, for making available information and documents as well as photographs.

Special thanks to Elizabeth Vizovono, Head of the Department of English, Baptist College, Kohima, and Rocus Chasie, author, for their help at different stages of the project.

And, of course, to all the interviewees and Naga elders who took time to share their stories with us, as well as all those who helped us in the different villages in various capacities, in some cases even though they did not know us.

A FEW WORDS ABOUT THE NAGAS

The Nagas are a Tibeto-Burman speaking people, of Mongoloid stock, made up of many tribes with different languages, customs, even cultures, and yet all claiming to be a people called 'Naga', a name given to them by others. The origins of the Nagas are still shrouded in mystery and conjecture. But this does not stop the Nagas from believing in a linear ancestry and descent, and that they are a people.

According to a Cambridge University study, 'the Nagas ... are representative of the forest dwelling tribesmen who once inhabited large areas of South-east Asia, the Pacific, South America and Central Africa ... First mentioned by Ptolemy in about 150 AD, it was clear that the Naga tribes had only coalesced recently in the patterns which the British discovered ... in the hills of the Eastern Himalayas' (Macfarlane, 'The Nagas').

The Naga tribes now live in north-western Myanmar and in the Indian States of Nagaland, Manipur, Arunachal Pradesh and Assam, along the Barail and Patkai mountain ranges lying roughly between parallels of 93 and 96 degrees longitude. All Naga tribes agree that they came to their present place of habitation from the East, although some also believe that their ancestors may have come 'east' from further north. Some like the Angami have legends that suggest they may have come from as far north as the Arctic Circle or beyond. The indications are that the tribes may have come through two or more migration routes and not just one.

Despite their diversity the Naga tribes can be broadly divided into two groups: the kilted Nagas, also called Tenyimi or Tenyimia, having similar cultural values and customs, and the other Naga tribes who are non-kilted, with some tribes that are tattooed. This division runs across tribe and state boundaries though even here there are grey areas. For instance, Lothas and Semas have similarities with the Tenyimia although these two tribes are not classified to be in the same group. Nevertheless, they believe they too migrated from Khezhakeno Village, like the other tribes of the Tenyimia group. The Sema and the Angami even believe they were brothers, a position acknowledged by both sides.

Given this ethnic Naga potpourri yet to be sorted, as well as the geographical location of the Second World War events in the region, we shall deal mainly with the Tenyimia group here. The Japanese routes from Burma to Kohima mostly passed through the lands of the Tenyimia, which became the main battlefields, so when we talk about the Nagas we would be referring largely to the Tenyimia group. It should however be noted that the battle routes crossed into other tribal villages especially in the Tangkhul area. The battles waged in Sangshak, Ukhrul and Kharasom turned out to be crucial for the defence of Kohima.

So who are these Tenyimia Nagas? A brief sketch of the Tenyimia Naga's life centred around the years of careful nurturing and preparing of the future members of the village society, for both men and women but especially for men, may best illustrate who they are. Females were raised to fill a broad range of roles, but the males were the focus of specialized training. The reason for this male emphasis becomes apparent when we look at the social life of the village community.

Naga society was patrilineal, not patriarchal, as many have mistakenly called it. Not patriarchal because the 'pure democracy' of the Angami/Tenyimia would not have allowed the presence of a patriarch; and life in a constant state of war with outsiders required multiple lines of fighters to protect the village, which a democratic patriliny was more likely to ensure than would a ruling patriarchal structure, hence the all-important position of the male-child lineage.

When a boy was born, there would be a series of stringent rites to be performed. These were sacred days for the household. They would not speak to strangers or even relatives if they had come from outside the village. They would naturally not participate in anything that would be considered 'work' or hunting. In fact, even those who had spoken to the household members during this period would not go hunting lest misfortune befall them. Among the many rites, the parental blessing of the boy and imploring God to make him a worthy son not just of the family but of the community as a whole was the most important. The blessing would continue to be pronounced even into adult life and so it is more commonly referred to as Elder's Blessing or 'Phichüja'.

The blessing would start with invocations to Heaven/Sky as the Father and Earth as the Mother:

May my son be filled with good health and attended by good fortune; May he be fleet-footed and not stumble against stone or stump; May he outperform his peers and rivals; May he be fierce and uncompromising; May he draw water from the well as long as others do; May the smoke of his fire be seen for as long as others are making fire; May he be a great warrior and bring honour to the family and community by bringing back trophies from war; May he live long with a lot of descendants ...

This list can go on. The blessing is also given when someone is setting out to do battle or on a journey. In the latter case, the blessing may slightly vary to something like this:

May the Spirits look after you and protect you; May good fortune attend you; May you always be in good health and directed towards your goal; May your achievements surpass that of your rivals; May you be fleet-footed and having achieved what you set out to do, may you return as quickly as the hand of Providence guides you.

Strengthened by such blessing, a Naga would set out with mental fortitude and psychological preparedness.

Returning home safely and as quickly as possible was always a kind of refrain of the blessing ritual. Here, mention may be made that when a child was born, the afterbirth was always carefully buried. There was a strong belief that when a person died, his/her spirit/soul always revisited the place where his/her afterbirth was buried. This could possibly point to the fact that although there were regular raids and wars, where taking the spoils of war and extending influence were part of the game, traditionally, the Tenyimia was usually not enamoured with increasing his territorial area of direct rule and was quite satisfied with what he had in his mountainous village, to which he would always return. It may also be worth mentioning that the Angami never considered himself as a 'chief', much less a king.

THEHU/KICHÜKI AND AGE-GROUP

When a boy reached 4–5 years, his father or elder brother/s would start taking him to the *Kichüki* (dormitory) and *Thehu* (meeting place). This was usually the home of a person in the clan that combined both as meeting place and male dormitory. The girls too would have their own separate dormitory in the home of an elderly woman (usually a widow) but it was not a *Thehu*. There they would learn social etiquette and the roles they would play in life as woman and mother.

Each clan had its own *Thehu/Kichüki*. This was where the boy's education and preparation for life began. He would become familiar with every member of the clan and what each was doing. He would learn clan and village history, folk stories, legends, songs, traditional customs and practices, and the duties and responsibilities of a member of the clan and village community. Any question could be raised and answered here. This was where every member was taught and thoroughly disciplined. From the *Thehu/Kichüki* would emerge the pride of the clan; this was where boys were fully prepared for life and to play their roles in society. They would have learned politics, diplomacy and the various ways of conducting oneself towards others, ready to compete with anyone in any field. They would give due regard to everyone, choose not to be the first to give offence lest it ended in bringing shame and loss of face to family and clan. But the members would not brook any insult when encountered. Each boy knew he was a valuable member of his clan/community and could practically do what he liked, even go against the decisions of his clan, khel and village, so long as he was willing to face the consequences. To this extent, he enjoyed veto power as no one could force him to do something he did not wish to. This was how the 'pure democracy' of the Angami became known. But he also knew that he had little or no life without his family, clan, khel and village. Once exiled, he literally became a non-person, without identity.

By the time a boy was about 7–8 years old, he would join a *Thesü* (age-group cohort) to which he would belong for life. The *Thesü* is a much larger conglomeration, encompassing at least the entire khel, which is a cluster of many clans. For the first time, he would come in contact with girls of his age-group in a formal way. The *Thesü* has a principal host-father by whose name the particular age-group would henceforth become identified with, and his house would become their 'headquarters'. The job of the principal host or host-father was to provide a meeting place and assist the group if they needed his help, but he would not interfere in any way. The age-group members would meet regularly, discuss things and plan their programmes.

All decisions of the age-group would be taken by consensus. If a decision was not possible, discussions would continue until it became clear what the vast majority of the members wanted. When such a picture had emerged, the members with contrary views would gracefully bow out. Then everybody would undertake whatever was decided by the age-group – with those who initially had contrary views usually trying to do more than the others to achieve the common goal. When such a 'consensus' was not possible, the idea or initiative would be abandoned.

The age-group cohort was where leadership was nurtured and groomed. Since the group decided everything for itself, those persons with ability began to be recognized by their peers.

Leaders thus emerged in a natural way through recognition of their organizational and persuasive abilities, common sense, wisdom and other qualities of leadership. Thus, leaders were accepted after being proven. The process may be spontaneous, as well as slow and long-winded, but it was also rigorous and free of so many of today's complications. But leader or not, everyone was valued. And everyone had equal opportunity to exhibit their qualities and abilities and also to achieve their highest potentials. Indeed, every member would try and help those who were 'slower'. It would seem at times that the weakest members in the age-group had the most friends – including girlfriends!

The age-group community was a place for enjoyment, competition, exhibition, even courting which may lead to choosing one's partner in life. Boy-girl relationship was totally open, and girls could also do what they wanted, but moral turpitude was never a problem. This was because an elaborate system of behaviour governed how one interacted with others, including members of the opposite sex, with the utmost respect. It was an unwritten law, known by all and not broken by anyone. Earning goodwill and contributing to the village community comprised the main activities of the age-groups. Constructing wayside rest places for people coming from or going to the fields, welcome gates and social work were usually done by the age-groups in turn. Each age-group would try to contribute the most to the khel or village community.

There was a lot of healthy rivalry and competition among the members within the age-group itself, each trying to outdo the others. The competition was to do more and to do better, never to pull down others, which was frowned upon with a social stigma attached to it. In your success, everyone in the cohort rejoiced and shared in your happiness. In failure, they supported and stood by you. Your peers in the age-group brooked no insult to you from anyone. This bond was a lifelong one. Short of a blood feud, which would lead to instant war, it was the dignified thing to be the most polite and to sacrifice the most even for your known enemy. The age-group community was a place of loyalty, of pride and prestige. It gave meaning to social existence.

So, while the family and clan provided identity, the *Thehu/ Kichüki* nurtured and grounded the members by providing the needed education and discipline for life, and the age-group was where boys and girls started to bloom and flower as mature citizens of the village community.

MARRIAGE AND SOCIAL LIFE

Against the background of wars and head-hunting that the Nagas lived in, ensuring the family line was very important. So a young man may marry by the time he was about 20 years old, if not earlier. Once he was married, he would live away from his parents with his wife and start his family. He would have his own home in an ancestral plot which would have been given to him by his father. His father would also have given him his share of agricultural fields, sufficient to live on. These two legacies, ancestral plot and fields, he would manage and use during his lifetime and improve upon them. He would one day, in turn, bequeath them to his sons, including any other properties he may have acquired during his lifetime. But the acquired properties can be gifted to any children, including daughters, or even be given to relatives although one's progeny always took precedence. Particularly in the initial years, the young couple would work very hard to cultivate and harvest enough.

The clan *Thehu/Kichüki* would continue to be an important place for the man – the education process here was a continuing one. Many would sleep there. Even those who did not would come in the morning and in the evening and sit around the hearth in the *Thehu* to socialize and share news. Everyone in the clan would know who was going where on which particular day and for what purpose. So if a member did not turn up in the evening, the clan would know where to go looking for him. They would also discuss what was happening within the other clans, khels and in the village community. Was someone having a dispute with another member of the village? What could be the possible ramifications? What should be the stand of the clan? This was a good opportunity for the younger people to learn from their elders about similar cases from the past and how they were settled. Basically these became case studies.

The sense of justice was highly honed. Settlement of the cases would depend on the circumstances of the case. Care would be taken, in each case, to see that even the guilty person is allowed to go without being totally humiliated. A lot of the punishment was allowed to hang on social stigma, castigation and ostracism. An unrepentant criminal may find that suddenly no one was willing to befriend him, or do things with him, and marriage partners would be hard to find. The severity of the social stigma would of course depend on the seriousness of the crime. There was no written law and no prescribed punishments except for the very serious crimes, but the procedures described above proved adequate.

Much of the time, the honour of the guilty person's family or clan would be taken into account so that the whole clan did not suffer for the wrongdoing of one individual. This was necessary because the individual's identity was totally integrated with that of the clan, and outside the clan the person had no identity to speak of. It was because of this that often the friendship between two persons resulted in the friendship between their clans, as would their enmity in that of the two clans. In minor cases, a simple apology was sufficient. Usually the guilty person's family would be the first to start chastising the culprit because this was the honourable thing to do. No one wanted the enmity of another clan because the road from there to a running blood-feud was not far. And once a life had been taken, it became a matter of honour for the clan and the filial duty of the descendants of the victim to avenge their loss. This often became an endless cycle of war.

In a case of wilful murder, immediate and permanent exile was prescribed. Often, the vengeance of the victim family was quicker. Even in cases of accidental killing, seven years' exile from the village was prescribed for the immediate family. After this period, the family could come back and resettle in the village. In cases like theft, seven times the value was prescribed except for the 'Thevo' or priestly clan, for whom the prescribed restitution was less.

In such a volatile situation with the possibility of a feud always imminent, the presence of third parties and their mediation was important. Within the khel it was easier to manage the problems that cropped up. They were usually settled by the different clan leaders without too much difficulty.

Inter-khel disputes were much more difficult to settle. There were numerous cases of different khels within the same village feuding and going to war with each other, particularly between the principal clans, for generations, each side wanting to be the one with the last to kill. This was why the presence of third parties, even from other villages, was a necessity. Each clan and khel, even individuals and families, had clansmen and friends in other villages. The mediating parties usually managed to work out a compromise solution, which was accepted because failure to accept the 'solution' could end in the mediating party losing face in front of both the feuding sides. But if the 'solution' was patently unfair, other parties would normally move in to see that justice was done. These were the kind of checks and balances that used to be in place. They proved effective in rendering justice in most cases.

Under such practices, and in the background of head-hunting, the right introduction and credentials from a villager would ensure a visitor or guest a warm and honourable welcome in the village. Without proper credentials, one would be suspect, even considered a spy or enemy, although usually no hasty actions were taken. Care always had to be taken so that no loss of face was caused. Understandably, most speeches were indirect, and frequently one had to make inferences to discern the meaning behind what was actually being said.

NAGA DIPLOMACY

A word on Naga diplomacy. In the old days, when you met a Naga for the first time he would, as a rule, speak in self-deprecating terms (today's Naga may be a different 'kettle of fish'!). There is a historical context for this behaviour. With so many running feuds and 'wars' between different clans and khels, plus personal disputes, there was no dearth of representatives needed to take on responsibilities on behalf of clan, khel and village. On such occasions, when one's name was proposed as representative of the clan, khel or village, one made protestations about one's unworthiness. This would continue until it became clear that the nomination was sincere and had the support of the vast majority. The selection process was long, but it helped build consensus. What usually happened in the event the mission was unsuccessful was that nobody lost face, and those who proposed your name were the first to come to your defence. In the event the mission was successful, everyone won.

There was a formal infrastructure to Naga diplomacy that may be described as the 'embassy system'. It existed mostly to regulate relations among the clans within a khel, but it also served the khel's purpose of putting up a common front against others. In the khel, each clan was allotted a plot of land around the khel fort. One family unit from each clan would live in this allotted space. The family living on this allotted plot would enjoy complete 'immunity' from any harm from the other clans, regardless of any running feuds at the time. This was an honoured practice in an environment where a drunken brawl could lead to a feud between clans and where, under normal circumstances, the 'ambassador' and his household may not even have time to run. Unbelievable but true. This remarkable custom must have evolved over a long period of time since there are no known models for it anywhere.

Another remarkable feature of the Angami Naga village society was the 'veto' power of the individual with the right to disagree with any decision of the clan or community. No man would be forced to do anything he did not want to do. The most the community could do was to ostracize the person as unruly and incorrigible. The next severe step would be exile, but this was not usually done. In practice, the punishment of exiling someone seems to be there more as a deterrent than as a legal instrument to be enforced, except in cases where someone was killed.

All the above together went to mould the image of the Naga society as a 'pure democracy'. They also raised a lot of questions about Naga origins and who they descended from. There is no clear evidence so far, not even definitive indications, about where Nagas came from, what they faced, or how they became a people. Some say that the colour combinations of the Naga shawls indicate they came from some highly developed societies. Others say the Naga ability to eat 'anything' is indicative of some harsh regions their ancestors may have passed through. There are also cultural similarities with some American Indian tribes and others. There was also a theory that the Nagas may have been part of those who ran away when the Great Wall of China was being built. As of today, no one really knows.

CULTURE AND IDENTITY

Throughout his life, the Tenyimia would live by a certain code so that his life was meaningful and purposeful in his eyes. He may be called superstitious, but his beliefs and cultural values were important to him. A popular description of culture is that it is an acquired behaviour of a people over a period of time. This is largely true but this seems too flimsy a definition. Even the dictionary offers several definitions of culture but none is definitive. And culture and civilization are things one cannot be too careful about. It would also be unwise to say one culture is 'superior' to another, although one can recognize which may be more modern. What we may ask, however, is whether a given culture is a complete culture or not. Meaning a complete culture ought to be able to provide adequate answers to all the basic questions of life for a particular society or people at a given period of time. Questions such as:

1. Who am I?
2. Where have I come from?
3. Where am I going?
4. What is the purpose of my life?
5. How do I live?
6. Is there life after death?

Obviously, there were no systematic philosophical explanations and answers to the above questions for the Naga. An easy example was that he did not know where he came from. But for all that, he was reasonably sure of most of the answers to the basic questions for him to live a meaningful life in his own eyes. His family, clan *Thehu/Kichüki*, age-group and village community, and the values he had been brought up to believe in had ensured these. They gave him confidence and a perspective beyond mere mortality. The Nagas believed in life after death and they have their own version of St Peter guarding the gate to the next world. A very poignant reminder is the epitaph of Saliezhü Angami at the Second World War Commonwealth Cemetery in Kohima, the only Naga plaque there:

Apau puo medozha chüterhü
Rükra themvü mevi lar pengutuo

'My beloved son, big of heart and true warrior,
I will see him return as a star in the sky.'

Naga belief was that good/great souls returned as moon or stars.

For the Naga, certain words attained paramount importance for his life and living so that they were meaningful in his eyes.

1. *Terhomia/Kepenuopfü*: This term means supernatural being or beings. The concept of good and evil was ingrained in the Naga. There was belief in one God (although the notion of plurality was there too, particularly of many evil spirits), and life after death, etc. A folk story was also told of God/Spirit, Tiger and Man, who lived together, as three brothers, with their mother. A Naga always lived very close to his God, sometimes to the point of becoming too superstitious.
2. *Mhosho*: An umbrella word that signified pride, integrity, honour, dignity, etc.
3. *Kenyü*: When something was *kenyü* it was taboo and just not done. Here arises the sense of the sacred and the sense of sin.
4. *Menga* or *Dzünga*: It is a very sophisticated notion of 'shame'. For instance, you could insult or humiliate a person but you did not do it because it was *menga* to do so. Here, *kenyü* may also play a role. In fact, *Menga/Dzünga* is an attitude and discipline

of life. *Dzünga* was a way of conducting oneself not just before fellow human beings but also before God. In many cultures in India, including the north-east, this is hardly ever seen. For instance, in a work involving portering, how many would consider themselves honour-bound to pick the biggest and heaviest loads to carry if they were the first to arrive on the scene and had the choice to pick the lightest load? Most would think only the foolish would pick the heaviest loads. But for the Tenyimia, it was *menga* not to do so.

5. *Peyu*: *Peyu* signified a man of wisdom, depth, statesmanship, etc. A *Peyu* was usually an elderly man commanding great respect within the community. One sometimes heard people say, 'He is rich, is he? So what? He is not a *Peyu.*' *Peyu* includes wealth but puts it in its proper place. Wealth is an important complement of *Peyu*, for without wealth a man may fail to reach the status of *Peyu*! There is an apt Angami saying that poverty is the killer of aspirations/ambitions.

These then were the concepts that became the driving forces in the life of the Naga and helped him to differentiate the things of value from things that were ephemeral, buttressed by his upbringing and training, from which he got his ideological moorings. He lived with purpose – to be a valued member of his community; and to that purpose he gave his best.

So what helped the Naga most in his life was a sense of self-worth in a living culture that offered him fulfilment and completion. The circumstances of his world were limited but adequate for his evolution as a complete human being. His community culture guided his growth and gave him confidence to the extent that he was prepared to sacrifice his life for his beliefs and what he considered a worthy cause. He could thus endure whatever difficulties came his way, and he did whatever he could for what he believed would be good for his progeny.

AGRICULTURE AND WEALTH

Agriculture was the mainstay of the village community, and the different seasons of the agricultural cycle decided the daily activities of the people. Basically, everyone did what everyone else was doing, depending on the season. For example, when it was time to plough and prepare the fields for cultivation, everyone would be doing that. Similarly, when time came to sow, plant, weed, or harvest, all would be carrying out those tasks. Of course, everyone would be competing to be the first to complete the season's particular set of works. There was no place for laziness. For instance, even hunting during work season in the fields would be considered as laziness. Hunting had its strict seasons – when there was less or no work in the fields, which was usually during the dry season. No hunting was done during the summer when there was work in the field, which coincided with the period when the animals were usually pregnant. The hunter also did not eat of his own kill. His family and relatives would enjoy the meat. Choice selections of the soft and delicious parts would be given to the elderly, particularly the old womenfolk (here the menfolk did not participate). A separate meal, perhaps a chicken, would be cooked for the successful hunter whose reward was to be praised and blessed by those who benefited from his successful hunt. Conservation of wildlife was a natural result. Even where edible wild plants/vegetables and medicinal herbs were gathered, people only took what they needed.

In the early days, the wealth of a Naga was measured mostly by how much paddy and cattle he possessed, and the gap between rich and poor was not so great. In any case, wealth itself was put in its proper place. People worked hard and aspired to become rich. But the end goal was not to keep the riches for oneself. The objective was to share one's wealth with others – clan, khel and village – in a series of feasts which came to be known as the 'Feasts of Merit'. This was because his only rewards were social acclaim and the right to sport/don certain decorations in his regalia and upon his dwelling. Wealth was seen as God's gift and only a passing phase. 'Beware in the days of prosperity' was a warning known to every person as that was when you made mistakes or committed social sin. So the rich did not look down on the poor; and the poor did not grudge the rich but aspired to emulate them.

After minutely observing the pure democracy of the Angami and other practices of Naga society, Captain John Butler was to comment, 'It is difficult to conceive as existing for a single day, and yet that it does exist here is an undeniable fact' (*Travels and Adventures*).

BEING WARRIORS AND MAKING WAR

How did wars and head-hunting start? Every Naga boy yearned to become a great warrior. Even the paternal blessing proclaimed over him included success in war, and to bring back enemy heads to the village. As all Nagas practiced head-hunting, some people may have the impression that it was a free for all, all the time. But, in fact, it was part of a complex system of social conduct and honour. A Tenyimia usually tried not to be the first to give offence. The most common manner in which he became involved in war and head-hunting was through supporting and defending relations in other villages, responding to someone's request for help or because he was being attacked. He usually made war and took heads to redeem his honour by seeking revenge. Profiteering was not his normal motivation. Profiteering was in fact usually considered taboo although spoils of war were also carried off. The Naga attacks on the British tea gardens, particularly from Khonoma, Mezoma and nearby villages, which finally forced the British to climb the hills, would appear otherwise to an outsider. Not from Naga eyes. From their perspective, they were getting back at the British colonialists for first violating their territory. Even in 1879–1880 when the British under Brigadier General Nation, with reinforcements from Dibrugarh and Shillong, and the soldiers of the Raja of Manipur, had laid a siege on their village for nearly four months, fifty-five warriors of Khonoma slipped out through the surrounding jungles and attacked the Baladan Tea Garden in Cachar, killed the manager and destroyed the estate, before quietly returning to their village to resume fighting the British and their allies. Avenging unprovoked attack was part of the honour code.

When war starts, particularly if killings had taken place, everything becomes fair game to the Naga, including what may be considered 'treacherous' and 'unfair' in Western eyes. It becomes ruthless with no quarters given or taken. When plans were made to attack one's enemy, support was sought from friends and clansmen in and outside one's village. Ambushes were part of the course of attack. In any such attack, any member of the enemy clan, khel or village – whether man, woman or child – would be considered an enemy on equal footing and killed if opportunity arose. But only identified enemies would be targeted and killed. Heads or other body parts would be brought back to the village and rites carried out. Any male member who took part in such rites, even if he did not take part in the actual fighting and killing, would earn the right to be considered as having taken a head!

What happened on the side of the victim's family? If someone had killed any member of your family, you became honour-bound to take revenge. If you were not able to do so in your lifetime, the duty passed to your sons and on down the line. The desire to seek, and actually take revenge, was not just a matter of pride for the Angami. It was linked to his belief system. The Angami believed that if vengeance was not visited on the enemy, the soul/ spirit of the diseased forebear would find no peace in the afterworld. So it became a filial duty to avenge one's forebears. And it became an endless war. It was because of this that J. H. Hutton, Deputy Commissioner of the Naga Hills, made the comment that 'the blood feud of the Angami is what the Corsican vendetta was' (*The Angami Nagas*).

But, even in war, the Tenyimia had a code of behaviour. Sometimes there were identified or recognized champion warriors in the opposing clans or feuding parties. In such cases, single combat duels could take place. This then became a well-planned affair, with other warriors not taking part. The two opposing warriors would schedule the date and time to fight each other. This was done with full knowledge of their kith and kin, who would remain bystanders during the fight, not taking part even if they could. When these two warriors met in battle they did it with mutual respect. So while taking 'trophies' (body parts) was normal, numerous stories are told of duelling warriors who agreed before the fight that they would not dismember the other's dead body. And such promises were always honoured by family and friends because this was the honourable thing to do.

At this point it may interest the reader to know how a Tenyimia prepared himself for war. 'Sekrenyi' (*Sekre* festival) is often described as a festival of self-purification and renewal of life. It was in fact a special rite of purification and preparation of the men for war. This was a 10-day 'festival' and considered the most important for the Angami and other Tenyimia tribes. One of the first rites is that every man would try to be the first to bathe in the village well while the water was still asleep – before anyone has disturbed it. He would bless himself thus: 'May this water cleanse me from all sickness and disease and may I become healthy and strong so that I may overcome all my adversaries, performing feats that others cannot and surpassing everyone in my achievements.' Implicit in this ritual blessing is the prayer to do what others would consider impossible; the greater the challenge the more the glory and the desire to achieve. The most important rite of the *Sekrenyi* was to consult the omens with a cock/rooster ritual. If the omens were bad, the ritual was repeated with a second rooster. The solemn part started with the liver and heart of the rooster, along with a little rice wine. The person would say, 'May my enemies remain in a stupor so that I may spear him while he/they are in such a state.' Other rites followed, but this one lay at the heart of the rites. For the whole duration of the rites, the man would cook his own food in new pots. During this time, and when preparing to go to war, he would abstain from any sexual activity lest he became defiled and displeased God. When the man was out at war, his womenfolk would not work in the fields and would abstain from certain proscribed activities even at home. And, naturally, they would remain chaste.

But death appears to be even more important to the Naga. The rites performed for the dead are far more stringent than any other, and scrupulously observed. Incomplete or wrong observance of rites was believed to bring misfortune and catastrophes. So rigorous were the rites that they were reason enough for many Nagas to become Christian! The rituals were observed for a period of 30 days; no other rite/ceremony lasted even half this long. The Naga belief in life after death was very strong. And his afterlife was important to him. His belief was not far from the Christian teaching of what does it profit a man if he gained the whole world but suffered the loss of his soul?

The belief in the afterlife also put a lot of earthly goals in perspective. Every Naga male wanted to be a great warrior and to be rich. But his desire for wealth was to share it with family and community and to gain social acclaim. *Peyu* was considered more precious than mere wealth. On the other hand, while being a great warrior had many benefits, taking too many lives was also discouraged. There was a warning that those who took too many lives may suffer the loss of their progeny and be left without male descendants to carry on their lines. The warning against taking too many lives extended even to the killing of animals, wild and domestic. Life itself was considered precious.

So when the British first arrived in the Naga Hills they might have thought they were facing a barbaric and savage head-hunting people, wild marauders who only understood force and the ability to enforce it. Indeed, even so many years later, General Grover, Commander of the British 2nd Division, during the Second World War, admitted that they had been taught to consider all Nagas as 'head-hunting savages' (Keane, *Road of Bones*, 295). Initially they would have found the Nagas to be an implacable enemy. But with the passage of time, the British would begin to unravel the deeper aspects of Naga life and values. They discovered that the Naga he faced was quite different from what he might have thought of him at first. The Nagas too learned to respect the efficiency of the British and their sense of justice.

According to a Naga elder, three things might have stood out about the Nagas in British eyes.

1. When there was a call for porter work, the villagers, eager to earn, would usually rush to find their loads. But instead of trying to find the lightest and easiest loads, those who arrived first would select the heaviest and most difficult ones to carry. This was in line with the Naga mental make-up of wanting to do more than any others, an action prompted by his sense of *menga/dzünga*.

2. Although there were numerous raids on the tea gardens and on other Naga villages, the Tenyimia generally had no desire to extend his territorial area. He was attached to his mountainous 'village republic', and being quite satisfied with what he had, he would always return home.

3. The 'pure democracy' of the Angami would have certainly intrigued the British. Here there was no ruler and ruled or ruling and opposition parties. There was not even rule by force of majority. The search was always for consensus. Neither was there any election. Leaders emerged naturally through recognition of their abilities. And, finally, there was the 'veto' power of the individual to be exercised according to his conscience.

The advent of the British colonialists in the nineteenth century started to dilute Naga traditional values as was bound to happen when an outsider, with different scales of values, rules a people who love their freedom and had never been conquered or ruled by anyone. Shortly after the British arrived, introduction of money began to cause deep rifts and divisions in the society, including new social strata. But on the whole the early British Administrators, some of whom were trained anthropologists, did not interfere too much in the culture of the people. But an unlikely storm was fast approaching on the Naga Hills in the form of the Japanese Imperial Army and the Second World War. For the Nagas this storm would prove to be a life-changing hurricane.

WORKS CITED

Butler, John. *Travels and Adventures in the Province of Assam* (1855). Reprinted. New Delhi: Vivek Publishing, 1978.

Chasie, Charles. *The Naga Imbroglio: A Personal Perspective.* Kohima: Standard Printers & Publishers, 1999.

Chasie, Dolhunyü. *Khwünomia Rüna Kechü Dze.* Kohima: Unpublished papers.

Chasie, Rovi. *The Quaint Little Village.* Kohima: Pen Thrill Publication House, 2016.

Elwin, Verrier. *The Nagas in the Nineteenth Century.* Oxford: Oxford University Press, 1969.

Hutton, J. H. *The Angami Nagas.* London: Macmillan, 1921.

Keane, Fergal. *Road of Bones.* London: Harper Press, 2010.

Khonoma Rüffüno, *Centennial Commemoration of Our Heroes.* Kohima: Private Publication, 1979.

Macfarlane, Alan. 'The Nagas of the Assam-Burma Border', Cambridge Experimental Videodisc Project, The Naga Database, alanmacfarlane.com/FILES/nagas, 2001. Accessed 2017.

Personal Interviews with Naga elders. Nagaland: 2016–2017.

PART I

A NOTE ON THE TEXT

₹ = Indian rupees
In 1947 13.33 Indian rupees equalled one pound sterling

Infantry ranks in the Indian and British armies:

Indian	British
Subedar	Captain
Havildar Major	Sergeant Major
Havildar	Sergeant
Naik	Corporal
Lance Naik	Lance Corporal
Sepoy	a soldier

ONE

NAGA EXPERIENCES IN THE SECOND WORLD WAR

The invasion of India was not only Japan's last bid for victory, but its last imperial land grab. It was also the last time Britain was forced to defend its empire.

– Robert Lyman

Armies of the world were killing each other in the forest clad mountain for no fault of [Nagas]. The Nagas had killed for sport, but this was plain savagery in their … eyes.

– Nirmal Nibedon

Had the approach of the Nagas been different, the battle might have been extended, the defeat of the Japanese might have been delayed and the casualties of the British might have been higher or the battle might have taken a different turn.

– The British-Governor-General-in-Council

Britain entered the Second World War against Germany in 1939. But it was following the outbreak of the war with the Japanese in December 1941 that the Japanese war machine began to roll westward through South-East Asia in quest of their so-called Co-prosperity Sphere. In 1942, the Japanese forces conquered Burma and were threatening to spill over into India, the jewel in the British Crown. Initially, the Japanese did not seriously consider entering India. But several factors seemed to have made them decide to march into India, chiefly two. The most attractive reason would have been the larger geopolitical goal of taking India from Great Britain. In this, they were encouraged by the formation of the Indian National Army (INA), consisting of Indian soldiers in the British Army who had surrendered and gone over to the Japanese side. Frequently described as 'renegades' by the British, this new Indian Army's mischief potential to the British was real, should the Japanese enter India. Not surprisingly, the INA promoted the notion of Indians rising up against the British to welcome the Japanese 'victors'. Another reason was the ease with which the Japanese were able to overcome the Allied Forces throughout South-East Asia and use their war supplies as they advanced. These factors made the Japanese overconfident and less cautious about what actually lay ahead.

So plans were forged to enter India in 1943. And the Japanese 15th Army, under General Renya Mutaguchi, was entrusted to undertake the mission under Operation U-Go. Facing them was the British 14th Army under General William Slim. The Japanese plan was to travel light, quickly capture British and Allied positions, as they did in South-East Asia, and capture the enemy's stores for supplies. Unfortunately for them, they failed to take into account General 'Monsoon' as they entered one of the heaviest rainfall areas of the world. The terrain was a big factor too, but even more so were the battle-hardened soldiers from previous encounters in South-East Asia now facing them. And then there were the new Assam Rifles and Assam Regiment, local boys who knew the terrain, the people and the jungle, and were born with an instinct for war.

At this juncture, the British and Allied Forces returned a big favour to the Japanese by, in turn, underestimating the Japanese. They expected a much smaller force to attack them and made preparations accordingly. There were also differing perceptions among the Allied Commanders as to the strategic importance of Kohima and Dimapur, which further handicapped them. So the ingredients were all there for bloody and prolonged fighting.

Although Operation U-Go, as well as the short-lived and failed Operation Ha-Go, were both about the Battles of Kohima and Imphal, this account will deal with only the Battle of Kohima, the furthest reach of the Japanese. As has often been said in narratives about the war, 'Before Kohima the British and Allied Forces faced defeat after defeat; after Kohima, they knew only victory!' (*Kohima: An Exploration of War, Memory and Gratitude*).

Because of the mistaken belief about a much smaller Japanese force attempting to enter India and the differences of opinion about the relative importance of Dimapur and Kohima, the 161st British Brigade was ordered to Dimapur on the eve of the Battle of Kohima. Only a token force was left behind in the Kohima Garrison, and even that may not have happened had Deputy Commissioner C. R. Pawsey not refused to leave Kohima. After realizing that Kohima was the main target of the Japanese, the brigade was ordered back to Kohima, but only the 4th Royal West Kents managed to reach Kohima before the Dimapur–Kohima Road was cut off by the Japanese. Thus despite the significant delays achieved by the battles in the Somra Tracts and particularly at Kharasom and Jessami, the Kohima Garrison found itself ill-prepared to face the Japanese when they arrived on 4 April.

The Japanese, on the other hand, seemed completely focused on reaching Kohima and waging the war there as quickly as possible. 'Kohima Masta', the Japanese would say and force any villager they met to carry their loads towards Kohima, according to Naga elder Pukoho Rolnu of Jakhama village. Their initial strategy seemed quite sound, approaching Kohima from three sides – east, south and west. But after this, things started to go wrong for them. It was quite clear they did not have adequate local Naga support and their intelligence system had broken down. Even worse, there was indication that something was seriously wrong with the planning, execution and coordination of the Japanese Army at the highest levels.

The Japanese probably had several chances to take Kohima. First, if the initial Japanese attacks on the Kohima Garrison had been carried out with more focus, they would, in all probability, have overwhelmed the Garrison. The British 2nd Division soldiers were just arriving in Dimapur and still in disarray. Except for the 4th Royal West Kents battalion, the 161st Brigade could not return to Kohima in time. So the Kohima Garrison was poorly defended. According to Robert Lyman, at this crucial moment one of the strongest Japanese units was sent to occupy Cheswema which, together with Meriema, represented the Japanese Right Hook.

The second reason Kohima did not fall to the Japanese was that they failed to execute their three-pronged attack on Kohima, which seemed to have been their original strategy. Had they taken Secü Village and controlled Zubza (now Secü-Zubza town), they would have practically blocked the Dimapur–Imphal Road, providing a better stranglehold on Kohima while also affording themselves an opportunity to effectively attack the British 161st Brigade before the 2nd Division arrived. But this move was done haphazardly without proper plan or determination. The Japanese attack on Secü Village turned out to be more of a 'probe' than an attack. According to eyewitness Naga elder and author Zapuvisie Lhousa, less than a company of Japanese soldiers arrived at Mezoma and some of them went and fought at Secüma. They returned without casualty.

Had the Japanese taken control of Secüma and Zubza on the left (western) side and Meriema and Cheswema on the right, they could have blocked the British 2nd Division coming to Kohima from Dimapur. But the Japanese preferred to withdraw to the high ground on Pulie Badze (above Jotsoma), from where they could not even fire their guns down at the 161st Brigade in Jotsoma, literally at their feet. The Japanese lack of supplies and adequate support of the local people were, of course, their biggest enemies.

Meanwhile, there was another route, on the western side, to the plains of Cachar, Assam, in the area where Ursula Graham Bower was operating with her Zeliang Nagas. This could be reached from Manipur, through Imphal. But the Japanese did not manage to take Imphal. The other route was through the Barail

Range, which the Nagas had used regularly to attack the tea gardens in Cachar. The 3,000 or so Japanese troops, or part of them that came to Pulomi (Poilwa) from across the Barak River, via Maram, could have used this route to reach Cachar, overwhelming Bower's Zeliangs. Cachar (next door to today's Bangladesh) was also much closer to Bengal and Comilla where General Slim had been ensconced most of the time. No doubt Japanese/INA forces pouring out through Cachar would have created a chaotic situation for the British/Allied forces. But it was obvious that the Japanese soldiers had no inkling of this route and no Naga told them about it. Nor did they have any orders to follow such a route.

Third, following Mutaguchi's order, a Japanese battalion of the 138th Regiment had started its march for Dimapur on 8 April, from Meriema/Cheswema, on the old Bokajan Road via Keruma (now Zhadima) and Phekerkriema Villages. But five hours into the march, they were recalled. This order, of course, came from the Burma Area Army HQ in Rangoon. But as author Robert Lyman commented, 'What might have happened if Sato had turned a Nelsonian blind eye to Kimura's order, or if he had delayed its official receipt for another 24 hours? ... Sato's hatred of Mutaguchi blinded him to the strategic possibilities offered by continuing his offensive through to Dimapur, and lost for the Japanese a crucial opportunity for victory in 1944' (*The Battle that Saved India*, 51).

Animosity between Lieutenant General Kotoku Sato, Commander of the 31st Division and his superior, Lieutenant General Renya Mutaguchi, Commander of the Japanese 15th Army, and lack of intelligence, resulting in absence of proper strategic planning and coordination, may have cost the Japanese a possible victory in the Naga Hills, before all the problems of logistics and supplies began to further bog them down. One could safely say that by the second part of April, the Japanese had sealed their own fate, particularly after the British 2nd Division had managed to come up to Zubza and set up their headquarters there. The only thing left to the Japanese was their fixation on Kohima. But the Japanese would soon face the greatest defeat in their history.

As mentioned earlier, if the Japanese had reached the plains, the Indian National Army (INA) would have become more effective in turning the local population to support the INA, if not the Japanese. In the Hills, the Nagas did not like the plainsmen. Furthermore, in the hills, a few soldiers could hold up many times their own number because of the nature of the terrain. But if the Japanese and INA had managed to reach the plains of Assam, it would have been just one more step to reach Bengal, INA chief Subhas Chandra Bose's home province/state (Bangladesh was then part of Bengal/India). And even in Assam, the feelings of the local population to the INA/Japanese forces might have been much more receptive than in the Naga Hills.

What might have been the scenario then? Would 'Indians' have risen against the British? Could Japanese supplies have come by sea through the Chittagong and other ports in Bengal, avoiding the impassable Naga Hills? In any case, food and people support for the Japanese would have been more than in the hills. Would the vast majority of the Allied 14th Army already engaged in the battle of Imphal be locked up in the Naga Hills and the Imphal plains, at least long enough for the Japanese/INA to temporarily achieve their objective of 'Delhi Chalo', thus reversing the position that the Japanese faced in terms of long lines of communication? What kind of impact would this have had in China with every possibility of the airbase in Chabua, near Dibrugarh, being shut down or made inoperable? Would that have turned what was later to be a brilliant Allied victory into a disaster? Probably not, at least not in the long term.

It is difficult to imagine that the Axis Forces might actually have won the war. Even if the Japanese had managed to reach the plains, the Allied Forces still had vast air superiority. The American focus, particularly their air force, would have shifted from China to the fighting in Assam, something the British had always wanted from the Americans. There was also the British 2nd Division which would have been quickly withdrawn to fight the Japanese in the plains. Plus, the Allied Forces in Imphal, avoiding the Kohima–Dimapur route, would most likely try and break out of the Valley and head for Cachar, the shortest route to Assam/Bengal, and possibly with the least resistance, rendering it very difficult for the Japanese to support and sustain their initial attack force. The Japanese would then have to depend quite a lot on what the INA could do in garnering local support. In the circumstances, only two things could be said with some certainty in the event the Japanese managed to reach the plains of Assam and Bengal: (i) the character of the war in India (Burma Campaign) would have changed and (ii) the future of India might have been very different from what it turned out to be. How far the ripples might have gone is a matter of conjecture, and must now lie in the byways of history. Such are the fortunes of war.

ADVENT OF WAR

As the war slowly approached, the Nagas could only wait, not knowing what might happen. They had some knowledge of the power of the gun because of wars they had fought with the British Colonial Army. They could guess it would be a terrible war, but beyond that they had little comprehension.

The first real inkling of the approaching war the Nagas got were through the arrival of the refugees from Burma which started in 1942 after the Japanese took over that country. With the passage of time, the flow of refugees increased. And by early 1944, it was in full flow.

According to K. N. Pusha, a respected leader from Viswema Village, who was about 18 years old at the time, many of the refugees died along the way from starvation and exhaustion. But many also made it to Dimapur and Assam. The 'Burma Camp' colony in Dimapur was where many of these Burmese refugees were resettled, hence the name, which is still in use today. Neilao of Kohima Village recounted the events thus:

We saw a lot of refugees from Burma dying or dead on the way. They were carried in by trucks and roped off on the way. They began to walk from where they had been left by the trucks and we saw that they had walked the flesh off their feet. Their bleeding feet were bound with rags. But many died so they were buried below the (present) Naga Bazaar church and they weren't properly buried so the jackals came and dug the bodies out and ate them. We saw them dead on the roadside as well. This was just before the Japanese came to our land and we called it the Burmese Retreat. These refugees were deposited at different places, at Sokriezie, at the DC's office ... and near the Hospital (Khate et al. 57–58).

Slowly, as the war crept nearer and nearer to them, the Nagas began to get news of the fighting going on. But they did not know what to do or how to prepare for it since they had no earlier experience of this nature. Most people interviewed said they did not do anything. Only a handful said they had buried some rice and smoked meat in the forest as their secret stash. On the whole, they simply waited.

The Pochuri/Meluri Nagas and some Kuki tribesmen were among the first to encounter the Japanese on the Nagaland side while the Tangkhuls, followed by Poumai and Mao, did so on the Manipur side. Some other Naga tribes like the Chang and Khiamniungan did have some experience of the war but they did not lie in the direct route of the Japanese Army's march to Kohima. Following the battles at Kharasom and Jessami, the Nagas in Phek, Chizami and Zhamai (now Zhavame) were among the first to encounter the Japanese in the Chakhesang area. Among the Angami in the vicinity of Kohima, Khuzama and Viswema villages were the first to encounter the Japanese.

K. N. Pusha recollected, 'On 2nd April, 1944, retreating British troops from Imphal side, reached Viswema. They stopped here and scanned the horizon towards Mao and Chakhesang side through their binoculars and then proceeded towards Kohima. Next morning, when we got up, we found the Japanese already in our village! I saw their uniforms were clean and their skin was fair. The same morning, they marched for Kohima.'

As the 1st Assam Regiment had vacated their post at Jessami

only on 2 April, it would appear that these Japanese soldiers at Viswema were not the same as those who fought at Jessami but had come from the Imphal–Mao side, most probably from Ukhrul and Gaziphema, even from Kanglatongbi, all north of Imphal. Corroborating this view, 85-year-old Neikhwere Noho of Kezoma Village (next to Chakhabama) said the Japanese came from the Mao–Maram side. Around the same time, 84-year-old Heuzieteusing Rao of Poilwa village, south-west of Kohima, said about 3,000 Japanese troops, along with INA soldiers, had appeared at their village, crossing the Barak River from the Manipur side. Such a route was possible through Maram, south of Mao, and away from the Jessami–Kohima direct route.

What appeared clear was that the Japanese were totally focused on reaching Kohima as quickly as possible and starting the war there. According to Pusha, the Japanese started for Kohima on the morning of 3 April without taking rest. Apparently, they reached Kohima the same day because from available accounts, (including in Fergal Keane's *Road of Bones*), we know that the first encounter between the Japanese and a British patrol took place at Aradura (Kohima) on the night of 3 April 1944. The next day, April 4, the Battle of Kohima began with the Japanese attack on General Purposes Transport (GPT) Ridge, just above the present official residence of the State Chief Minister, where an Assam Rifles camp was located.

Obviously, leaving rear troops to take over and consolidate the villages in between, the Japanese had frog-marched to Kohima. Corroborating this possibility are accounts of the people of the area. For instance, the Japanese arrived in Jakhama, just a stone's throw away from Viswema, only after the party for Kohima had left. Some villagers say the Japanese came to Jakhama on 3 April while others say on the 4th. Similarly, they arrived in Kigwema, Mima, etc., all very close-by southern Angami villages, on 4 April. Likewise, on the east of Kohima, from the Chakhesang side, the Japanese arrived at Cheswezu on 3 April and Chedema the next day. They appeared in other northern Angami villages later.

The Japanese had approached Kohima from south, east and west; the north side was towards Dimapur, which was not possible. And soon the British 2nd Division, which reached Dimapur on 4 April, would arrive and set up headquarters at Zubza, covering and cutting off the northern routes towards Dimapur. The old Bokajan route, across the Dzüdza River, to the east, was still open and was used by a battalion of the Japanese 138th Regiment to march towards Dimapur on 8 April, before they were recalled.

Meanwhile, at Viswema, the Japanese established their ration/supply headquarters at Mr Vinol's house, adjacent to the Dimapur–Imphal Road. Nearby villages would bring their paddy and other foodstuff to this place. At the next village, Jakhama, Lieutenant General Kotoku Sato, Commander of the 31st Division, set up his headquarters at Sokhaphezu, then a thickly forested area believed by the villagers to be haunted. Throughout the Kohima campaign, this would be General Sato's headquarters. Viswema and Jakhama were the villages from where the Japanese printed their wartime paper money according to local accounts. The denominations were 50 paise (note) and rupees 1, 2, 5 and 10.

According to Pukoho Rol (Rolnu), a respected elder of Jakhama, and one of the first teachers in the area, the Japanese were obsessed with the idea of reaching Kohima as quickly as possible and starting the war in Kohima, their obvious objective. He also heard the Japanese say, 'Tomorrow Kohima finish, overcome Khonoma!' The mention of Khonoma, he said, was obviously because the Japanese had heard of the 1879–1880 Battle of Khonoma against the British where the first Victoria Cross in north-east India was awarded to Captain Richard Kirby Ridgeway of the Bengal Staff Corps.

EARLY NAGA REACTIONS

On the whole, Naga reaction was one of incredulity, incomprehension and fear. For instance, how do you react when you get up one fine morning and find your village completely overwhelmed

with Japanese soldiers, as happened in Viswema? Or when 3,000-
plus fully armed fighting soldiers descend on your village of probably 100 households or less as happened at Poilwa? In Cheswezu
Village, Besuveyi Swuro says, 'When we first saw the Japanese arrive, they looked like an army of ants!' In Kigwema Village, someone shouted, 'The whole forest is moving! So many of them have
come!' According to Viketu Kiso, a scout for the British, 'Men
poured out of the tree copses, from behind every rock and green
plant … the Japanese soldiers with guns out-thrust, they made a
terrifying sight …' In most cases, quiet submission and cooperation were the only ways out. In many villages, there was no time
to react as the Japanese were 'rushing' to Kohima, leaving other
troops following them to take over the villages.

Even the British, with all the intelligence at their disposal and
months of planning, found themselves ill-prepared. The scene in
Kohima was one of utter chaos. The civil and particularly the military authorities were confused and unsure and often worked at
cross-purposes. Just as the Japanese were approaching Kohima,
the British Army was withdrawn to guard the Dimapur stores.
This almost cost the British the loyalty of the Nagas.

According to Khriezotuo Sachü, retired educator from Kohima
Village, 'When the Japanese were almost reaching Kohima, the
British Army left, leaving the Nagas to face the Japanese. The
Nagas felt betrayed and felt that they could not trust the British
any more. So, many people started leaving Kohima to seek shelter
in nearby villages.'

Luckily for the British and Allied Forces the unflinching stand
of the then Deputy Commissioner, C. R. Pawsey, not to abandon Kohima and 'his Nagas', earned the loyalty of the people and
saved the day for the British because all the 'dobashis' decided
to stay with him. The other government servants also remained
steadfast in their loyalty.

NAGA ATTITUDE AND POSITION

How did the Nagas view the war and position themselves? In recent times, some may give the impression that all the Nagas supported the British and this helped the Allied Forces to win. This is true to the extent that the vast majority of the Nagas sided with the British. There were many Nagas who looked on the British favourably. Those who went to France as part of the Naga Labour Corps during the First World War and their descendants who were serving the British Government at the time were loyal. The return of what was due to the men of the Labour Corps, long after their return home, without a single rupee coin missing, had created a very favourable image of the British among the Nagas, as the stories soon spread. Evidently, the power of money had arrived among the Nagas, giving those who had it greater influence in the society.

But as a people, the Nagas had no position in the war and remained neutral. Many also helped the Japanese. The Nagas had little or no reason to fight for the British. Battles with the British colonialists, hardly a generation ago, were still fresh in their minds, and the relationship was in a 'blow-hot, blow-cold' state. And they had no reason to fight for the Japanese who they had never before encountered. As was his custom the Naga only fought and killed identified enemies for specific reasons. If someone insulted him or brought death to his family and kin, vengeance was the only answer he knew. In such situations, he could be duplicitous and would employ all the worst in human character. But if someone was good to him, he would be good to that person. And, if someone was loyal to him, he would be ready to go the extra mile, even sacrifice his life for that person, as had happened in the case of Deputy Commissioner Pawsey. But as far as the Second World War was concerned, the Naga thought it had nothing to do with his world. He was neutral and had simply got caught in this terrible war.

This neutral position was the main reason why when the Japanese first arrived the Nagas were good to them. There was fear too, of course. But in Naga culture, a stranger in their midst could be an enemy but was also a potential friend. And it was clear that the Naga villagers initially provided food and shelter to the Japanese when they entered their villages. Sadly, because of the desperate situation of the Japanese and probably partly because of cultural differences, Naga feelings of empathy for them were often not returned. Their rude and sometimes even atrocious behaviour became unacceptable. This was the ultimate point of rupture and departure in Naga–Japanese relations in the 'Battle of Kohima'.

What turned the tide in British favour? It was mainly the one, single act of friendship by C. R. Pawsey, rendered in the language the Nagas understood. The Japanese approach towards Kohima was an uncertain time, indeed a momentous and fear-filled time. The British Army had left, abandoning the Nagas to their fate with the Japanese. Many Nagas, disappointed with the British, left Kohima to seek shelter in nearby villages. The only remaining fatherlike British figure, Deputy Commissioner C. R. Pawsey, declared in no uncertain terms that he would not leave Kohima. He would not abandon the Nagas. All the Naga dobashis (interpreters) and other government servants spontaneously responded in typical Naga fashion, and to a man stayed with him, determined to face his fate come what may.

At the heart of the Naga support to the British (as opposed to the Allied Forces), because of Pawsey, were the salaried Naga government servants, who represented a new social stratum, earlier unknown in Naga society but nevertheless powerful because of the money they earned! This money, plus proximity to the seat of power, gave the dobashis and other salaried employees of the government, influence over other Nagas. They were of course men of influence in their village communities to start with. The fact that almost every village had at least one dobashi helped to carry their collective influence to every corner of the administered Naga areas. When the dobashis and other Naga employees decided to help the British, this was no mean support. Added to this structural advantage was the support of those who had served in the Labour Corps during the First World War and their descendants, as mentioned above. Furthermore, the Naga educated class were supportive of Pawsey because of his efforts to bring the disparate Naga tribes together. Before such a phalanx, even the Naga Nationalist leader Zapuphizo, later crowned 'the Father of the Naga Nation', found himself helpless in his effort to get Nagas to help the Japanese and throw out the British colonialists.

As Thepfülhouvi Angami IFS, former Principal Chief Conservator of Forests, Nagaland Government, explaining Naga support for the British, said, 'Their friends' war became their war!' The life of the Naga was simple and largely uncomplicated. He did not like complications.

WORKS CITED

Government of Nagaland. *Heralding Hope: 125 Years of Kohima.* Kohima: Govt of Nagaland, 2004.

KET. *Kohima: An Exploration of War, Memory and Gratitude.* DVD, 2017.

Khate et al. *Battle of Kohima.* Kohima: Ura Academy, 2007.

Ltu, Khrienuo. 'World War II in North East India: A Study of Imphal and Kohima Battles', Unpublished Paper, 2014.

Lyman, R. *Japan's Last Bid for Victory: The Invasion of India, 1944.* South Yorkshire: The Praetorian Press, 2011.

_____. *Kohima 1944: The Battle that Saved India.* Oxford: Osprey Publishing Ltd, 2010.

Nibedon, N. *Nagaland: The Night of the Guerrillas.* New Delhi: Lancers Publication, 1978.

Personal interviews of Naga Individuals. Nagaland: 2016–2017.

Swinson, A. *Kohima.* London: Arrow Book Ltd, 1956.

TWO

NAGAS UNDER OCCUPATION AND RELATIONS WITH THE JAPANESE

As the Japanese descended on village after village, most villagers fled to the jungles and/or their fields, afraid to stay behind. Large numbers of villagers were also caught unawares. For instance, according to Vimedo Rutsa, many from Kohima Village were working in their fields when the Japanese arrived. Messages were sent to them in their fields not to return to their homes but to seek shelter in nearby villages. So, with just the clothes on their backs, they made their way to other villages closest to them.

The long period of living through the war began for the Nagas. From interviews of elders, accounts in village after village said the Japanese were polite when they first arrived. They tried to make friends with the Naga people. In many instances, they tried to point out the racial affinity between the Nagas and the Japanese, stressing that the British were so different. They said they had come to liberate the Nagas and promised much economic development after they won the war – the same pitch was made by the INA. However, because their supplies were slow in coming they requested the Nagas to help them with food stocks. They said this was only a 'temporary requirement' until their food supplies arrived.

Initially, the Japanese paid for whatever they took in their own (war) currency which, of course, was useless. Nevertheless, the gesture was appreciated. The villagers gave whatever they could. This was a part of the season when the villagers were still having enough food stock from the last harvest and feeling generous. But when the requirement from each village, having to feed several times the usual population, stretched on week after week, and there seemed no end to it, it became unsustainable. Besides, the Japanese requirement was not just paddy/rice. They needed meat, vegetables, and so many other resources which were scarce even for the village population. Normal life for the villagers came to a standstill. They quickly found that their entire occupation had become one of trying to help and sustain the Japanese soldiers. In some villages, the village authorities organized a rota for different khels/clans to perform various functions such as providing and pounding paddy, picking wild vegetables, etc. The rota was done mainly so that the villagers could have a little respite, in turns, to do their own work in order to survive. But often this objective became redundant because the Japanese would force anyone they found to do porter duty, carrying ammunition and supplies.

Meanwhile, as the Japanese 'temporary requirement' of food-stuff kept stretching longer and longer, their promise to the Nagas for development after they won the war seemed too far off to make a difference in the present situation. But what was even worse was the continued relentless fighting and bombardment of Naga villages by the British. Most homes were bombed out or burnt. Many were killed; many others injured or maimed. Food stocks ran out and life became very difficult. Politeness soon disappeared and harsh reality set in on all sides. Hunger and losses in the war initiative exacerbated Japanese behaviour. As the Japanese became more extreme and arbitrary, the Naga villagers increasingly resented their attitude and turned against them.

Some comments are given below about the situation the Nagas faced.

Zhovire, of Jakhama Village, was about 11 years old when the Japanese came, led by a long-haired officer (identified by some villagers as General Shiroki, 'the man in charge of the administration'). According to Zhovire:

*After they had camped in the village, they came to the houses
... and asked for food ... Some of the soldiers were so famished
they ate the gruel meant for the pigs ... [Nagas usually boiled/
cooked pig food]. Everyday ... people pounded paddy grain for
the Japanese and steadily grew rebellious. One of these women
had her hands covered with blisters from the daily pounding
of grain. She also had to clean the grain before giving it to the
soldiers. In anger, one day, she stopped cleaning the rice and
muttered, 'Eat the husk too and choke on it'. (Interview)*

Zhovire also said, 'Apart from the soldiers, the horses had to be
fed regularly and women watched with tears in their eyes as their
granaries were emptied for horse feed! In anger, some villagers
started to secretly kill the horses.'

Vingotsore Natso of Jakhama Village was around 20 years old.
She used to help the family by herding cattle, besides doing all the
other work womenfolk usually did. She remembers carrying paddy three times to Viswema, the Japanese ration headquarters in
the southern Angami area. She said that as the village was living
under Japanese occupation, with General Sato's own HQ set up
there, the village authorities had set up a rota for different clans
and khels to carry out different responsibilities. Supplying paddy
and livestock, vegetables, labour, etc., were the main tasks. The
Japanese became very fond of the local tobacco and consumed
even the stems and stumps.

Vingotsore was not happy with the Japanese. 'I was angry when
the Japanese started doing whatever they liked with our food
stocks and took them whenever they liked. But I was really hurt
when they fed my entire standing crops to their horses – crops
that were meant to feed my family for a year. Taking food from
starving people and feeding animals is incomprehensible to us
and considered an extreme taboo!'

Her husband, Nohol Natso, was a driver and mechanic for the
British and for a time lived at the British motor vehicle workshop.
When the Japanese arrived, the British left. Nohol was still under
British employ, and was loyal to them, but he said, 'What to do,

we had to learn to be friends with both British and Japanese in order to survive!' He still vividly remembered his days with the British as well as the Japanese. He said, 'When British planes flew over us, Japanese soldiers would come and hold us tightly so that there was no movement. They said if there is no movement the pilots cannot see us.' Nohol was part of the Naga delegation to the Allied Victory Parade in Delhi in 1945. He proudly shows the Naga delegation's photo of the occasion to visitors.

Pukoho Rolnu said there was a case where a Jakhama person got very angry when Japanese horses ate all the grain in his fields. He complained. But the Japanese seemed to be solely interested in asserting their authority, and they decided to punish him and make him an example. Some leaders of the village pleaded with the Japanese authorities saying the man was a psychologically disturbed person and not to be too harsh on him. 'That was how his life was spared!'

Besuvei Swuro, a respected elder of Cheswezu Village, just above Chietheba, in the Chakhesang area, well-known as 'the friend of Subhas Chandra Bose', said: 'In the beginning the Japanese were polite but later they became difficult. Apart from taking paddy, they killed a lot of cattle and killing pigs was an everyday affair. When food became scarce, they would sometimes line up the villagers and make them kneel, threatening to behead them. Some villagers would challenge them to do it. Luckily, only one man was actually killed.'

In Khonoma Village, in the western Angami area, the Japanese were not there for long. They arrived at Khonoma on their way to Pulie Badze, Jotsoma, from Poilwa. Some Japanese soldiers also went to Mezoma and Secü Village, just above Zubza (now Secü-Zubza town), where they fought the British soldiers and withdrew. But most villagers in Khonoma had left the village to live in the jungle in 'camps'. One woman who stayed in the village lamented, 'A Japanese soldier came and took away my hen that was sitting on her eggs, about to hatch!'

In Rüsoma Village, northern Angami area, the Japanese were entering people's homes and taking whatever they wanted. In one home, the family hid the rice under a chair and put a pumpkin on top. A Japanese soldier bayoneted the pumpkin and took it away with him. The head of the family muttered, 'Eat that and die early!' In another incident in the same village, the villagers complained to the Japanese officer because killing their cattle had become too much for them to tolerate. The officer, who was staying in the Gaonbura's house, punished the guilty soldiers. But that same night, the soldiers came and shot their officer dead. Next morning, the villagers buried the officer's body.

In nearby Jotsoma Village, both Japanese and British soldiers held great strategic positions. The Japanese because of their position on Pulie Badze peak, and the British through Warren's 161st Brigade and their 12 field guns which were located on the lower side of the village near where General Grover's memorial now stands. Jotsoma became a kind of last resort battleground for both sides. For the British, Jotsoma was the staging ground to relieve Kohima. For the Japanese, having abandoned their attack on Secü Village, above Zubza, and their 8 April march to Dimapur on the old Bokajan Road from Meriema/Chieswema, on the opposite bank, the only high ground they now held to do battle for the Kohima Ridge was Pulie Badze. The loss of Pulie Badze in the second week of June signalled the end of the Japanese in Kohima.

Savito Nagi has detailed Naga narratives from village after village as the Japanese entered them. His book titled *Kijürü Kenieu Nu Kohima Rhüu Rükralakeshü* (Remembering the Battle of Kohima in the Second World War) runs somewhat on the lines of Julian Thompson's *Forgotten Voices of Burma: The Second World War's Forgotten Conflict*.

NAGA–JAPANESE RELATIONS

With all of the above going on, one can imagine what Naga–Japanese relations were like. All over the Naga areas, the Nagas first accommodated the Japanese, partly because of fear and because this was their way of receiving any guest. There was evidently much goodwill for the Japanese in some areas. The Naga

Nationalist leader, A. Z. Phizo, had apparently already made a pact with the Japanese in Burma to help them in return for Japanese help to throw out the British from the Naga Hills. So when the Japanese arrived, they spoke about both Nagas and Japanese being of Mongoloid stock and that they would help the Nagas to regain independence from the British. Another propaganda in use at the time was that the Japanese were the elder brothers of the Nagas. What may be more relevant was that villages like Meriema and Viswema had stories about being related to the Japanese. This was reflected in the reception given to the Japanese when they arrived. The INA too tried to turn the Nagas against the British, but this did not make much headway because the Nagas generally did not like the plains people and felt no affinity with them. Moreover, their bad behaviour, in several cases, would soon turn the Nagas against them.

Meanwhile, stories of some early encounters with Japanese soldiers are interesting. For instance, in Pfütsero, Neikhalo Kapfo, a retired teacher said, 'The Japanese arrived on a day when the age-groups were having a feast. When the young men heard of the arrival of the Japanese, a few of them hurriedly ran off to help carry their loads. But soon, they came back having received severe beatings from the Japanese soldiers! Apparently, inability to communicate one's intention was the reason.'

Mrs Kapfo related another incident. Some Japanese soldiers were trying to kill a pig. The owner, a woman, tried to protect her animal. The soldiers behaved rudely towards her. The woman went and complained to the commander whereupon the CO lined up his soldiers and in front of the villagers, publicly punished the culprit soldiers.

In Chedema Village, a stone's throw away from Kohima, Khetso Pienyü was about 30 years old when the Japanese arrived. 'The Japanese said we were all Mongoloid people and asked us to help them. Some Nagas also said the Japanese were our older brothers. So I used to help them, even staying in their camp for days at a time.' He did this despite the vast majority of his villagers supporting the British. But in spite of his sympathy for the Japanese and the help he actually gave them, Khetso did not hesitate to confront a Japanese officer when he showed bad faith. One morning a Japanese officer came and asked for rice indicating that he would pay for it. So Khetso gave him some rice (about 3 kilograms), but after receiving the rice the officer showed no inclination to pay. Khetso got angry and wrestled the Japanese officer to the ground. He then forcibly took the money/insignia which the Japanese officer had shown him initially as payment. Years later, he felt contrite that he had forcefully taken money from a man in a desperate position. He tried to return the things he took from the Japanese officer through a Naga who was travelling to Japan. In Naga society, a man could always be traced through the name of his village where everyone knew everyone and Khetso thought this might be possible in the Japanese case too. According to his son, Kelhoulevo, headmaster of a school, several mementoes were brought back including a Japanese fan and a piece of cloth with Japanese writing on it which greatly moved them. Sadly, all these have been lost.

In nearby Meriema, the villagers even welcomed the Japanese soldiers with a basket of eggs, symbolic of great friendship. Here, for some reason, the villagers believed they had kinship with the Japanese people. Prior to that, it was reported that in many villages, the Japanese had asked where Meriema was. Meriema, of course, was strategically positioned opposite Zubza and a long stretch of the Dimapur–Imphal Road. They placed their field guns here to fire on the Allied vehicles coming up the road. The Japanese had three camps in the village.

Unlike most other villages, where the soldiers had their own camps, it appeared that in Mima many Japanese soldiers were billeted in homes, with the villagers feeding and looking after them like any guests. According to Vimese Tsochü, who hosted four Japanese (his father hosted another), 'Our relationship was very cordial and there was never any unpleasantness. My guests used to go and fight in Kohima during the night and return in the morning. One of them even claimed he killed a lot of British Indian soldiers with his sword. They would sometimes sing to us and teach us 1–2–3 in Japanese. The doctor gave medicines to the villagers before leaving while the Japanese (military) Commander Hamoto gave our family a shirt as a memento.'

In Poilwa Village, Heuzieteusing Rao was about 12 years old and used to collect hay for the Japanese. He recalled being paid for his efforts. Incredulity and shock were the first reactions when about 3,000 Japanese troops plus Indian National Army (INA) soldiers descended on their village, crossing the Barak River from the Manipur side. He recalled with some glee that when the Japanese first arrived, they did not know what 'zu', the Naga rice beer, was. Of course, when they realized what it was they took to the drink with zest. Likewise, he said some Japanese soldiers at first did not know the stinging nettle plant. He saw a Japanese soldier, who had obviously been stung by it, calling a number of his comrades and making them touch the plant. The first soldier, naturally, was laughing his head off! But the British were not far behind and soon started bombing the village. INA soldiers told them to dig bunkers/trenches and hide. This they had never done before. Nor had they needed to in the kind of warfare they were used to.

In Kohima Village, Khriezotuo Sachü, retired educationist, found the Japanese curious and was pleasantly surprised. 'We had heard about Japanese atrocities before their arrival. But when they came they were surprisingly pleasant and polite to our people. They asked for our help and offered to pay for everything. Naturally, our people helped them.'

But others in Kohima Village had different views. According to Noumvüo Khruomo, the night the war began they buried their grain and fled to their fields. But soon they learned that, 'The Japanese were eating our grain and they killed and ate our domestic animals while the British threw firebombs and torched our village.'

According to Neilhou Dzüvichü, who was around 24 years old at the time, 'The Japanese were very cruel to us. They killed our pigs and chickens and they ate our grain … They killed people and they frequently took men away to carry their loads.' He was a porter to both the British and Japanese.

In some villages where members were in the British India Army, particularly in the newly established Assam Regiment, the Naga–Japanese relations were sometimes not cordial even if there had been no village community decision taken as such. This was because the Naga soldiers fought as soldiers on the enemy side. In Phek Village, for instance, Sepoy Zashei (Huire), later President of the Naga Federal Government, led Japanese soldiers into an ambush. Likewise, Sepoy Pungoi of Porba Village, originally from another village but teaching in Porba at the time, did the same at Sakraba Village. Both of them received gallantry awards from the British.

Khusoi of Porba Village, a respected Chakhesang elder, was a young boy at the time and often accompanied Sepoy Pungoi. He would also visit the Japanese camp on his own. According to him, there was a bonus to visiting the Japanese camp. He would find the Japanese soldiers killing the cattle and pigs of the villagers. But they would not eat the entrails and threw them away. These were delicacies for the Nagas and he would carry them away to feast on them with his family.

In Phesama Village, as at Pfütsero, the Japanese officer in charge, a Colonel, maintained strict discipline. Upon discovery of a soldier behaving improperly, and a commotion taking place, 'The Colonel ... quickly surmised that the soldier was at fault ... the burly Colonel angrily picked him up and ... flung him through the air to land in a heap on the ground.' With such disciplining, 'Incidents of soldiers misbehaving were few and far between ...'

In many places, when the British came, the Japanese would pretend to be Nagas. Pastor Kiezotuo said, 'There were so many Japanese soldiers in our village (Rüsoma), but if the British came, they pretended to be Nagas and would ask our ... clothes so they could cover themselves ... and look like us.'

There was even a romantic story in Rüsoma. According to Pastor Kiezotuo, a very handsome Japanese officer started living with a young Naga woman named Rüzeü. They did not know each other's languages and communicated through sign language. The Japanese officer stopped wearing his military uniform and cut his hair in the Naga style. 'He was a very nice man. He would make the children play the high jump and then give money to the one who jumped the highest. Rüzeü addressed him in her tongue and he spoke in his. But they were happy together.' They did not have children. This Japanese officer went to fight in nearby Dihoma Village and never returned. According to Mhalelie Vimera, a village elder, this Japanese officer was Iwaichi Fujiwara. He said that, before Iwaichi left, he had told Rüzeü to wait for him and that he would come back for her. Rüzeü lived to a ripe old age and died only about four years ago. Iwaichi Fujiwara was the intelligence chief to the 15th Japanese Imperial Army and Operation U-Go under General Mutaguchi. Through his F. Kikan, a special unit he established to encourage independence movements in British India, Malaya and East Indies, Iwaichi was instrumental in setting up the Indian National Army (INA). He was one of the very few to make the transition to post-war Japanese Ground Self-Defence Force and retired in 1964 as Lieutenant General.

But as Japanese cruelty towards the Naga villagers increased, and British generosity and supply of rations continued, the Nagas turned more and more pro-British which made the Japanese even more desperate. As Japanese war correspondent Yukihiko Imai would report, 'As soon as we reached a village we caught the women and children and locked them up. We then asked the menfolk to guide us to the next village, promising to release their families as soon as they had done so.' This, not surprisingly, did not earn the friendship of the Nagas. On the other hand, it roused the Naga sense of honour and vengeance. The Japanese were often given wrong information or led into ambushes. Some even joined the Japanese deliberately to report to the British, as did two members of Ursula Graham Bower's team in north Cachar.

Colvin even wrote about 'a Naga, probably an Assam Rifleman

who was in the bunker, delighted in going out by himself for several hours each night, returning at first light with a wide grin to show his trophy of Japanese ears threaded on to his bayonet.'

In Jakhama Village, where General Sato had his HQ, people cited an instance of a public beheading of a British officer who had been taken captive. As most villagers had not seen a public beheading earlier, out of curiosity, many went to witness the execution. As the sword went through his neck, blood gushed out and much of it splashed the Japanese officer who had executed him. With a show of distaste, and muttering to himself, he wiped the blood away. According to Pukoho, 'The blood of the victim splattering the executioner was a bad omen and the people felt the Japanese were going to lose the war!'

According to Razhukhül Kechü, son of Vinol (in whose house in Viswema Village the Japanese had set up their 'ration headquarters' for the southern Angami area and where Japanese war money was also printed), it was General Sato himself who had beheaded the British officer. He said General Sato had first asked two of his Naga interpreters, Visar Angami of Jakhama (later NNC President) and Vipratso Pusa of Viswema, to do it, but when they refused he himself carried out the beheading. Razhukhül said this was told to him by his elders.

As Japanese atrocities and bad behaviour mounted to intolerable levels, even the Naga civilian dobashis for the British and ordinary Nagas everywhere became very active in reporting Japanese movements and also started capturing, and even killing them.

The reports on Japanese given to the British by Nikhalhu Makritsu and Zhuikhu Zhimomi, two 'dobashis' (interpreters) at Piphema, were typical and won them both the coveted British Empire Medal (BEM). Author Asoso Yonuo, in his book *The Rising Nagas*, said that at one point the Nagas had the distinction of having captured more Japanese than the entire Fourteenth Army.

The dobashi network and general Naga support for the British became so powerful that the Japanese could not do a single thing, or go anywhere, without the British knowing about it. According to Havildar Zhavise Vihienuo: 'As people got fed up of the pestering for food by Japanese soldiers, they began to report their every movement to the British. This made it impossible for the Japanese to fight back.'

But there was also, among the Nagas, great respect for the Japanese ability to survive and fight. Havildar Sovehu Nienu, 1st Assam Regiment, who fought the Japanese at Jessami, Pulie Badze and all the way to Burma, was of the opinion that: 'The Japanese were really great fighters. If their supplies had come, they would probably have won the war!' There were other Nagas who thought similarly.

Pukoho Rolnu of Jakhama, who was the first Naga vocational teacher at John High School, Viswema, said: 'The Japanese became cruel and our people turned against them. But we must understand that desperate people begin to do desperate things. I have even seen them eat plants which our people considered poisonous. They would add a 'medicine' and consume it. I think their medicine was very powerful.' Similar expressions were made by others.

NAGA SITUATION

Meanwhile, most Nagas were themselves not in much better position than the Japanese soldiers were during the war. Fortunately, there was no report of any deaths from starvation. Most Nagas lived either in the jungles or in their field huts, fearing to stay in the villages. Those who stayed in their villages were pestered to an extreme extent. Others had to seek shelter in various villages as refugees. Food stocks were no longer available; their cattle and domestic animals and fowls were consumed by the Japanese soldiers. Luckily for the Naga, he was used to the forest and knew what was edible. What further helped was the Naga ability to eat most things that might make some people puke! His knowledge of herbal medicines, too, was extensive. They would frequently eat raw whatever food they could find. And there was a shortage of salt which sometimes caused complications and sickness. There were reports in some areas of much suffering due to diarrhoea, dysentery, typhoid and so on.

The arrival of the British 2nd Division, and the headquarters they set up at Zubza, made it possible for the British to offer shelter and food provisions to the Naga villagers who were asked to move to western Angami villages. Most did so quite quickly although this meant displacement and abandonment of their ancestral homes, fields and villages, a rupture no person would undertake willingly, and certainly it was most difficult for Nagas whose identity was tied to their village and ancestral home.

Internal displacement, as can be expected, was very high. For instance, people from almost the entire southern Angami area, and many northern Angami villagers, moved to western Angami villages for protection and food. Daily rations were distributed, particularly at Teiziepe (Teizie bridge), over the Dzüdza River, for those staying in nearby villages like Jotsoma, Khonoma and Mezoma. Without British rations, the Naga situation would surely have been so much worse.

JAPANESE ATTITUDE TOWARDS WOMEN

The overall Japanese attitude towards Naga women was a real curiosity, quite different from the stories one had heard about their behaviour further east before their arrival in the Naga Hills.

In village after village, those interviewed said the Japanese did not misbehave with Naga women. It must be kept in mind that the general man-woman relationship in Tenyimia Naga society – largely the route taken by the Japanese Army from Burma to Kohima – was and is quite free and open, although what was considered inappropriate would be visited with severe strictures and punishment. The story told above of Rüzeü and the Japanese officer at Rüsoma Village is a case in point.

Zhovire of Jakhama said he 'noticed that the Japanese soldiers studiously avoided the presence of (Naga) women. Japanese soldiers trying to enter a house would retreat if they saw women in the courtyard. One soldier halted in his tracks when he saw a young woman at the doorway of the house he wanted to enter. Muttering to himself, he retraced his steps.'

What we did encounter in many places were reports about a meeting of Naga Nationalist leader, A. Z. Phizo, and his brother Keviyalie, with the Japanese in Burma in 1943. Khrienuo Ltu writes: 'Phizo and his brother agreed to help the Japanese without financial assistance. The Japanese in return gave a guarantee to safeguard the independence of Nagaland ...' Whether such a pact included good Japanese behaviour towards Naga women is not clear. But Japanese behaviour during the entire time they were in the Naga Hills was quite remarkable in this area, particularly given their reputation elsewhere.

There were, naturally, exceptions although in most cases, the perpetrators turned out to be those accompanying the Japanese. According to an interviewee, there was a suspected case in southern Angami of a Naga woman giving birth to a Japanese child. But the people did not make an issue of it because the woman concerned was said to be psychologically disturbed. In northern Angami, there were probably a few cases. In Kohima itself, there was a report that, 'Some Japanese soldiers even started sleeping with the women.' One case that has already been published is that of Neiputhie Rutsa, a leader of Kohima Village, involving an INA soldier. Neiputhie was away in another village while his wife and mother were working in their paddy fields, on the banks of the Dzü-ü River, staying in their 'pru' (field hut), like most other Nagas at the time. Some INA soldiers assaulted them and tried to rape his wife. His mother started shouting for help. She was shot dead. As a warrior, and in Naga tradition, Neiputhie was said to have wreaked his vengeance on the Japanese, obviously holding them responsible, by taking about a half dozen Japanese heads. He even brought a severed Japanese head as proof to show British authorities what he had done!

JAPANESE WOMEN SOLDIERS

According to several accounts, there were 'women soldiers' who accompanied the invading Japanese Army. These women wore military uniform, 'with short hair like the men' and carried guns, although their guns were much shorter than those carried by the men.

How did the Nagas become aware of the presence of women in the Japanese Army?

In a Chakhesang area, there was the story of two friends having an argument. One expressed his surprise that there were Japanese women soldiers. His friend was sure there were none. The first friend said, 'But I saw her breasts!' This silenced the latter.

In Viswema Village, K. N. Pusha said the villagers became aware that some soldiers were women when these women took off their outer shirts and started pounding paddy!

In Jakhama, where General Sato had his headquarters, Pukoho Rolnu said that the villagers first became aware of the presence of Japanese women soldiers when the villagers saw them bathing! According to Zhovire, the women were separately put up in Nizol's house.

In Mima Village, out of the four Japanese hosted by Vimese Tsochü's family there were 'two women soldiers named Matinu and Hokhinu.' According to Vimese, both the men and women wore military khaki uniforms but their shoes were different. They were all accepted and hosted like any other guests. At night, their beds were made on bamboo mats (*tsopie/zoprie*), the same mats which were used for drying paddy. Did he see any behaviour that may be considered inappropriate or interpreted as intimate when they were in his house? Vimese was confident there was no such thing. Of course, he did not know anything about what may or may not have transpired during the day after they left the house in the morning. But he had no suspicions.

In Kohima, too, their presence was first noticed when two Japanese soldiers went into the bush to pee. Elsewhere, in the east towards Burma, there were stories of some Japanese women who could not keep up with the rest and had to be carried by Naga porters. In many villages, however, the presence of women in the Japanese Army was unknown.

A little indiscretion was observed in Kigwema Village when a villager witnessed Japanese soldiers sleeping with the women who accompanied them. According to Viketu Kiso: 'Some soldiers among them slept with women and shot at sleeping pigs and missed them! So some elders said " … what kind of war are you going to fight when you cannot even shoot a sleeping pig?"' In Naga tradition, sexual relations were taboo during war and both the warriors and their womenfolk would remain chaste lest they displease God and bring his wrath on to themselves.

Were these really Japanese women or part of the infamous 'comfort women' for which the Japanese have been hauled over the coals in places like China and Korea? Or could they be Burmese women or some other South-East Asian nationalities? People like Vimese Tsochü, who saw them at close quarters and observed everything about them including their communications, insist these were Japanese women and not from other nationalities. In the Chakhesang areas, some people were quite convinced that these women were Japanese. They remarked, 'The only difference between the men and the women was that the women were fairer than the men.'

Some inquiries with Japanese friends about whether there were women soldiers in the Japanese Imperial Army during the Second World War have elicited negative answers or ignorance about it.

SOME JAPANESE PECULIARITIES NAGAS SAW

It would be presumptuous for anyone to talk about another people, particularly one that was a stranger, and while engaged in a war. There is no claim that what follows was universally practised by even all the Japanese soldiers who were in the Naga areas during the war. Different villages also had different experiences. These are just a few personal observations of individual Naga elders who saw the war, and were kind enough to share their experiences as these would be of immense interest to younger Naga generations today.

According to Khetso Pienyü, the Japanese were expert skinners of animals. They would not only skin cattle but even pigs, which Nagas never do. Nagas carefully clean the dirty outer layer. The skin of pigs and cows are included in the Naga pot after being chopped into smaller pieces, roasted and cleaned thoroughly; leather-making was not a Naga tradition. Khetso went on to say, 'When Nagas kill cattle, we normally use grass or something else beneath to prevent the meat from getting dirty. When the Japanese kill an animal, the skin becomes the layer between the ground and the meat. And they do it so quickly and smoothly!'

As to the animal parts they consumed, it was uniformly said that the Japanese did not eat the entrails of the animals they killed. In Poilwa, Heuzieteusing Rao said the Japanese did not even eat the fat of pigs but used it as 'oil' for their guns and other purposes. In Chedema, Khetso said they did consume the fat but not the skin or entrails. In the Chakhesang area, Khusoi's account has already been given above.

As to Japanese eating habits at the time, there were few compliments apart from surprise at their use of chopsticks, which the Nagas saw for the first time and could not imagine how anyone could eat with two small sticks!

In many villages, people said that Japanese soldiers carried their individual pots and pans and they were very possessive of these. Sometimes, a few of them would cook together and eat. But everyone said the soldiers would start dipping their chopsticks into the pots as soon the pot started boiling and would begin to eat. This was the same whether it was rice or any kind of meat. Was this a habit picked up on the war route? Most possibly. But it made someone like Khetso Pienyü remark, 'Probably because they ate so much improperly cooked food that they used to fart so much!' It would appear they were also impervious to any smell or stench of rotting flesh around them and would quite happily eat their food next to a rotting corpse, sometimes even making jokes. War does unusual things to people.

The consensus Naga opinion seems to be that 'You cannot eat Japanese food because they never cooked (food) properly.' This was one reason why many Nagas doing porter work for the Japanese would slip away as soon as they could. In any case, most times, they were not offered food at all. But there was another habit of chewing a leaf with a nauseating smell. According to Khetso Pienyü, 'After every meal, they chewed this leaf we call "Nhasa", new plant/leaf, or "Japan nha" (Japanese plant/leaf, *Eupatorium adenophorum*). This plant was not indigenous and apparently made its appearance only during the Second World War, and hence the name. The Japanese soldiers would invite us to chew the leaf. One day the soldiers became quite insistent. So one of my friends chewed it and immediately emptied his lunch in front of everyone. After this incident, they never asked us to chew it again!'

The Japanese soldier's ability to make a fireplace very quickly won the admiration of Pukoho Rolnu. He said, 'In no time, a Japanese soldier would make a three-point fireplace and start cooking! He would use three sticks, make a fire and hang his pot above the fire.' Most of the time, the Japanese soldiers would use their helmets to pound paddy. They would either chew the rice raw or cook it later.

Khetso Pienyü thought there were two categories of Japanese. The Japanese buried their dead whenever they could. And this they usually did in the forest, away from the main thoroughfares. But while some Japanese soldiers were fully buried, some had their heads exposed above ground. One day, Khetso came across one of the latter category. The flesh had all rotted away and the hair had fallen off. Only the skull and nerves remained. Intending to give the village womenfolk a scare by placing the skull at the village gate, Khetso tried to remove the skull. He even put his two feet on the shoulders and twisted and pulled. But the head would not come off. He was surprised how tough human nerves are. 'Unfortunately for me, I had not carried my dao that day!' he said.

Another custom seemed to be to send back home body parts of the dead Japanese soldiers. According to Zhovire of Jakhama, his father was given this distasteful task in their village. 'He had to cut the small finger off from the hands of dead Japanese soldiers and roll it in cotton wool and keep it aside in a basket for the officer to take back to Japan. He cut off hundreds of fingers for many days but could never quite get over the distasteful task.'

INFESTATION

This last is not a peculiarity of the Japanese alone. It could happen to anyone. It also showed the kind of situation the Japanese soldier faced during the war. More than distaste, it raised feelings of empathy, even admiration, for the soldier who had to endure such tough situations. It is from this perspective and what war does, that this section has been included here.

It was noticed in Rüsoma Village (northern Angami area) that wherever Japanese soldiers camped, there was an outbreak of bugs and scabies. According to Pastor Kiezotuo, 'Wherever the Japanese camped, the place would be infested with scabies. In Kohima, too, everyone had the scabies. People bled from the scabies sores.'

Thirteen-year-old Neidilie Kuotsu of Phesama Village, in the southern Angami area, had a similar story. He and his friends, as boys of that age, used to go everywhere and they liked to mimic the Japanese who were in their village. The character most visible, and seemed popular among the Japanese soldiers, was the quartermaster, who went around the village wearing a Gaonbura's blanket and also carrying a gun and a spear so that he looked like a Naga from a distance. They would mimic the Japanese calling him 'O Medosa!' One day, they visited his private quarters, below a waterfall and were jumping up and down on his bed when they discovered his blankets were 'infested with maggots!' They ran away in alarm.

NAGA IMPRESSIONS OF JAPANESE

So, what impressions did the Japanese leave on the Nagas? Warm in a few exceptional cases, respect in some for their fighting ability and bravery, but anger in most, and many even despised them towards the end of the war. However, with the passage of time, Naga feelings have mellowed and have come to be replaced by understanding as the immediate feelings have had a chance to heal. The soldiers were just soldiers, obeying to the best of their ability what they were told to do. The lasting impression they left behind was their bravery and ability to not only fight but also face very harsh conditions.

According to Havildar Zhavise Vihienuo, 'The Japanese first came through the southern Angami side. At first, we liked each other. They even opened Japanese schools and our people also helped them to the extent possible. However, because their supplies did not come, they started pestering our people for food. Their attitude and behaviour also changed. Some Nagas also died at Japanese hands. As a result, the Nagas turned against them and began reporting Japanese camps and movements to the British.'

As Vimedo Rutsa said, 'The Japanese lost the war because they did not bring their tiffin!' That, for him, encapsulated the story of the Battle of Kohima for the Japanese.

Today, Naga attention has switched towards present-day Japanese generations. Japan has become one of the most advanced countries in the world and was, for a long time, the second biggest economy in the world after the United States. It surprised the Nagas that the Japanese seemed to care so little about their history. Vimedo Rutsa, who is a respected Naga elder, asked, 'Why are the Japanese still not talking to the Nagas? We knew the Japanese were fighting the British in a war but surely the Nagas were not their enemies. Our people helped them too. But till today, they have neither justified themselves nor apologized to the Naga people. Their forebears still lie in our brooks and alleys without final closure. Is this arrogance or foolishness? What kind of people are they?' For people like Vimedo, the concern is more for final closure and peace for the departed souls.

WORKS CITED

Colvin, J. *Not Ordinary Men*. London: Leo Cooper, 1994.

Interview with Mhalelie Vimera, Rüsoma Village elder and APO Office Bearer.

Keane, Fergal. *Road of Bones: The Epic Siege of Kohima 1944*. London: Harper Press, 2010.

Khate, *et al. Battle of Kohima*. Kohima: Ura Academy, 2007.

Ltu, Khrienuo. 'World War II in North East India: A Study of Imphal and Kohima Battles', Unpublished papers, 2014.

Personal Interviews, Nagaland: 2016–2017.

Yonuo, A. *The Rising Nagas*. Delhi: Manas Publications, 1992.

THREE
NAGA–BRITISH RELATIONS

What of Naga–British relations? It was not too long ago that the Nagas were fighting the British colonialists. The British first made their appearance in Naga territory in January 1832 under the command of Captains Jenkins and Pemberton when they tried to trace a land route from Imphal to their Assam headquarters. The party of 700 soldiers and 800 coolies (porters) was attacked and chased all the way down to the plains. Intermittent wars continued and the British had to change their policies from time to time as they saw no economic benefit in entering the Hills. It was the constant Naga raids on the tea estates that finally forced the British to climb the Hills.

Only in 1880, following the final Battle of Khonoma, after almost fifty years of war, and two years after shifting their headquarters to Kohima, the British gained some confidence to 'rule' or 'administer' the western Naga areas. Their administration did not include the Free Nagas in the unadministered zone adjacent to Burma.

As foreign colonial rulers, the administrative officers protected British interests but they were also cautious. They knew the wars they had fought with the Nagas were still fresh in the minds of the people. They were also conscious of the constant Naga warring among themselves, which was a major Naga vulnerability they could exploit. Various Naga groups were approaching the British for help to defeat their Naga enemies. But if push came to shove the Nagas would fight back, regardless of numbers or inferior weaponry. This probably was largely the reason why the British administration did not interfere much with Naga traditions, customs and culture. So long as the Nagas acknowledged British rule and paid their house tax, they were largely left to pursue their own devices. The fact that many of the early British administrators were also anthropologists or anthropological enthusiasts further helped the situation. This was how the British generally conducted affairs and consolidated their power over the Nagas – with minimal interference.

The first great test in British–Naga relations was the so-called Great War (the First World War), a little over 35 years after the Battle of Khonoma. Relations were still tentative. The generation that fought in the 1879–1880 Battle of Khonoma, and those Angamis who laid siege to the British Garrison in Kohima, were still alive. Their feelings towards the British were understandably not that warm.

The Nagas knew the British were a powerful people but the War was a time of crisis for them and they needed help. It was also an opportunity for Nagas to earn money, and by then they had learned from the British what money could do! The promise of new experiences in strange lands, too, was very inviting for the adventurous Nagas. Of course, there was danger but this had never deterred the Nagas from doing what they wanted. So when the call came, many Nagas volunteered to serve in the Labour Corps, including some from Khonoma Village, although the majority seemed to have come from non-Angami tribes who did not take part in the 1879–1880 battles.

The accounts of how many Nagas actually went as part of the Naga Labour Corps to Europe has become hazy, with so many claiming different figures. The official figures we could find are that about 2,000 Nagas went to France. The Nagas of Manipur went as part of the Maharaja of Manipur's contingent. Most of the Naga labour went to France. The other posting was Mesopotamia (present Middle East). There is an unconfirmed report of an Ao who went to Germany.

After the war, those who served in and survived the Labour Corps returned home. While the returnees may have had a lot of stories to tell, there was not much else apart from exciting stories of adventure, and venereal disease surfacing in Naga society for the first time. But the moment the 'salaries' of the Labour Corps members arrived in big trunks, everything changed. What surprised the Nagas, including those who got paid, was that not a single rupee (silver coin) was missing. This made a great impression on the Nagas across the board and their faith in British integrity and justice system grew enormously.

As respect for the British and their justice system grew, adventurous Nagas began to venture out to do business in other parts, sometimes armed with knowledge of only their mother-tongue! It is told that at least one of these businessmen, from Khonoma, who traded in beads in Cambay (present Gujarat), used to carry pebbles in order to bargain the price! As in any new venture, only very few ventured out at first. But as their trade became successful, more and more followed in their footsteps. Soon Nagas were trading in places like Dacca, Burma, Maharashtra, Gujarat, Ceylon (Sri Lanka), etc. Many times these traders were compelled to entrust their goods and/or money to the official British India Post. And each time a person's earnings were returned without any loss, respect for the British grew exponentially!

Mention has been made of how senior British administrators, being anthropological enthusiasts, facilitated a non-confrontational British–Naga coexistence. In some cases the administrators seemed to have carried their enthusiasm for preserving Naga culture in pristine form a bit too far. For instance, Kumbho Angami MBE, who had been working with the missionaries in Mokokchung district as a teacher, was asked to go and teach in the Sema area (Atoizu). He agreed. But the SDO, Mokokchung, insisted that he had to be able to dress in traditional Sema style in every aspect. Kumbho, who was always attired in knickerbockers and knee-length socks, refused and so he was not allowed to teach there.

The degree of this fetish of wanting Nagas to dress traditionally seemed to have been a peculiarity with some administrators. In Kohima, there are stories of certain administrators not permitting Nagas to wear western clothes. Havildar Zhavise Vihienuo spoke about a Lotha gentleman who had come to Kohima in connection with a scholarship. He had come sporting a pair of shorts. The British officer who he went to meet chased him for quite a distance and tore his shorts off! What was worse was that Nagas, particularly the government servants, were often forced to wear 'dhotis', something that was completely distasteful to Nagas, according to Zhavise Vihienuo and others. Khriezotuo Sachü said there were two kinds of dhotis; one was white, the other was black.

The Nagas were also forbidden to use western names and the administration threatened that those with western names would not be allowed to study in school. This became awkward vis-à-vis the missionaries and the early converts. Many times the missionaries' wives with some knowledge of nursing and midwifery would assist in deliveries of the early converts. They would also name the newborns after Christian saints they venerated. There were many cases of Nagas having to change their names back to Naga names although Kumbho refused to change the names of his children, according to his son, Thepfülhouvi Angami IFS, former Principal Chief Conservator of Forests for the Government of Nagaland.

But, all in all, life returned to a semblance of normality. The 'riches' the Labour Corps members had received had begun to make a difference in their lives and even up-scaled their place in the traditional social order. Many of them were either the first educated members or simply the more adventurous. When they went to a foreign country, they all became 'Nagas' as opposed to this or that tribe. Meanwhile, the Naga Club was formed in Kohima as a social club to meet and interact on a regular basis. This was initially set up by the Naga Government servants. Basically, all the educated Nagas became members of the club.

A branch was opened in Mokokchung as well. Before long, because of the weight of the historical responsibility they felt at the time, this Naga Club would become the crucible of Naga nationalism. Their submission of the Naga Memorandum to the Simon Commission on 10 January 1929, asking the Nagas to be left out of the Reformed Scheme of India, is now the stuff of Naga history. The Government of India Act, 1935, put into effect the Naga desire to be left out of the Reformed Scheme of India.

Meanwhile, Deputy Commissioner C. R. Pawsey's efforts to bring the disparate Naga tribes together were much appreciated by the educated Nagas. So, while the British–Naga relations were still not fully healed, general Naga feelings were not only on the mend but positive towards the British. This was the kind of situation prevailing on the eve of the Battle of Kohima and the Japanese advance towards Kohima during the Second World War in 1944.

The British Army, for whom Naga feelings were dubious at the best of times, did not cover themselves in glory when they decided to withdraw from Kohima as the Japanese were reaching the vicinity of the town, leaving the Nagas to their fate at the hands of the Japanese. Many Nagas started leaving Kohima to seek shelter in nearby villages. They were used to sudden moves like this from their head-hunting days, but this was different. They thought the British had betrayed them. The army's reported request to the Deputy Commissioner to leave Kohima for security reasons was the last straw. As Nagas were beginning to think of how to respond to this unexpected turn of events, word of Mr Pawsey's opposition to the withdrawal of the 161st Brigade from Kohima began to circulate. He had argued against the withdrawal to no avail. According to K. N. Pusha, Pawsey reportedly told the British Army, 'If you want to leave, go, but I will not leave Kohima; I will not abandon my Nagas!' This was the kind of language the Nagas understood and appreciated from their most trusted man. Here was a friend who was willing to share their fate. Their response was immediate and unanimous. They could never abandon their friend come what may. Naga elders believed the Kohima Garrison was not totally abandoned because of Pawsey.

Several authors have commented on the importance of the role played by Deputy Commissioner Pawsey in garnering Naga support to the British/Allied cause.

According to Murkot Ramunny, in his book, *The World of Nagas*, Charles Pawsey 'stayed with the people ... His behaviour at a critical time enhanced the prestige of the British administrators and justified confidence Nagas had in them' (18).

According to L. C. E. Philips, when all others had gone from Kohima, Charles Pawsey stayed behind, 'So that his Nagas should not lose faith in the British cause nor feel that he had abandoned them' (*Springboard to Victory*, 156).

Arthur Swinson had no doubts that Naga loyalty to the British was because of Charles Pawsey. 'It is doubtful ... if the Nagas would have undertaken any of this difficult and dangerous work if it had not been for the extraordinary character of Charles Pawsey, the Deputy Commissioner of Kohima.' He went on to say that, 'The Nagas trusted him and knew that in no circumstances whatsoever his word would be broken' (*Kohima*, 145).

Swinson continued, 'When Mutaguchi's thrust against Kohima began, the Nagas remained loyal to the British cause, despite the loss of their homes and territory, despite danger and death ... [because of] the part played by Charles Pawsey ....[This] should never be forgotten' (146).

While endorsing the above views, Christoph Fürer-Haimendorf included the friendships built by other administrators such as J. H. Hutton and J. P. Mills that accounted for Naga loyalty to the British.

The British Governor-General-in-Council acknowledged that 'Had the approach of the Nagas been different, the battle might have been extended, the defeat of the Japanese might have been delayed and the casualties of the British might have been higher or the battle might have taken a different turn' (Govt of India, 'A Report on the Measure of Rehabilitation').

Once committed, the dobashis gathered round DC Pawsey and their network went to work. There was at least one dobashi in every village, but if a village did not have one, the dobashis in nearby villages had influence over it. Usually the dobashi was an influential man in the village and the position was further fortified by a salary and proximity to power. In addition, the educated and concerned segment of Naga society rallied around the administration. The vast majority of Nagas, from then on, fought for their friend Pawsey and did what he told them to do.

So, what roles did the Nagas, particularly the civilian segment, play? They became scouts and spies, guiding the British and gathering intelligence for them; they became porters carrying supplies and ammunition; they became stretcher-bearers, trench diggers, etc. Slowly, as Japanese behaviour became more and more intolerable, even this civilian segment of Nagas would become warlike, leading the Japanese into ambushes, giving them wrong directions, and even killing them. In the process, some Nagas also lost their lives. Meanwhile, those Nagas in the British India Army for example, the Assam Rifles and the Assam Regiment, fought as soldiers. They were joined by the Naga Levies, many of whom were also inducted and given ranks in the soldiery. Their participation has been covered in the second part of this book.

And, of course, the Naga friend Pawsey was never left alone. A coterie of dobashis and other Naga leaders would always surround him. His head dobashi at the time, Mhiesizolie, who doubled as his driver, was with him in his bunker the whole time that they were under siege from the Japanese. The bunker was at the present war cemetery site, which was where the DC's bungalow was. Mhiesizolie would slip down to Sanyühu Dzüluo, a spring well, at night (there is a timber mill there now) when there was a lull in the fighting, and bring drinking water. They were in the bunker for about two weeks. According to Mhiesizolie's brother, Lhusiekolie Chasie, after the battle, Pawsey took Mhiesizolie down to Dimapur so he could rest and recover his health. In another account, Vatsümvü Kirekha said that Dr Neilhouzhü Kire was also with Pawsey during this time. When the British soldiers reached them, Pawsey said, 'We haven't had water for three days!' The situation, according to Kirekha, was immediately remedied with a water bottle.

Some examples and comments on the participation of the Naga civilian segment are provided below for better appreciation of the roles played by the Nagas to help the British. It must be kept in mind that these roles had to be performed under conditions that required stealth and speed along steep hills, dense forests, incessant rain, narrow passages, and marshy villages infested with mosquitoes and even snakes.

Kelhikhrie Angami was a guide for the British throughout the war. Jasokie Angami, former Chief Minister of Nagaland, was also a scout for the British. His youngest son still has a pistol that his father used as a British scout during the war. Viketu Kiso, also a British scout, recalled that one of their colleagues was shot dead by the Japanese. At the time, they did not know, but they later recovered his skull in the forests near Japfü peak.

Another scout was Kumbho Angami. His son, Thepfülhouvi Angami, said his father was a scout for Chindit Column 76, and they travelled through many parts of the Northern Angami areas and some parts of Chakhesang areas. At one point, Kumbho carried a British soldier/officer who was so weakened by sickness that he could not walk any more. 'Maybe because of this, my father was awarded the MBE,' said Thepfülhouvi. He also recalled his father telling him that when it came to payment, the Nagas preferred coins to paper money.

Jon Latimer recorded that, '80 walking wounded and 100 non-combatants were guided to safety from Jail Hill in just seven hours' (*Burma: The Forgotten War*, 263).

Lieutenant Cleland stated that, 'Naga village after village rose up to help the British – men, women, even children sometimes. For instance, Mao village provided 100 labourers, Khuzama 200 and Viswema 500 etc.' (Govt of India, 'Tour Diary of Lt. Cleland').

Some other comments are given below:

Arthur Swinson: 'At a signal from the column commander, the grinning Nagas eased forward with the first stretcher, gripped the cliff edge with their toes, and shuffled happily along it' (*Kohima*, 213).

John Colvin: 'Without Naga help in the evacuation of the wounded British and Indian troops up and down the sodden hills, the death rate among the Allied battalions would have been much higher' (*Not Ordinary Men*, 37).

A. J. Barker: '(British) rations and ammunitions were carried up to the new positions and casualties carried down mostly by the Naga porters – the tough hillmen who negotiated the 1,500 feet into the Zubza valley and 2,000 feet up again on the main road with only one rest, while British stretcher-bearers took something like eight times as long, and were completely exhausted after a single journey' (*The March on Delhi*, 19).

J. H. Hutton: 'Porters in hundreds helped the British 23rd Brigade ... They carried things for 2nd Division in the attack on Aradura Spur and evacuated the wounded ... Nagas engaged as porters and scouts rendered invaluable assistance for the 7th Division who advanced along Kezoma-Kidima range' ('Problems of Reconstruction in the Assam Hills', 36–7).

Hutton went on to say: 'A Naga Government interpreter located a Japanese ammunition party of nine men, organized a band of villagers who surrounded and captured them. Another interpreter, hearing of an advance Japanese patrol of 15 men, guided the British to ambush and capture ... the party' ('Problems', 3).

As Assistant to the Deputy Commissioner of Kohima, Honorary Captain A. Kevichüsa acted as interpreter for the British and organized Naga labour. He also surveyed various roads between Dimapur and Kohima. An area in which the British used the Nagas quite extensively was in intelligence gathering where Kevichüsa was involved. Most of the Naga government servants were sent to their villages for intelligence purposes. The intelligence gathered by Ziechao Whuorie, for instance, which enabled a whole British brigade to reoccupy Kohima Village has been covered elsewhere. These Nagas faced threats to personal safety. The Japanese would shoot any Naga acting as guide for the British. Even the porters were subjected to punishment. Swinson reported a case where, 'Three Naga porters, on the 4th Brigade supply route, were met by a Japanese patrol which was evidently lying-up waiting for them. Their loads were taken; they were beaten up, and left tied to the trees' (*Kohima*, 174).

Swinson went on to say that, 'No European could possibly have taken stretchers over that country. All the troops knew, when they first encountered the Nagas, was that they were head-hunters ... But soon they were struck not only by their cheeriness and eagerness to help but by their intelligence. Most officers had to be trained to "read" air photos, but when Grover showed a set to some Nagas they understood immediately exclaiming: Yes, do you see – that's my village' (*Kohima*, 145).

General John Grover had commented that they had been taught to regard the Nagas as 'savage head-hunters' (Keane, *Road of Bones*, 295).

According to Hargovind Joshi, 'Cheerfully facing torture and death they [Nagas] organized an efficient intelligence system for the services of the Allies, they operated tirelessly around, behind and across Japanese lines, they inflicted formidable casualties on the enemy ... They cheerfully placed all they had, whether of men or material at the disposal of the British' (*Nagaland*, 58).

The Nagas, in turn, respected the British soldiers for their courage and fortitude. According to Neichieo, who carried British wounded and dead, 'The British soldiers did not know how to hide, they would simply walk in the open and the Japanese would easily kill them. But the British soldiers, though wounded, never complained and would say, "Thik hai! Thik hai!"' (Interview).

Havildar Sovehü Nienu, of the 1st Assam Regiment, regretted that a lot of British soldiers were not used to warfare in a terrain like the Naga jungle and so many died unnecessarily, particularly during the assault on Pulie Badze, the north-westernmost tip of the Aradura Spur and the last defence of the Japanese in Kohima.

A Naga eyewitness (a porter) on the battle at the Kohima water source, above the present Norfolk Regiment memorial in Kohima, commented: 'The British were sometimes not careful at all, but there was no question about their courage. As soon as one soldier was shot dead, another would immediately jump in and take his place. The Dzüvürü became a river of blood!'

The Naga goodwill towards the British continued and grew stronger as the war continued. Eric T. D. Lambert, the then Chief Civilian Liaison Officer in charge of intelligence, attached to the 14th Army, would himself say, 'Naga loyalty, particularly of our old enemy Khonoma, had to be seen to be believed' ('Naga Loyalty During the Japanese Invasion', 143–4).

British rations were available without fail while Japanese behaviour became more and more atrocious as their military situation deteriorated. As a grateful people tried to show their gratitude for British rations and protection, the Japanese situation would become even more desperate. They would be forced to withdraw. The war had also reduced Naga feelings of suspicion and uncertainty towards the British soldiers, because protection and rations were supplied by the British Army. And by and by, they soon discovered that they had become comrades-in-arms, trusting each other with their lives.

So, what lasting impressions did the Naga people have about the British? Tremendous respect surely. But there have also been a lot of disappointments. At the level of the Naga veterans – some of them were still in Burma serving as soldiers when the British transferred power to Indian hands – they had expected to be taken care of and adequate provision made for their welfare. This was not done. Many of these soldiers represented some of the most influential families in their village communities, coming as they did from well-to-do families. They were among the higher social strata and the first generation of Nagas with some education. But they returned home from the war to find they were not as well regarded by their village communities as they used to be.

The second and deeper hurt was felt by all Nagas. This was because the British Government left the Nagas under the new Indian Government without saying a single word about Naga sentiments of wanting to be left outside India. Across the board, regardless of village or tribal affinity, the Naga people felt let down by their British friends when they departed from India in 1947.

Of course, there were the earlier proposals like the Crown Colony Proposal (also referred to as the Coupland Plan). Sir Robert Reid, then Governor of the Assam Province, had suggested that the tribes of Assam and Burma together be made a protectorate under the British because these tribes have 'neither racially, historically, culturally, nor linguistically any affinity with the people of the plains or with the people of India proper. It is only by an historical accident and as a naturally administrative convenience that they have been tacked on to an Indian Province.' Governor Reid feared that unless protection was given to these tribes at least for some time to develop on their own lines without outside interference, the chance may never come to them again (See Syiemlieh's *On the Edge of Empire* and D. Chasie's *Khwünomia Rüna Kechü Dze*).

However, the proposal did not work. Tribes in the region like the Khasis and Mizos were not too keen while the Nagas were more interested in having a Naga nation of their own rather than being clubbed together with others. So while several British administrators were very concerned for the Nagas and their future, nothing happened officially. In recent years, some authors including David Syiemlieh have tried to show that the British had all along planned to leave the region, including the Nagas, within India. If the Nagas had known this at the time, they would most probably have considered it a deeply cruel cut from their war comrades.

It may be recalled that in 1929, in a memorandum to the Simon Commission, the Nagas had made clear their wish to remain

outside India. The British Government at that time gave due con-
sideration to the Naga plea and left them outside the Reformed
Scheme of India through the Government of India Act 1935.
Considering the assistance that the Naga people had given the
British during the Second World War, the Nagas had thought
their British friends would be more sympathetic to their cause.

The post-war world was no longer as simple, or straightforward,
as it used to be for the Nagas. Tragically, for them, their world
would soon be plunged into another long 'Night of the Guerrillas'
because Britain did not speak on their behalf. This was how the
vast majority of the Nagas would henceforth interpret the events
of Naga–British history. The words of Naga elder Vimedo Rutsa
captures the general Naga sentiment: 'The British should have
told the Indians that they (Indians) are different and Nagas are
different and both should respect each other. But the British did
not tell the truth and left the Nagas under the Indians. Therefore,
for so many decades, Nagas have been fighting the Indians and
thousands upon thousands of Nagas have been killed.'

WORKS CITED

Barker, A. J. *The March on Delhi*. London: Faber and Faber. 1994.
Chasie, Dolhunyü. *Khwünomia Rüna Kechü Dze*. Kohima:
    Unpublished papers.
Colvin, J. *Not Ordinary Men*. London: Leo Cooper, 1994.
Elwin, V. *Nagas in the Nineteenth Century*. Bombay: Oxford UP,
    1969.
Fürer-Haimendorf, C. *The Naked Nagas*. Guwahati: Spectrum
    Publications, 1946.
Government of India. 'A Report on the Measure of Rehabilitation
    and Reconstruction undertaken by the GoI in the Naga Hills
    and Manipur State in 1944.' Confidential Dept, File No 497,
    NSA, 1944.
Govt of India. 'Tour Diary of Lt Cleland.' Secret Department, File
    No 455 NSA, 1944.

Hutton, J. H. 'Problems of Reconstruction in the Assam Hills', *The Journal of the Royal Anthropological Institute of Great Britain and Ireland*, Vol. 75, No 1/2, 1945, pp. 1–7.

Joshi, H. *Nagaland Past and Present*. Delhi: Akansha Publishing House, 2001.

Keane, F. *Road of Bones: The Epic Siege of Kohima 1944*. London: Harper Press, 2010.

Khate, M. et al. *Battle of Kohima*. Kohima: Ura Academy, 2007.

Kohima Museum Papers, York, UK.

Lambert, E. T. D. 'Naga Loyalty During the Japanese Invasion,' *Man*, Vol. 46 (November–December, 1946).

Latimer, J. *Burma: The Forgotten War*. London: John Murray, 2004.

Ltu, Khrienuo. 'World War II in North East India: A Study of Imphal and Kohima Battles', unpublished papers, 2014.

Pawsey, C. R. 'Relief in the Hills.'

Personal interviews with Naga Elders.

Philips, L. C. E. *Springboard to Victory*. London: Heinemann, 1966.

Ramunny, M. *The World of Nagas*. New Delhi: Northern Book Centre, 1993.

Syiemlieh, David. R. *On the Edge of Empire: Four British Plans for North East India, 1941–47*. New Delhi: Sage Publications, 2014.

Swinson, A. *Kohima*, London: Arrow Book Ltd, 1956.

Wilcox, W. A. *Chindit Column 76*. Longmans, Green & Co. Ltd, 1945.

FOUR
KOHIMA AFTER THE BATTLE

After the battle Kohima was completely devastated and reduced to rubble. The once thick forests were totally denuded. Even the tree stumps and remains of buildings were pockmarked with bullet and shell holes. The most intolerable thing at the time was the terrible stench of rotting corpses.

As the Japanese started retreating from Kohima, Havildar Zhavise Vihienuo and his 2nd Assam Regiment were brought up to Kohima as reinforcements. 'Kohima was totally destroyed and seemed devoid of all life. The few people we met were shell-shocked and seemed unable to speak even. The trees had no leaves or branches while the stumps were full of bullet and shell holes. It was the same for the few houses left standing. Kezieke area was completely bombed out and Kohima Village was burnt to ashes. Kohima looked like a ghost town' (Interview).

Pukoho Rolnu of Jakhama said he had come to Kohima soon after the war. 'Kohima was completely destroyed. I saw a lot of rotting corpses, many of them had maggots climbing out of boots. In some the feet had come apart at the ankles. The stench was horrible. I also saw a lot of rifles and other weapons piled up and burning like funeral pyres' (Interview).

The battle for Kohima was a massive fight to the bitter end. Its savagery shocked the head-hunting Nagas who found it difficult to comprehend. Sepoy Mukom Khiamniungan, a soldier attached to the Assam Regimental Centre in Shillong but who fought in Kohima, was so affected by the battle that even decades afterwards he would try to avoid coming to Kohima. He lived in Noklak, Tuensang District, on the Myanmarese border, and sometimes he had to go to Dimapur. But from Mokokchung he would go to Dimapur via Assam without passing through Kohima. He could not even take tea in a restaurant in Kohima as he would always see the dead and rotting corpses in his mind's eye. His son, Ningbao Khiamniungan, said his father told him that the war was 'like a night!' (Interview).

MODERN WEAPONS AND MILITARY TRAINING

It was during the Battle of Kohima that the Nagas were exposed to modern warfare and weaponry for the first time. Intense bombardments from planes and widespread, indiscriminate havoc unleashed by tanks, machine guns made them aware of the devastating effects of modern weapons. They saw everything and experienced everything first-hand, even the villagers. Those who worked as porters, stretcher-bearers, scouts and guides and interpreters experienced the events even more closely and observed military tactics as well. Such experiences would never be blotted out of the collective and personal memories of the Nagas.

But of even more consequence in the long run was that for the first time large numbers of Nagas had become part of the soldiery, either as full-time soldiers or as Levies, who were more soldiers than civilians and fought in the war over long periods. The soldiers received military training and applied them in action. They learned military tactics and how to handle modern weapons. The discipline and knowledge they learned, and the experiences they got in the Army, became an integral part of their lives.

After the war, the entire Naga Hills area was strewn with weapons. The British administration tried to collect all the weapons back and even applied reward and punishment methods to do so. But while many were returned, it became quite clear that a sizeable quantity was not returned. It seemed there were also quite a lot of Japanese weapons and ammunition left behind in their camps which were not disclosed to British authorities, according to Naga elders in different parts of Nagaland. Because of such weapons some Naga sympathizers of the Japanese would later claim that the Japanese gave a lot of their weapons to the Nagas. In truth, it was more likely that the Japanese had neither the strength nor the resources left to carry their weapons back. At the end of the Battle of Kohima, they hardly had any physical strength left to carry themselves across the Chindwin and back to Burma.

According to author Savito Nagi, the weapons left uncollected after the Second World War were initially used to arm the Naga Army cadres in the new Indo-Naga conflict. It was also because of the military training and experience in handling modern weapons that the Naga veterans of the war would soon be wooed by the Naga Nationalists while also becoming suspect in the eyes of the newly independent Indian Government and Army. In some instances, former comrades would become enemies and fight in the field of battle again.

REHABILITATION AND RECONSTRUCTION

Once the Japanese withdrew from Kohima, how to restart life in the post-war period became a big question. The biggest issues with the Naga people were the most basic. Internal displacement and destruction of their homes and villages were the most critical problems. Many had been refugees in other villages. Those who were not refugees in other villages had been living in the jungles or their field huts. All of them had little or nothing to come back to. Some could not even recognize their ancestral plots and where their houses had stood.

Food and shelter were the most pressing needs. The British continued supplying their rations in a very generous way. They also gave medicines, clothes, blankets, etc. They brought house building materials such as bamboo, timber, tin sheets, plus cooking pots and pans, plates, winnowing trays and so on. Vimedo Rutsa recollects, 'The British supplied us with everything, even spoons and ladles.' Agricultural implements like axes, hoes, plough-shares, daos were distributed to the people as the Japanese had thrown all these away so that they could not be used by the Nagas as weapons against them.

Relief centres were opened to help the people. According to Khrienuo Ltu, Khonoma Village was chosen as 'the first relief centre in the Naga Hills because it was the centre for villagers of Kohima, Phesama, Kigwema and various other southern Angami villages' (Ltu, 189). Food supply depots were also opened at various places like Kohima, Phesama and Khuzama. New store houses were built for the storage of rice, depots were opened near motor roads, and clerks were appointed to issue food to the people on time. A record of the number of people fed by the British is available:

Kohima and Chedema:	4,665 adults and 2,472 children
Kidima:	434 adults and 312 children
Khuzama:	407 adults and 283 children
	(Ltu, 190–91)

It is quite possible that these figures may include people from nearby villages too, but they are by no means exhaustive.

According to some reports available, the quantity of rice imported at the time (1944) into the Naga Hills was 60,088 maunds and imported paddy was 63,914 maunds (a maund is roughly 40 kilograms).

Compensation was also paid. It was determined that about 2,780 houses were destroyed due to the fighting and bombing in the Naga Hills. Of these, the biggest sufferer was Kohima Village with an assessed 913 houses destroyed and assistance was given accordingly. This was followed by Kohima town with 318 houses destroyed, Viswema 293, Chizami 217, Khonoma 62, Phesama 34, etc. Other villages are also listed but the figures are lower. Even then the list, again, could not have been exhaustive.

Wherever possible, the British encouraged people to rebuild their houses with local help and offered some cash assistance. 'It was obviously impossible to give the Naga, even the poorest, a house equal to that which he had lost, but it was determined that the materials to be provided would be on a scale, if not extravagant, at least adequate to enable him to return to normal life' (Govt of India, 1944, 23).

'People who lost their houses and who were looted by the Japanese were given ₹400 and ₹200 by the British' (Govt of India). Other figures and stories by various people abound. According to Neiselie, for instance, 'If the Japanese had not come, there would be no village road. People were given compensations of ₹100, ₹200, ₹50, ₹60, ₹20 and ₹30' (Interview).

Vimedo Rutsa narrated this humorous story in Kohima Village. Vimedo's grandfather was a rich man and had dependants living with him. Curiously, when the damage assessments were made, and the sums paid out, one of his dependants received more money than he did! With a chuckle, Vimedo said, 'I can still see my grandfather cursing!' (Interview).

Most villages could not get their fields ready for paddy cultivation that year. Quite ingeniously, the British arranged and brought paddy plants ready for transplanting. This was a new species of rice and the people called it 'rosholha', meaning ration rice! This, plus other assistance distributed to villagers, ensured self-sufficiency in food so that life could resume with some semblance of continuity.

IMPACT OF THE WAR

A modern war of such intensity, with modern weapons, could not but be devastating for the people in whose lands it was fought. It was even more so for the Nagas who, for the most part, were still living in their traditional village-world having little or no contact with the outside world when it happened. True, some Nagas who went abroad as part of the Naga Labour

Corps during the First World War had gained some exposure. But this time, the outside world had brought war to their lands. They had little choice but to face it and go through it. Many times, they also had little choice but to help either one or the other of the antagonists.

They would see and experience many new things. For many Nagas aeroplanes were a novelty. For instance, Noumvüo Khruomo recalls the first time he witnessed planes while working in the field: 'Are we to witness this in our lifetime!? We stopped working and returned home.'

Hutsonyu Chuzo from Phek said, 'Japanese planes came ... from Burma side. Since people saw the plane for the first time ... thought it was a big bird. Since it was an extraordinary sight the next day was declared taboo (*penie*) to work in the fields.'

Neilhou Dzüvichü saw four kinds of planes, 'One was the ration carrier, another was the striped aircraft, then there was one that photographed and drew maps and the last was the aircraft that carried bombs ...' He also said, 'The Japanese could fly aircraft better than the British and the Japanese airplanes made less noise ... we watched all the air-fights from the ridges opposite the fights' (Khate, *et al.* 61).

For Viketu of Kigwema: 'Bombing at Kohima was like a cinema from my village ... The green and red lights hit the ground and exploded' (Interview).

There were several reports from interviews of Naga elders and veterans that Japanese aircraft managed to reach Kohima a few times. Khetso Pienyü, for instance, talked about seeing a Japanese plane being shot down. He went to look at it and was stopped by a British soldier but not before he had seen a lot of bombs and ammunition strewn around the fallen aircraft.

What were some of the comments about the war from the villagers?

Lhoutuo Shüya said, 'In a way I am (grateful) for the coming of the Japanese because after 1940, life became better economically ... the highest (wage) was ₹1 ... when the Japanese entered our land everything was thrown out of order and our daily wages were increased' (Interview).

According to Vatsümvü Kirekha: 'The Japanese war was a turning point for our people. Before the war, we had no tin houses and no one used locks on their doors. All houses were made of thatch. No one used matchboxes; people dried cow dung and ... burnt these and carried them to the fields to make fire' (Interview).

Asoso Yonuo remarked that: 'Subsequently a tiny petty bourgeois class of the native people who had made their fortunes out of the profit of the battle had risen on the modern capitalistic basis' (149).

After the war, the most visible and major sign of change was the disruption in traditional community life. Earlier, everyone in the community would be carrying out the same activities that revolved around the agricultural cycle. If one was preparing the fields for sowing seeds, everyone else in the village would be doing the same work although they may all be competing to be the first to finish it. The same for other activities like planting, weeding, harvesting, observing festivals, etc. Basically, the activities were season-based and individual activities did not differ much. After the war, individual activities changed and varied so much they became unpredictable. No one was sure any longer who might be doing what on any given day. The first erosion in the life of the community-based society had taken place.

How did this come about? In one word 'Money'. With the coming of the British colonialists, money had been introduced. Initially the scale was small. Most villagers were still paying their house tax with paddy. Then the return of the Labour Corps members from the First World War with their accumulated salaries was quickly followed by the earnings of adventurous Nagas who started trading in places like Burma, Dacca, Cambay, Ceylon, etc. The government servants who earned regular salaries also added to the new economic trend. But the event that brought about the biggest change was the Second World War with a war economy unperturbed by any thought of inflation or its possible after-effects on the barter economy of the Naga society. Its impact was decisive and did real damage to Naga traditional values. A new class of moneyed Nagas, earlier unknown, soon emerged. Their proximity, in many cases, to the administration brought them influence. The combination of money and power would cause further erosion of the traditional authority structure.

With increasing numbers of people moving from rural to urban areas, trade and commerce also surfaced and became a part of daily life in towns like Kohima and Dimapur. In the new emerging society money spoke with such new power that old-time values began to be diluted. The first casualty was traditional morality.

Former Principal Chief Conservator of Forests Thepfülhouvi Angami stated: 'The war affected the lives of the Nagas considerably, not least of which was the sudden awareness of a much bigger world. For the first time, many were seeing aeroplanes, bulldozers – monsters that could even level hillocks! And with so many people coming and going, etc., it started affecting the moral character of some men and women and their depth of feeling and perception, making life a little shallower, if easier' (Interview).

The change in sexual mores and flouting of traditional authority, referred to above, was just the tip of the proverbial iceberg. It went much deeper and began to corrode the traditional Naga character from within. And once the poisonous corrosive set to work, it would continue to destroy and remain an uncompromising fifth column that the Nagas would keep fighting in a losing battle even to the present day. The Nagas would retain the shell of their culture, but the core would have melted down and they would keep drifting even while clinging on to the hope that someday things would become better.

Deputy Commissioner, C. R. Pawsey observed that Naga honesty was the first casualty of the war.

Meanwhile, life continued in Naga society and people tried to become rich, ostensibly in their traditional quest to earn and share wealth and gain name and fame by throwing 'feasts of merit'. Traditionally, the rich Nagas shared their wealth with the village community and the poor did not begrudge the rich but tried to emulate them. But slowly the search for money began to be the driving force for many people, and a goal in itself. While the desire for a good name in the community was still a factor, more and more the focus became advancement of self, family and progeny. Soon the larger goal of sharing wealth with the community practically disappeared.

The new drive for individual wealth acquisition led to 'selfishness' in Naga society. And with it, traditional values like *peyu* (statesmanship, wisdom, etc.) began to play a diminishing role. This in turn negatively impacted the traditional authority system that had worked so well until then. Money would slowly become all important and reduce everything, even people, to 'purchasable' commodities (*kenyü*). The moneyed individual family unit began to take precedence over the community. In traditional Naga society such a perspective would have been intolerable and considered an extreme taboo (*kenyüthor*). Was this the point where the traditional Naga 'sense of sin' began to be peeled off and the sense of the sacred began to dissipate? The traditional Naga was a God-fearing person, if superstitious most of the time. While change is inevitable, it will do the Naga people good to dissect the things that have happened to them, assimilate them where needed, and strategize an adequate plan to move on. The Nagas need to ask tough questions of themselves to avoid the Naga journey from sliding backwards. Their very peoplehood is at grave risk at the present time. Without a proper understanding of the past, and who they were, the Nagas, like anyone else, may play a lesser role than they were meant to.

But if money had created a small new stratum in Naga society and changed values, how were the monies used? What did those who had money do with their new-found wealth? The most noticeable effect was the 'purchase' of education for one's children. 'Legacy' was a very important part of a Naga's life, as amply shown through the bequeathing of ancestral property. But now 'education' was replacing 'ancestral fields' in the lexicon of Naga legacy, especially in the context of money economy and salaried employment that formal education could bring. Tragically, as 'family' replaced 'community', the search for certificates and degrees would become all important not only for employment but for personal status. This came at the expense of the respect for traditional wisdom and culture.

There is another side to this story. Despite the 'selfishness' pointed out above, many Nagas began to get quality formal education, with some venturing out to Indian cities, mostly Guwahati and Calcutta to start with. With education came increased church membership, which generated a sense of common identity among Naga tribes as a people. It was a different kind of community from earlier times, but also reminiscent of it, which was probably why Christianity took a hold on Naga soil so rapidly.

In a roundabout way, however, the definitive transition of the Naga barter economy into a money economy at the behest of the Second World War quickly produced inflationary trends, which would later be artificially sustained by the 'Naga Insurgency' through the Government of India 'pouring in money' to contain it, according to many writers on mainland India. The entire shift in the Naga economy through the medium of 'money' and the utter disruption in the traditional authority system, which had kept Naga society glued together at least at the village community levels, would cause a paradigm shift and make Nagas unbalanced and vulnerable to all kinds of manipulation and exploitation by vested interests both within Naga society and outside forces. This trend continues today.

The war affected Nagas in other ways too. Kohima was firmly placed on the world map. As Vandanshan, son of Naga veteran Yambhamo Lotha MM, MID said, people came to know about the Nagas because of the Battle of Kohima. The Nagas were largely

incidental to the war but suffered all the same. When two elephants fight, as the African saying goes, the grass gets trampled.

Struggles though painful often help growth in people. Vimedo
Rutsa commented: 'Although the war brought so much misery
to our people, without it our people would have remained ignor-
ant for so much longer.' Echoing this view, author Savito Nagi of
Jotsoma said: 'Even though the Japanese took our (food stocks)
and the British burned down our villages, (the war) woke us up
from our sleep of ignorance and fear … After the war, our people
became brave like the Japanese and educated like the British'
(Interview).

Meanwhile, very significant events were unfolding in the
southern Angami area. As soon as the Battle of Kohima was
over, the leaders got together and formed the Southern Angami
Council (SAC), consisting of representatives from all the southern Angami villages. Explaining this, K. N. Pusha of Viswema
Village said, 'Earlier the southern Angami people used to be
divided along clan lines, particularly Zoüno and Keyhono. But
the Second World War had shown our people that we cannot afford to continue to be divided as this was destructive and did not
benefit anyone. So, our people came together.' The SAC took two
major decisions. The first was to start a Polytechnic educational
institute, which resulted in the establishment of John School at
Viswema, in 1945, named after John Angami, a contractor during the war and prominent leader of the area who also financially
contributed the most. Very soon, the school became a high school
and provided education not only to the entire southern Angami
area but also to some Chakhesang villages. Today, it is one of the
oldest educational institutions in Nagaland.

The second decision was the construction of a hydroelectric
power station at Kehorü, the major river between Jakhama and
Viswema villages. At this time, even Kohima did not have electricity. There was report of a generator that was used by a mis-
sionary in Kohima and generator-operated film shows were
sometimes held but houses did not have electricity. But Viswema
and Jakhama Villages had electricity. Apparently, even Kigwema

Village got electricity from a second hydro project. The plan was to provide electricity to the entire southern Angami area. Sadly, before the plan could be implemented fully, the Indo-Naga conflict caught up with the Nagas. Eventually, the generating unit at Kehorü disappeared while the people, once more, fled to the jungles, some to fight and some for survival.

The above examples show what was possible when people kept their personal interests aside, came together and did things together for the common good. Several people said that even DC Pawsey would come to Kehorü, whenever he could, and watch with keen interest the progress being made at the hydro project. He also donated tin sheets from the Kigwema Hospital for the sheds at the power plant. The hospital is in the present Japfü College area which at different times became a hospital site for Japanese and Allied forces because it could not be bombed from the air owing to the high hills around it.

At the socio-political level, things were moving rapidly for the Nagas. By and large, they were still recovering from the ravages of the Battle of Kohima, but history was not going to wait for them. They had to wake up and decide what they wanted. The various exposures and experiences, both at home and abroad, had also begun to bring them together as a people.

As Chotisüh Sazo, Honourable Speaker of the Nagaland Legislative Assembly, said:

> We know that several thousand Nagas went to France during World War 1. This gave a little consciousness of Naga identity which led to the formation of the Naga Club in 1918 and, later on, the submission of the Memorandum to the British Simon Commission (10 January 1929). In 1944, the Battle of Kohima brought total transformation to Naga society. It also led to formation of Naga National Council (NNC) in 1946, Nine-Point Agreement in (28 June) 1947, Declaration of Naga Independence Day on 14 August 1947, followed by the Naga Plebiscite in May 1951. Our people suffered a lot, and so many changes were brought about in various fields including

*education, economy and Naga identity. These are all impacts
of the Second World War. (Interview)*

The Nagas would soon be immersed in another conflict with the
Government of India, still awaiting a final settlement. Meanwhile,
the majority of the Naga people would continue to feel sadness
that the British Government, before leaving, did not say a word
about the Naga people's desire to stay outside India. This grouse
of the Naga people would continue to run alongside the gratitude
and respect they felt for the British. But this is a no-win situation
and ought to be resolved in a spirit of voluntary forgiveness and
hope for a better future.

WORKS CITED

Government of India. 'A Report on the Measure of Rehabilitation
and Reconstruction undertaken by the Government of India
in the Naga Hills and Manipur State in 1944–45, in order to
repair the ravages caused by the Japanese invasion of 1944',
Confidential Department, File No 497, 1944, p. 23, NSA, 1944.

Government of Nagaland. *Heralding Hope:125 Kohima*. Kohima:
Govt of Nagaland, 2004.

Khate, Mekhrie, *et al. Battle of Kohima*. Kohima: Ura Academy,
2007.

Ltu, Khrienuo. 'World War II in North East India: A Study of
Imphal and Kohima Battles', Unpublished Papers, 2014.

Personal interviews. Nagaland: 2016–2017.

Yonuo, A. *The Rising Nagas*. Delhi: Manas Publications, 1992.

FIVE

FOR YOUR TOMORROW

Sometimes people ask, 'Who and how many Nagas were involved in the Second World War?' When an elephant walks through your family house and someone asks you, 'Which members of your family were affected?' What do you say? The scenario in most parts of the Naga Hills was like that.

The Second World War was like a hurricane where warnings became available only a little while before its arrival with an intensity no one could have predicted. Naga attitudes and inclinations have been covered above. Some Naga participation, including those who won gallantry awards, has been covered in the second part of this book including the Appendices.

What still needs telling are the conditions of the Second World War Naga veterans of the British India Army and what happened to them afterwards. Many of them died in the war. Others followed them in the intervening decades, some in the 'Indo–Naga' conflict. Very few of them are alive today.

Many of the Naga veterans came home from Burma only in 1947, some after the transfer of power to India and British departure. Most of them had joined the army in the prime of their youth, but in the span of a few years, after fighting in the war, they came back as 'old men', discharged from the army and as retirees, to pick up the threads of their lives and resume life in their village communities. Most of them had expected that the British India Government would have made some economic provisions for them to restart their civilian lives. They were forgotten as the British Government was apparently in a hurry to leave India. Not surprisingly, many of the Naga veterans, experts in warfare, felt totally disoriented, confused, and often felt useless as civilians. A few years of warfare had seemed like a lifetime to them. Some who got married soon after their return were more fortunate than the others because new responsibilities gave them fresh purpose even though their wherewithal was always difficult.

For most of them, before they could really have adequate time to settle down, they were once again caught in another conflict, again, not of their choosing, and making things no easier. The Second World War had not been their war. This time was different. Naga nationalism was more personal for them and the pressure to fight another war, this time for Naga iIndependence, was urgent and the pressure almost always came from their kith and kin. Some like Sovehü Nienu were quite clear and were able to withstand the pressure despite offers of high office in the new Naga military and civilian set-ups. But many others did not have that luxury. Thus, when the Naga National Movement turned violent and the Naga Nationalists raised the Naga Army to fight for independence, Yambhamo Lotha, who was Naik during the Second World War, became a General in the Naga Army. He later died at the hands of the Indian Army.

Whether or not they joined the Naga Army, because of their military background the veterans became suspect in the eyes of the new Indian Army and Indian Government. Their already difficult lives were further torn apart, and many of them did not survive the crosshairs of this new conflict as both sides considered those who did not join them as their enemies. Some died at the hands of the Indian Army while others were killed by the Naga Nationalists. Subedar Satso-o Yhome of Kohima Village, perhaps the one Naga who did most of the Naga recruitment for the Assam Regiment in the Second World War, was killed by the Naga Nationalists. His grave still lies in the heart of Kohima, next to the Traffic Police Stand at Centre Point. Even those who did not die suffered intimidation, imprisonment, harassment and in a few cases even abduction, from both sides.

For instance, Havildar Zhavise Vihienuo, who did not join the Naga Nationalists, was imprisoned for 16 months by Indian authorities without any charge against him. He was not given any reason for his imprisonment despite his best efforts to ascertain why.

Today, only very few of those who fought in the Battle of Kohima are alive, and none of those who won gallantry awards is left. Among those who are still living, there were hardly any records that we could uncover, either in the UK or in India. Only those who still had their documents and medals could show some proof of their gallant deeds. We managed to reach many of those still living. Some had become very old and so infirm that they could not even move around within their own homes. One such case was Keduchü Kupa of Kami Village. We could not even talk with him although his family very kindly carried him to the kitchen for us to see him in early January 2016. Happily for us, he maintained a diary which the family graciously shared with us.

It was fascinating to listen to the stories of the veterans. Different reasons seemed to have attracted young Nagas to join the British India Army. Some like Sovehü Nienu and his friends abandoned their studies in Kohima and ran away to join, without informing their parents, because they thought army life would be adventurous and fun.

A second category was the Nagas who joined the army because of poverty and the need to earn. Quite similar to this category were those Nagas who, though not poverty-stricken, joined the army to better the economic conditions of their families.

There were also Nagas who joined the army or became Levies because they could not refuse the requests of their kinsmen who were already helping the British. On the other hand, there were Nagas who helped the Japanese Army on request by the Japanese or their Naga relations/friends, or in some cases because there was no choice. Sadly, unlike those who helped the British, those who assisted the Japanese were totally forgotten partly because the British continued to rule after the war, and partly because the Japanese themselves had forgotten their friends who had helped them at great cost to themselves at the time. To be fair to the Japanese, after losing the war, they were facing enormous difficulties at home.

For all the above Naga groups, financial stability for themselves after the war, or if they died, financial stability of their families, was important. Clan and kinship went a very long way; those in responsible positions with the then British Government carried a lot of responsibilities that could not be easily described or defined. Only a person within the Naga cultural context could fully understand the enormity of these responsibilities that each Levy or soldier was burdened with. Those in the civil category like the interpreters (dobashis) carried even greater responsibilities for their kith and kin, more because of their standing in the community and proximity to power. For each Naga who became employed by the British in some way, the loyalties of their family and clan turned towards the British, while this was not so much the case for those who helped the Japanese. One reason was that the Japanese had allied themselves with the Indian National Army (INA), and the Nagas on the whole did not like the 'Indians' or 'plainsmen' as mentioned before.

CONDITIONS OF VETERANS

The conditions of the veterans and their expectations from the British India Government after the Second World War have been briefly touched upon. Many Naga veterans, especially the strictly non-army personnel, had come home after the war or very soon after. But most of the army men returned home much later. Those from the Assam Regiment, particularly those in the 1st Assam Regiment, returned from Burma only in 1946–1947, and some after India got its independence. These were soldiers who had staked their lives in a life-or-death struggle, given the best of their youth, and they did not expect to be forgotten by their 'bosses'.

Sadly for them, everything had changed and what they found back in their village communities left them totally disoriented. They had no role to play within their village communities as others had assumed positions of authority in the period between the war and their return. They had nothing with which they could establish themselves as influential members of their communities – which their families were before the war. These young men knew what to do in the war: fight the enemy and kill them. It was straightforward. Back in civilian life and in post-war Naga society, nothing was clear any more. They did not know what to do and often felt useless. Their time in the war completely turned their lives topsy-turvy. They lost their bearings. So it is hardly surprising that few Naga veterans' descendants occupied positions of influence in post-war Naga society, while many remain semi-literate or illiterate even today.

Here are a few statements to showcase what the Naga veterans felt:

Havildar Sovehü Nienu of Phek village, 101, 1st Assam Regiment, 3-inch mortar unit, fought at Jessami, Pulie Badze and Burma till 1947 (post Indian independence): 'We thought we would be well taken care of. But we were totally forgotten' (Interview). He and his wife were blessed with 11 children.

Naik Saishe Swu of Ighanumi village, 93, 3rd Assam Regiment, joined the army in 1943 and fought the entire war in Burma, returning only in 1947:

I came back in 1947 and the only reward I got for my years of war was that I returned home alive while so many of my friends died. I had expected some assistance to restart life as a civilian. There was nothing. Soon the Naga Nationalists wanted me to join them while the Indian Army started harassing me. Two Naga Indian Intelligence personnel were always following me. On one occasion, an Indian army patrol came to my house and even took away all my army papers and war medals. I could not fathom what benefits they got from taking away my documents and medals but they took them away and never returned them. I was so fed up with all these harassments, and my pride as a veteran soldier was so hurt, that at one point I even joined the Naga Nationalists. Years later, I went to the Indian Army CO at Chakhabama and pleaded. He was kind to get my army papers back but my medals were lost forever (Interview).

Sepoy Khetozu Sema, 1st Assam Regiment, 90, now settled in Kuhuboto, Dimapur, joined the army in 1943. He had fought in Burma the entire war period, returning to India in early 1947: 'I had joined the Assam Regiment at the age of 16. We were taken to Calcutta and then flown to Burma where many of my friends died fighting the Japanese. Only three of us returned home. We were soon discharged and told to go home. I went to Mokokchung as the Semas were then under Mokokchung. My papers and medals came afterwards but nothing else; not even the pay that was due to me! This made me very sad' (Interview).

Havildar Lemayanger Ao, 97, 1st Assam Regiment, from Changki Village (Mokokchung), now settled in Dimapur, was in the Assam Regiment from 1941 to 1947 when he was discharged. He was in charge of 75 vehicles in the Motor Transport department and moved rations to wherever it was required in the Battle of Kohima theatre. He recalled his CO was Colonel Brown. 'I was disappointed that the pension we were promised was not given.' We met him and his wife, a very gracious woman. He said, 'I am old and living in this condition. One son is mentally disturbed and a daughter has been sick for a long time. If there is any way you can help, please help us' (Interview).

Sepoy Shitozu Sema, 92, of Litsami Village, now settled in Thilixu, Dimapur, joined the 3rd Assam Regiment in 1943. His is one of the most colourful stories we encountered. Shitozu was living in the village with his parents as a farmer. He recounted how he joined the army:

My older brother was in the British Army and posted at Jakhama. I went to visit him ... I heard recruiting was going on at Ghokiye village, next to my village. So I went to Ghokiye village but by the time I reached there the recruiting team had left! Later, when I heard that recruiting was going on in Kohima, I left to join the army without telling my parents. Subedar Satso-o Angami was my recruiting officer (Interview).

Initially, Shitozu was rejected because his height fell short of regulations (5 foot was the requirement and he was only 4 feet 11 inches). But he refused to abandon his dream of being an army man and refused to return home. Seeing his determination, a compromise solution was evolved and on the consideration that his chest expansion was above regulation, he was accepted into the Assam Regiment. But disappointments seemed to pursue Shitozu, as he was kept under training in Shillong, the regimental headquarters for the entire duration of the war. His keenness to join the fighting in the Battle of Kohima made no difference to his superiors. So the man who wanted so much to be an army man never actually saw action. But his strong determination was, once again, later manifested when he became a university post-graduate long after he attained senior citizenship rank.

Havildar Chenchungba Amer, 94, 1st Assam Regiment, Changki Village, now settled in Dimapur, joined the army in 1943 and fought in present-day Nagaland, Manipur and Myanmar, receiving a monthly salary of ₹12. He returned home in 1946. He remembered Eric Lambert, Chief Civilian Liaison Officer who also looked after intelligence. He recalled his duties this way:

As the Japanese withdrew from Kohima, we were sent pursuing them to Imphal and then to Pallel, Moreh, Chindwin and on to Mandalay, crossing the Irrawady River. The places I remember in Burma where we fought were Sikpur, Sibu, Tanku,

Harsi, Kaleo, Kalemyo, Maymyo, Chin and Arakan, as well as Mandalay port. After the capture of Mandalay port, we were ordered back to Chin and Arakan areas for defence and security duties. I was happy with the British. They were fair in their dealings with us. Later they tried to help us with whatever was possible. (Interview)

Sepoy Tuochalie (Kemp) Rengma, 89, 3rd Assam Regiment, Phenshunyu Village, Kohima, joined the army in 1943. He was only 15 years old then but registered himself as 17. He was physically well-built but obviously his youth showed and the recruiter wanted to accept him as a 'Boy'. He refused as he wanted to be a fully fledged soldier. As there was no doctor at Tseminyu, they were taken to Mokokchung for physical examination. 'After final training in Shillong, I was assigned to the Demonstration Platoon at the training centre. Those who were physically fit were usually selected for the Demonstration Platoon. Our job was to teach each batch of new recruits how to fight war.' But much as he wanted to fight, he was kept at the Shillong Training Centre for the entire duration of the war. He recalled ten of his Rengma friends who had joined the army and gone to war. 'All my friends died in the war. Who knows, I may have died also if I had gone to the frontlines' (Interview). He married after the war and was blessed with ten children.

Sepoy Khakhu (Khing) Rengma, 105, 1st Assam Regiment, Tesophenyu Village, Tseminyu, Kohima, joined the army in 1943. After training in Shillong, they were taken and stationed at Mariani

As the war raged in Kohima, we were brought to Zubza. From there we took part in the counter-attack (British Left Hook). We climbed the slopes to Meriema village and fought a pitched battle at the present High School area. I also remember fighting in what is now Chandmari area of Kohima, which was then occupied by the Assam Rifles. We went to help them as the Japanese were attacking them (Interview).

Khakhu also recalls chasing the Japanese all the way to Burma via Imphal and walking long distances for many days. He does not remember the names of places but he recalled that on one occasion they captured 60 enemy soldiers. 'We are now old and living in a difficult situation. Please tell people that we need their help now.' When we met him in his village home in 2016, he was living alone and looking after himself. His friend's daughter, now a school teacher, comes in and takes care of the most essential needs in housekeeping and accompanies him when required to functions he has to attend. Sepoy Penthungo (Ezung) Lotha, 92, 1st Assam Regiment, Longsa Village, Wokha, joined the army in March 1944, just before the Battle of Kohima. He was recruited by Subedar Satso-o Angami. Prior to that, he worked as a Naga Levy in 1943 working on the road to Burma. Penthungo recalls going to Burma and fighting the Japanese in the jungles, but he does not remember the names of places. 'My pay was ₹18 a month but they used to give us only ₹8 or ₹9. Towards the end, my pay was increased to ₹26.' He further explained that at the end, 'We got only medals and no compensations. We took home the clothes we were wearing – one shirt, one pair of trousers, shoes, and one blanket, that is all. They told us to go back, so we came home' (Interview). He returned home in 1947 when they were discharged. All his comrades from his village have died and he is the only survivor.

Sepoy Nyimchamo (Odyuo) Lotha, 90, 1st Assam Regiment, Pyangsa Village, Wokha, joined the army in November 1944 after the Japanese had retreated from Kohima. After a short training in Shillong, they were taken to Calcutta and onward to Rangoon by ship in the early part of 1945. 'I saw roads, bridges and houses damaged by bombs. I also saw many Japanese soldiers, both men and women, captured and imprisoned' (Interview).

Nyimchamo was a driver. 'On one occasion, we were driving from Makilie to Maymyo town when we had an accident and the vehicle plunged down a ravine about 200–300 feet below the road. By God's grace we survived.' Nyimchamo also recalls being stationed at Mandalay for about seven to eight months. 'I stayed in Burma for two years and returned only in 1947. From Rangoon, we came by ship to Goa where we had five days holiday!' He remembers his salary was ₹50. He also recollected getting three medals but all have been lost except one, which he said was 'made into a (finger) ring by my youngest son!' (Interview).

When we met Nyimchamo, he was unwell and we interviewed him in bed. The pension he was receiving was not enough, but the bigger complaint was that old and sick people have to physically present themselves before appointed authorities to prove they are still alive so that they can receive their meagre pensions.

This was a common grouse among the veterans because this was something that really hurt their pride and manhood. They who were 'lions' in their younger days and had fought their enemies with no quarters asked or given, had now to prostrate themselves before people who never saw war for a small amount of money. The humiliation went deep with all of them and their families, who had to carry them to appointed centres. It is difficult to understand why the pension authorities could not depute employees to go to the homes of the veterans. Hopefully, this will be done, particularly now that there are so few Second World War veterans left. This, of course, is relevant for post-Second World War veterans too.

The above reminiscences and comments by the Naga military veterans have been offered here as examples of what the Naga veterans felt in general. How many Nagas actually joined the army and/or fought as soldiers in the Second World War? There is no way of knowing now. We are only aware that we could not cover all. We did make the effort and even advertised in newspapers, but there were hardly any responses. Only when we 'discovered' them and approached them personally did they respond.

Many Levies were also promoted to the soldiery. But there are no records of who and how many participated in the war as soldiers. We made a search through various means and places where we thought we might get help. One useful way was to try and find out through the gallantry awards given out during the war or soon after. We uncovered many names through this method, but in most cases there were no further records, including of the veterans still alive, although we were shown the medals in their possession. In many other cases documents were simply not available with the children of Naga veterans. Even medals they once had have been lost. In some cases, however, we had great satisfaction where we were able to return lost citations for gallantry awards to the rightful owners or citations to veterans who were unaware they had been awarded them.

Many family members of veterans did not know anything about the war experiences of their fathers, such as which army unit they were in, where they fought, the harsh conditions they had faced, etc. In some cases, they heard for the first time the experiences of their fathers when we interviewed them. It would seem that one of the worst impacts of the war was this breakdown in communication within the family.

The situation seems like a common post-war experience throughout the world. It can be immediate, as Havildar Zhavise Vihienuo said about Kohima after the Japanese withdrawal: 'the people were shell-shocked and looked as if they could not even speak or communicate'. And the silence can last a lifetime. It can take generations to heal. For the Nagas, the prolonged conflict with the Government of India in the wake of the rise of Naga nationalism made things worse as families were once more plunged into an abyss of violence and struggle for survival that Indian author Nirmal Nibedon has described as 'The Night of the Guerrillas'.

A sad discovery was that a good number of Naga veterans, including those who had won gallantry awards, had no male descendants or no descendants left at all. This sometimes gave rise to interesting conversations with elders. In a patrilineal society, where the family tree is based on the male line, the male progeny was important for its continuance. This would bring up the traditional Naga/Tenyimia warning that those who took too many lives may suffer the loss of their progeny.

Our efforts to find out how many Naga soldiers died could not be ascertained although we found the records of some, and these are listed in the Appendices. The veterans themselves could not remember all their friends who died in the war. What was clear was that a lot of Nagas died both at the hands of the Japanese and the British, particularly because of their bombing. It is quite certain that more Nagas died at the hands of the British. It was clear that many Japanese too died at Naga hands.

NO. 533 SEPOY SALIEZHÜ ANGAMI

When talking or writing about the Naga soldiers in the Assam Regiment, one cannot bypass the story of Saliezhü (Linyü) Angami, of Kohima Village, the only Naga soldier whose plaque is available at the Kohima War Cemetery although at least fifteen other Assam Regiment sepoys of his battalion were killed at the siege of Kohima. The other sepoys killed during the siege are commemorated on Panel 53 of the Rangoon Memorial which is located inside the Taukkyan War Cemetery north of Yangon, Myanmar.

Saliezhü Angami, of the 1st Assam Regiment, was the son of Nuboü and Perheilie Linyü of Kohima Village. He had fought at the battle of Jessami and was lucky enough to be one of those who managed to make his way back to Kohima after the battalion finally managed to get news, from Lieutenant John Corlett, that the order to fight to the last man and last bullet had been rescinded and they could retreat. The first thing he did on reaching Kohima Village was to go home. From his village, he could see the entire fighting going on in present Kohima town, and he was troubled that while he was safely staying in his village, his comrades were fighting the Japanese in a desperate struggle, with their lives on the line.

In the midst of the confusion of war, there were no clear orders and summons to action he could receive in the village. He had no idea who among the 1st Assam Regiment soldiers who fought alongside him in Jessami may have reached Kohima town and were engaged in the fierce battle below. But propelled by his sense of solidarity with his comrades, and against the advice from some Naga friends, Saliezhü Linyü, rejoined his battalion for the defence of Kohima. Not much more information is available about his wartime experience except that he was reported to have been a very effective grenade-thrower.

Saliezhü was buried in Kohima and lies in a dignified and well cared-for cemetery where family and others can easily visit his grave. What is equally important about this grave is that it carries a cultural message for younger Naga generations. The epitaph of Saliezhü reads as follows:

Apau puo medo zha chuterhü
Rükra themvü mevi lar pengutuo

Which translates to something like: My beloved/favourite son, big hearted and true warrior, I will see him return as a star (in the sky).

The Tenyimia/Angami believed in life after death. They also believed that when good persons died, they would reappear in the sky as a moon or star.

SURVIVING VETERANS' CONDITIONS

What are the conditions of the surviving Naga veterans and their families today? There were, naturally, individual problems that each veteran faced which were specific to them, but there were also several commonalities. Some of them are summarized below.

1. All of them are now old and most are also infirm. Some of them were lying in their beds but their families very kindly allowed us to meet them. When we asked about the Second World War and their roles in it, their eyes would light up and they would

tell whatever they could remember or came to their minds at the time. A proper organized interview was often difficult because of their physical condition. Most of them had also become hard of hearing. Happily, a few were still very sharp mentally and even physically able.

2. Apart from a few fortunate ones, who were well looked after by their children or extended families, the majority of the veterans were in poor economic circumstances. In a society that used to be community-based, it was sad to see at least one veteran living alone. Thankfully, he was still mobile, looking after himself, doing his own cooking and other necessities, when we met him.

3. The veterans had given the best of their youth to fighting the war. As soldiers, they learned to fight and kill people. In civilian life, their military training was of little help to them. When they got married and raised children they had to shoulder new responsibilities. But these veterans had little or nothing to rebuild and restart their lives with. Economically impoverished, they could not afford to sponsor their children's education. So the cycle of poverty was all some of them were fated to. In many cases, their children were semi-educated, a few even illiterate. Many of them had come from families of influence in their village communities before the war and now they were not counted any more. More than anything else, their pride and manhood were hurt. Not surprisingly, this went very deep.

4. The Naga veterans after returning home and finding themselves forgotten by the British Government had no time to nurse their grievances. Very soon, Naga nationalism and the ensuing violence propelled them into another era of active conflict and warfare. They were caught between the Naga Nationalists and the new Indian Army and Government. The Naga Nationalists had declared Naga Independence on 14 August 1947. Many of the Naga veterans returned home from Burma after this date. In the absence of a political resolution, military conflict began.

Many of them did not survive the Indo-Naga conflict, which is still begging for a proper settlement.

5. After the worst of the conflict, and establishment of Nagaland State 1963, the Government tried to help the veterans with a pension, disbursed through the State Rajya Sainik Board. But the pension was a pittance and, frequently, it was more trouble for the veterans to travel long distances to receive it. What made it worse was that the veterans had to regularly prove they were still alive. This meant they had to go to the District Headquarters and physically present themselves. How much this may have hurt the pride and dignity of the veterans was totally lost on the Board. In the case of Keduchü Kupa of Kami Village, the family complained that because the veteran was not able to do this, his pension was discontinued for a time and restored only later. We met him in January 2016, and in March we got the news that he had passed on.

According to Havildar Zhavise Vihienuo, the veterans' pension was raised from ₹500 to ₹3000 a month, after their meeting with the Duke of York, during his visit to Kohima in 2012. As of 2016, the pension has been increased to ₹6000/- per month in accordance with Brigadier Roy-Choudhury, the new Rajya Sainik Board Director and Secretary.

6. The veterans have lived through turbulent and trying times. Many expressed disappointment in being forgotten by the British India Government. But there was no bitterness in any of them. Neither was there any expression of regret about the past. Only in two cases we detected a note of 'if only' from the children of veterans who were no more. The veterans themselves were all very gracious in their bearing and attitude. And most of them happily recounted their stories.

7. A breakdown of communication between the veterans and their families about the war that we had observed earlier was tragic. But there were exceptions, and they delighted us.

8. Most veterans did not know how to react when we told them about the Kohima Educational Trust (KET), set up by the British

veterans of the Battle of Kohima to assist with the education of their descendants. Many said, 'How good of them!' Some even thought they would get immediate economic 'relief'! We had to explain how the entire initiative came about and that this was a non-government people-to-people charitable initiative with an educational mandate. The KET-KES made sure that at least one descendant of theirs got the KET school scholarship.

BRITISH VETERANS AND KOHIMA EDUCATIONAL TRUST

What about the British veterans, the Naga veterans' counterparts? From stories retold and reports available, their own situation was not much better. Most British veterans of the Battle of Kohima felt they had been forgotten by their Government. They have even been described as 'The Forgotten Army'.

In the wake of such apparent neglect, it was remarkable that the British soldiers who fought in the Battle of Kohima, and who initially did not figure positively in Naga consideration but who eventually became their comrades-in-arms during the war, would be the only ones today who have remembered the Naga people.

Gordon Graham of the Queens Own Cameron Highlanders fought in the Battle of Kohima as a Captain. He was twice awarded the Military Cross. He was promoted to Major and retired as a Colonel. He worked as a journalist before the war and returned to India after the war as a journalist. His experiences are beautifully recounted in his book, *The Trees are All Young on Garrison Hill*, 2005 (www.kohimaeducationaltrust.net). Later, he became a famous publisher, representing some of the biggest publishing houses in the world. He was also founder-editor of 'Logos', the acknowledged international legal publishers' magazine.

A humble and deeply spiritual man, even after having become a great success as a publisher, Gordon Graham thought about the Naga people and how they had helped the British soldiers during the Battle of Kohima when most others, British and Japanese, had apparently forgotten Kohima. Gordon did not want things to end there. He believed that the British soldiers carried a debt of honour to the Naga people for the help they received during the war. This was regardless of why and for whom the Nagas had helped the British. He was not questioning the motivation; he only saw what was done. And he was not thinking of how his own government may have neglected the British veterans. His thoughts were more about British pride and honour to a people far away, and how to maintain the bridge between two peoples that was forged in the fires of battle during the Second World War. This was a most rare and exceptional example of someone trying to use history to propel peoples into the future, trailblazing a path for anyone, anywhere, to follow if they wished to. Gordon Graham did not preach but showed British civilization and set the bar for others elsewhere to follow.

Gordon, it was obvious, had been working on his idea for a long time. One of the first formal steps he took was to write in 2000 to a Naga journalist friend he had hosted in his home in 1993. By 2003, his idea seemed firmly in place. In 2004, during the last reunion of the British 2nd Division veterans, he suggested to his comrades that they commemorate their war history in a more meaningful way by setting up a trust to assist with the education of the descendants of their Naga allies in the Battle of Kohima – a documentary on the same theme has his interview. His comrades liked his suggestion and unanimously adopted it. Thus the Kohima Educational Trust (KET) was born as a charitable educational trust in the UK to assist with the education of Naga children. In 2005, Gordon and his wife Betty, along with daughter Sylvia and her husband Robert May, travelled to Kohima to set up the Kohima Educational Society (KES) as the Nagaland counterpart of the KET. By 2007, the initiative was not only in place but started operating with Naga educationist Pheluopfhelie Kesiezie as the first chairman of the KES.

The KET was initially sponsored only by the veterans of the British 2nd Division. The funds trickled in through generous British veterans donating five or ten pounds out of their meagre pensions, accompanied by very touching letters, scanned photos of which Gordon Graham would kindly forward to Kohima from time to time to his Naga journalist friend. These donations were not unlike the widow's mite parable in the Bible. Today, the KET has been embraced by the wider British public and HRH, the Duke of York, Prince Andrew, became Patron of the KET in 2012.

KET trustees work voluntarily to raise funds. They feel responsible to carry out the objectives of the Trust and work very hard, even travelling to Kohima at their own expense while undertaking Trust work. The KES members too work voluntarily and try to raise funds whenever possible as this is a project for assisting the education of Naga children. One example was a musical concert in Kohima in November 2015 by leading Naga musicians which raised about ₹5 lakhs. There have also been donations from prominent Naga citizens. Donations, naturally, are always welcome from anyone who would like to participate in assisting with the education of Naga children. Those who wish to know more about the KET-KES can visit or write to KES: www.kohimaeducationaltrust.net; kohimaeducationalsociety@gmail.com.

WORKS CITED

Graham, Gordon. *The Trees are All Young on Garrison Hill*. KET, 2005.
Kohima Educational Society.
Kohima Educational Trust.
Personal interviews of veterans and their family members. Nagaland: 2016–2017.

SIX

THE KOHIMA WAR CEMETERY AND BATTLEGROUNDS TODAY

When you go home
Tell them of us and say
For your tomorrow
We gave our today.

(The stone on which these words were inscribed is said to
have been brought from Maram, now in Manipur State)

This epitaph was borrowed from the historical battle of
Thermopylae even if many visitors may not know its origins. But
today it may be fair to say that the inscription has become more
widely known because of the Battle of Kohima. With the passage of time, the Battle of Kohima is becoming more and more
part of world history. Kohima is no longer just an obscure place
somewhere in north-east India, close to Myanmar. A recent case
in point was in 2013, when British historians voted the Battle of
Kohima–Imphal as the most significant battle in the history of
Britain.

The Commonwealth War Cemetery at Kohima has become a
must-visit for anyone coming from outside, regardless of whether
it is a VVIP dignitary on an official visit or tourists. The Kohima
Cemetery also has some remarkable features that make it unique.
It is one of the few in the world where the cemetery is situated

on the actual site of the battle. Indeed, it was the 'heart' of the Battle of Kohima during the Second World War. Second, because of the crucial nature of the Battle of Kohima and other aspects of military importance, this battle is taught both at Sandhurst (British Military Academy, UK) and at the Indian Military Academy, according to Atuo Mezhür, former Senior Manager of the Commonwealth Cemeteries in north-east India.

Imphal was the bigger battleground, encompassing a bigger land area and with more troops deployment as well as war infrastructure. Imphal was the focus of both the Japanese Army and the Allied Forces, with the opposing army chiefs having their frontline HQs there or close to it. The Allied Forces also clearly had their doubts initially about the importance of Kohima. Next to Imphal, they thought Dimapur may be the more important and strategic place. And they withdrew their forces to Dimapur just as the Japanese forces were reaching Kohima, leaving the little town abandoned, with only a skeleton garrison, reinforced by the tired and battle-weary soldiers of the 1st Assam Regiment from Jessami who straggled in, feeling lucky to have survived the journey to Kohima. But soon, realizing that the Japanese were coming to Kohima in force, the 161st Brigade was reordered back to Kohima but only the 4th battalion of the Royal West Kents managed to reach Kohima before the Japanese cut off the Dimapur–Kohima road.

Interestingly, although early on, most Nagas had not considered the Second World War as their war, time is moving fast, particularly in the Naga case, and tremendous changes and new thinking have been taking place. British historians voting the Battle of Kohima–Imphal as the most significant battle in the entire history of Britain, the visit of HRH, Prince Andrew, to Kohima to lay a wreath for the fallen soldiers, the establishment of the Kohima Educational Trust (KET) by the British veterans of the Battle of Kohima, now embraced by the larger British public, the widely publicized commemoration of the 70th anniversary of the Battle of Kohima, the wider consciousness of war tourism potential in Nagaland, etc., have all given rise to objective thinking and awareness among the Nagas. There is a new consciousness too of how much the Second World War had cost the Naga people, and how firmly the Battle of Kohima had become embedded in the pages of Naga history. Furthermore, not saddled with the baggage of the past, the new generations of Nagas are willing to look at everything with rational and objective eyes.

THE GUARDIANS

The story of the Battle of Kohima would be incomplete without a few more words on the Kohima Commonwealth War Cemetery.

The Kohima War Cemetery is a prominent feature on the Dimapur–Imphal Road and it is positioned near the centre of Kohima town. The cemetery rises in terraces that cover areas where bitter fighting took place, and the old tennis court can still be seen marked out towards the top end. The grave markers in the Second World War cemetery number 1,421. There is also a cremation memorial commemorating 917 Hindu and Sikh soldiers.

Any coverage of the Kohima War Cemetery would be incomplete without a few words on the 'guardians' who have lovingly taken care of this cemetery over the decades. First mention must be made of the contractors who worked with the British Army Engineers. According to Atuo Mezhür, there was one Bassi and his assistant Pritam Singh. Then there was one Rawla who appears to have worked at the memorial around the tennis court. There was, possibly, another Sikh contractor by the name of V. M. Malhotra. How many contractors were actually involved is not clear. What does seem clear is that a lot of Bihari labour was involved, even in the early 1950s. Those who built the cemetery with careful precision in the footsteps of the British Army Engineers (MES) are to be commended. Likewise, the Naga family from Kohima Village who have maintained it with loving care through three generations now.

ATUO'S STORY

Atuo Mezhür, former Senior Regional Manager of the Commonwealth Cemetaries in north-east India, says:

I was born and brought up at the Kohima War Cemetery as my father (Samuel Mezhür BEM) was the Caretaker. As such the War Cemetery has always been a part of my life. I know most of the graves and where they are located.

The Kohima Cemetery was started in 1945 by the Army Engineers. It was only in 1947 it was felt that some people with horticultural knowledge were required. My father, a graduate of agriculture, took responsibility of the War Cemetery as Group Supervisor, taking charge of all the graves in north-east India, including a small grave in present-day Darjeeling. He actually helped exhume many remains of British soldiers in the jungles of what were then Burma and the Naga Hills. On his retirement in 1986, I took responsibility of the Commonwealth War Graves in NE as Regional Manager.

The Kohima War Cemetery is today a must-visit site for any dignitary visiting the State, whether it be the Chief of Army Staff, president or prime minister or other foreign dignitaries, etc. I had the singular satisfaction of taking around President Abdul Kalam, Prime Ministers Deve Gowda and A. B. Vajpayee and HRH, the Duke of York, Prince Andrew, etc. We even had an army general from Nepal whose regiment had fought in the Battle of Kohima. I also take much satisfaction in meeting with relatives of soldiers whose graves lie here which are always deeply touching or even local Indian tourists who are just curious.

The Kohima War Cemetery is one of the few cemeteries in the world where it was located on the actual site of the battle. And because of the military significance of this battle, it is taught both at Sandhurst (UK) and at the Indian Military Academy as a subject. It gives me great pleasure to see young Indian army officers come and witness what they had been taught at the Academy about the Battle of the Tennis Court.

On my retirement, my son Lhouvi Mezhür has taken charge of the management of the Kohima War Cemetery. Like me, he was born and brought up at the cemetery and it is so much a part of his life. Three generations of my family have looked after the Kohima War Cemetery and we feel proud to have worked with the Commonwealth War Graves Commission (CWGC) all these years.

THREE GRAVES AND TWO VCS IN KOHIMA

Three graves in the cemetery are of special interest. Two graves contain the remains of recipients of the Victoria Cross, the highest British military gallantry award; one of these men was killed during the siege of Kohima and the other was killed later during the fighting to clear the Japanese out of the Kohima area. The third grave contains the remains of Saliezhü Angami, a Naga sepoy, and he is the only Naga buried in the cemetery. His story has been covered elsewhere.

A previous Victoria Cross award for fighting against Nagas

Interestingly the first award of the Victoria Cross in the Naga Hills occurred for gallantry displayed in November 1879. It was given to Captain Richard Kirby Ridgeway of the Bengal Staff Corps for leading an attack against Khonoma Village. His citation reads:

For conspicuous gallantry throughout the attack on Khonoma, on the 22nd November, 1879, more especially in the final assault, when, under a heavy fire from the enemy, he rushed up to a barricade and attempted to tear down the planking surrounding it, to enable him to effect an entrance, in which act he received a very severe rifle shot wound in the left shoulder. (TBNA)

Following that campaign, which had included a siege of the British garrison in Kohima by the Nagas, the British extended their administration into the Naga Hills. The primary objective was to prevent the Nagas from terrorizing the Cachar tea estates.

Lance Corporal John Pennington Harman VC

Twenty-nine-year-old John Harman moved into Kohima on 5 April 1944 with his unit, the 4th Battalion of The Queen's Own Royal West Kent Regiment, the only British battalion that managed to squeeze in before the Japanese blocked the Dimapur–Kohima road, after withdrawal of the 161st Brigade to Dimapur on the eve of the Japanese arrival in Kohima. His rifle company was responsible for defending the Bungalow area. The fighting progressed to the higher grounds around DIS/FSD, on the northern side below Jail Hill, which was where he was killed after displaying the highest level of gallantry and a total contempt for death. His citation explains his actions:

In Burma at Kohima on 8th April, 1944, Lance-Corporal Harman was commanding a section of a forward platoon. Under cover of darkness the enemy established a machine gun post within 50 yards of his position which became a serious menace to the remainder of his Company. Owing to the nature of the ground Lance-Corporal Harman was unable to bring the fire of his section on to the enemy machine-gun post.

Without hesitation, he went forward by himself and using a four second grenade which he held on to for at least two seconds after releasing the lever in order to get immediate effect, threw it into the post and followed up immediately. He annihilated the post and returned to his section with the machine-gun.

Early the following morning, he recovered a position on a forward slope 150 yards from the enemy in order to strengthen a platoon which had been heavily attacked during the night. On occupying his position, he discovered a party of enemy digging in under cover of machine-gun fire and snipers. Ordering his Bren gun to give him covering fire he fixed his bayonet and alone charged the post shooting four and bayoneting one thereby wiping out the post.

When walking back Lance-Corporal Harman received a burst of machine-gun fire in his side and died shortly after reaching our lines. Lance-Corporal Harman's heroic action and supreme devotion to duty were a wonderful inspiration to all and were largely responsible for the decisive way in which all attacks were driven off by his Company. (TBNA)

Captain John Niel Randle

Twenty-six-year-old John Randle was fighting with his rifle company of the 2nd Battalion of The Royal Norfolk Regiment on General Purpose Transport (GPT) Ridge when his company commander was wounded and evacuated. John Randle immediately took over command of the company, displaying great tactical acumen and bravery to the point of sacrificing his own life to ensure that a Japanese bunker was silenced. His citation reads:

On the 4th May, 1944, at Kohima in Assam, a Battalion of the Norfolk Regiment attacked the Japanese positions on a nearby ridge. Captain Randle took over command of the Company which was leading the attack, when the Company Commander was severely wounded. His handling of a difficult situation in the face of heavy fire was masterly and although wounded himself in the knee by grenade splinters he continued to inspire his men by his initiative, courage and outstanding leadership, until the Company had captured its objective and consolidated its position. He then went forward and brought in all the wounded men who were lying outside the perimeter.

In spite of his painful wound Captain Randle refused to be evacuated and insisted on carrying out a personal reconnaissance with great daring in bright moonlight prior to a further attack by his Company on the positions to which the enemy had withdrawn. At dawn on 6th May the attack opened led by Captain Randle and one of the platoons succeeded in reaching the crest of the hill held by the Japanese. Another platoon, however, ran into heavy medium machine gun fire from a bunker on the reverse slope, of the feature. Captain Randle immediately appreciated that this particular bunker covered not only the rear of his new position but also the line of communication of the Battalion and therefore the destruction of the enemy post was imperative if the operation was to succeed. With utter disregard of the obvious danger to himself Captain Randle charged the Japanese machine gun post single-handed with rifle and bayonet.

Although bleeding in the face and mortally wounded by numerous bursts of machine gun fire he reached the bunker and silenced the gun with a grenade thrown through the bunker slit. He then flung his body across the slit so that the aperture should be completely sealed. The bravery shown by this officer could not have been surpassed and by his self-sacrifice he saved the lives of many of his men and enabled not only his own Company but the whole Battalion to gain its objective and win a decisive victory over the enemy. (TBNA)

OTHER BATTLE SITES IN KOHIMA

What about other areas of Kohima? All parts of Kohima and its outskirts were affected and no part of the town was left untouched by the war. The Japanese had approached Kohima from three directions. The first was from the southern side, on the Imphal–Kohima Road, and here they made their first appearance at Viswema on the night of 2–3 April 1944. This group probably came through Ukhrul, crossing Gaziphema and Maram/Mao to southern Angami area to reach Kohima. This group branched out to send about 3,000 troops from Maram to Poilwa. There is a possibility that some Japanese troops may have come via Kanglatombi, which they overran, as Maram is south of Mao, to present a second direction of attack and approach Kohima from the western side via Khonoma and Pulie Badze/Jotsoma. This second group also marched to Mezoma and Secüma, above Zubza. This group would withdraw and finally meet with the southern group at Pulie Badze, the north-westernmost tip of what the British called the Aradura Spur, although no Naga recognized Pulie Badze as part of Aradura. The third direction was from the eastern side, coming after the well-known battles of Kharasom and Jessami. There were at least two routes they took in the Chakhesang area to reach the Kohima-Phek-Thevopisü-Chozuba-Ciesezu route and the Chizami-Zhavame-Pfutsero-Kikrüma route. There were also some who were believed to have gone via Kezhakeno, Kezoma, etc. Some from the southern group would also join those from the eastern group at Meriema/Cheswema.

While the attack group on the southern side, which included the Commander of the 31st Japanese Division, General Kotoku Sato, who set up his headquarters at Jakhama, concentrated on the attack on Kohima, the eastern and western attack groups, while supporting the Kohima thrust, seemed to have worked as the Japanese Right Hook and Left Hook. These were strategic moves and could have ensured Japanese victory at least in the Kohima area, which would literally mean their victory in the Naga Hills, and help them in their intended march to Delhi or what the INA called 'Delhi Chalo!' Unfortunately for the Japanese, things did not quite work out that way and they got bogged down in Kohima.

The places in Kohima where the bitterest fighting took place are now dotted with British memorials. The present Commonwealth War Cemetery (DC's bungalow) and Raj Bhavan (Garrison Hill), including above the present hospital area (IGH Spur), the Heritage Hotel (Kuki Piquet), the Second World War Tank just below Kuki Piquet, Indoor Stadium (FSD), Assam Rifles' Officers Mess area and towards the Imphal Road (DIS), present Police Headquarters area (Jail Hill), etc., together represent the concentrated fighting belts of the battle for what is today Kohima town.

Then there was the Aradura Spur, which covered a long distance, starting from above the cathedral area to Dzüvürü River (where the Norfolk Regiment Memorial is located just above the Imphal Road and further on the Royal Scots memorial), to GPT (General Purposes Transport) Ridge, above the Chief Minister's residence and all the way to Pulie Badze. The Queen's Own

Cameron Highlanders Memorial stands in Kohima Village, just below the tower, at the highest point in the village. All the above mentioned areas, including the present Police Reserve areas saw scenes of some of the most entrenched fighting in the Battle of Kohima. No part of Kohima, and its vicinity, was left untouched.

WORKS CITED

Arthur, M. *Symbol of Courage: A Complete History of the Victoria Cross*. London: Sidgwick & Jackson, 2004.

Fecitt, H. 'Fighting the Nagas 1832–1880. The Naga siege of Kohima and the British attack on Khonoma.' www.kaiser-scross.com/304501/544622.html.

Keane, F. *Road of Bones: The Siege of Kohima 1944*. London: Harper Press, 2010.

Nagi, S. *Kohima Rhüu*. Kohima: NV Press, 2016.

Personal interviews. Nagaland: 2016–2017.

The British National Archives (TBNA). London, UK.

PART II

NAGA PARTICIPATION AS SOLDIERS IN THE SECOND WORLD WAR

BY MAJOR HARRY FECITT MBE, TD

SEVEN

THE DECLARATION OF WAR IN 1939

The Naga response and the formation of the Second World War Naga labour corps

NAGA INVOLVEMENT IN THE FIRST WORLD WAR

Memories of the Naga involvement in the 1914–1918 Great War strongly influenced the Naga reaction to the British declaration of war in 1939. In 1917, British officials had recruited around 2,000 volunteers from the Assam Naga Hills to go to France and serve in the 21st Naga Labour Corps. The men were organized into four companies, the 35th, 36th, 37th and 38th (Naga) Labour Companies and were commanded by the British Deputy Commissioner for the Naga Hills. The Nagas worked on military labour duties in Mametz, Le Transloy, Haute Avesnes, Contalmaison and Guillemont. Some went to Mesopotamia. They performed duties such as salvaging war material for reuse and on road maintenance, but they probably also constructed camps and loaded and unloaded trains and trucks whenever required. They knew that they would be working in a war zone but they were assured that they did not have to fight.

A total of 1,680 men arrived in France in June and July 1917, and probably the other 300 that had been recruited were found to be unfit or unsuitable. The men returned to Assam in 1918 and interestingly some of them, along with other Naga Government servants in Kohima at the time, formed an association called the Naga Club in Kohima with a branch in Mokokchung, making it the primary association where the educated Nagas met on a regular basis. On 10 January 1929, the Naga Club members, feeling the weight of the responsibility on their shoulders, as the only educated Nagas at the time, gave a representation to the Simon Commission, when it visited Kohima, asking that the Naga people be left out of the proposed Reformed Scheme of India and to have the right of self-determination, as they did not want to be part of India. (For text of the Representation see Appendix 5.) The Commission took cognizance of Naga sentiments and left them out of the Reformed Scheme of India as per the British India Act, 1935, terming the Naga areas as 'Naga Hills Excluded Area'.

Further recruitment took place in 1917 but a draft of 810 Naga Hills recruits that should have gone to France was diverted to take part in the Kuki Rising, when British troops operated against Kukis who rose up in arms against attempts to recruit more men for the Manipur Labour Corps that was also serving in France. The sub-tribal statistics of this draft was: Angamis 480; Aos 120; Zemis 90; Lothas 60; and Kukis and Kacha Nagas 60. This draft was used for portering duties and at one time during the operations against the Kukis, some of these men went on strike, but after a few floggings had been handed out – which often provided entertainment for the men not receiving the lash – calm was restored and everyone got back to work.

In the Indian Princely State of Manipur, the Maharaja, Sri Churachand Singh, raised the 22nd Manipur Labour Corps of 2,000 men but it was likely that compulsion was used to obtain many recruits, with chiefs and headmen being told to find certain numbers of 'volunteers'. The men were organized into the 39th, 40th, 65th and 66th (Manipur) Labour Companies and were commanded by the British Political Agent to the Princely State. The communities/ tribes recruited were Meiteis, Tangkhuls, Koms and Kukis. R. S. Ruichumhoa, one of the first Tangkhuls to receive a thorough education and one of the earliest evangelists, led the Tangkhul contingent numbering 1,200. In late 1917 when the Maharaja attempted to raise another 2,000 men, many Kukis rose up against him and the British.

The men of the 21st Labour Corps who died in France or on the high seas, and who are commemorated by the Commonwealth War

Graves Commission, are listed in an Appendix at the end of this book. The Tangkhul casualties from the 22nd Manipur Labour Corps have not yet been identified. Regrettably the records in Manipur of this Labour Corps were destroyed in the Second World War by Japanese bombing.

SECOND WORLD WAR

In September 1939, when Britain declared that it was at war with Germany there were many enquiries from Nagas asking if recruitment was to commence for a Naga Labour Corps. British officials discussed this until July 1941 when they decided that a Labour Corps would not be activated as their priority was recruitment for the Indian Army. Nagas volunteered to serve both in the Assam Regiment and the paramilitary Assam Rifles, and around 400 tribesmen had been enlisted by the time that war broke out with Japan in December 1941.

When the British decided that a good road had to be built from Manipur into Burma about 3,000 Nagas were recruited to work on this project. The men assembled in Kohima bringing their own equipment of bamboo mats, cooking pots, clothes and as much rice as they could carry. The project was popular, and around 1,500 Lothas turned up instead of the 1,000 requested along with 1,633 Aos instead of the 1,500 requested. There were reports of men from other tribes but the records are not clear. Three thousand men were put to work on the Pallel–Tamu Road and the remainder were used on various jobs around Imphal. When the Japanese bombed Imphal, some Nagas absconded back to their villages, but the vast majority faithfully continued their road work, and kept the Tamu Road open until the last refugees and soldiers from Burma had reached Manipur.

The Nagas were then dispersed along the Dimapur–Kohima Road to keep it open during the monsoon. But the rains in June were heavy, while the sleeping arrangements were insufficient as not enough tarpaulins had been provided, and sickness developed. The men from the Pallel–Tamu Road work were suffering from having eaten a diet of highly polished rice and this led to the development of beriberi. Many of the Aos working below the 42nd mile slip died, and the Ao contingent was disbanded in groups from August onwards. From September, batches of eastern Angami (now called Chakhesang) recruits arrived, and they worked on the road from the 42nd mile up to Kohima.

In that month, the USA Air Force and the Royal Air force established a chain of watchtower observation stations in the Naga Hills; these stations reported any aircraft that they saw and sent weather reports to the airfields in Assam. On the whole, the Nagas cooperated with this project and provided labour, but in the Trans-frontier area, fighting occurred in which the Sub-Divisional Officer from Mokokchung was wounded by a poisoned arrow; he would have died if a fellow officer had not sucked the poison out of the wound.

It is likely that in 1943 the British continued to use volunteer Naga labour as and when required, but not on a massive scale. In 1944, when the Japanese invaded Manipur and the Naga Hills, the situation changed dramatically and Naga assistance to the British became directly linked to military operations, as will be described. Tribute must be paid to ünilhu Angami of Khonoma Village who was the 'Headman' of the Naga Porter Corps; his influence and efforts made the Porter Corps a successful military support unit. He later became an officer in the Naga Levies and was awarded the prestigious Military Cross.

WORKS CITED

Chasie, C. *The Naga Imbroglio: A Personal Perspective*. Kohima: Standard Printers & Publishers, 1999.

Lambert, E. Copies of papers deposited in the Kohima World War II Museum, York, UK.

Pratap, C. 'North East India and the First World War'. The Centre for Hidden Histories, 4 February 2016. www.hiddenhistorieswwi.ac.uk/uncategorized/2016/02/north-east-india-and-the-first-world-war.

Starling, J. and Lee, I. *No Labour, No Battle. Military Labour during the First World War*. Stroud: Spellmount, 2009.

EIGHT

UNEXPECTED STRANGERS PASSING THROUGH AND DROPPING IN 1942–1945

Refugee and military visitors to Naga Hills during British and Chinese retreat from Burma.
'V' Force operations in the Naga Hills.
The Chindit operations.
The USA military operations.
Allied aircrew who parachuted into Naga territory.

ESCAPE ROUTES FROM NORTHERN BURMA IN 1942

In 1942, war came with a sudden and savage fury to the British colony of Burma as Japanese troops invaded the country which was defended by British, Indian, Burmese and Nationalist Chinese troops and by USA aviators contracted by the Nationalist Chinese Government. Because the lowland Buddhist Burmans preferred rural agriculture to industry or military service there were many Indian workers, soldiers and policemen in Burma. Additionally, there were Indian businessmen and money lenders who were often detested by the Burmans, as was the British colonial presence. Very soon, gangs of Burman thugs known as dacoits were attacking and killing Indians, and looting Indian properties and possessions. Burman nationalists quickly sided with the Japanese although the hill tribesmen mainly preferred British rule and protection.

As British troops retreated before Japanese attacks, wealthy Indians sailed from Rangoon to Calcutta or Madras whilst poorer Indians trekked to the Arakan coast and made for Chittagong in British Indian territory. But many Indian Government, dock and railway workers were persuaded to stay in Burma by British officials who promised safe evacuation if Upper Burma could not be held against the Japanese invaders. However, Japanese air attacks devastated wooden-built Burmese towns and villages, causing panic and the flight northwards of thousands of Indian, Anglo-Indian, Anglo-Burmese and British civilians. Meanwhile many Indian and Burmese police and sepoys deserted from their units; the Burmese went home but the Indian deserters fled northwards, carrying their arms and often acting as brigands.

Most of the British, Indian and Burma Army troops and some of the Chinese troops who marched out of Burma ahead of the Japanese invasion in 1942 took the route north along the Irrawaddy River, then up the Chindwin River to Kalewa, and finally up the Kabaw Valley to Tamu, from where the Indian Princely State of Manipur could be reached by a mule track. Other Chinese troops marched eastwards into Yunnan. British and Indian refugees mainly marched with their own troops on the Kabaw Valley route, suffering enormous privations; thousands died from Burman dacoit attacks, starvation and exhaustion.

But there were groups of Allied soldiers and refugees who had marched or been moved by road or train to Myitkyina in northern Burma; they were evacuated by air to India until 6 May when Japanese air attacks closed down Myitkyina airfield. The people who remained at Myitkyina when air evacuations ceased were mostly ill-clad and poorly prepared Indian clerical and general workers, and their families who then had the option of walking over wild terrain to Assam; the routes available used to be the Hukawng Valley leading to the Pangsau Pass, and the Chaukan and Diphu Passes further to the east. None of the routes were pleasant and only the fittest survived as monsoon weather descended on to the Patkai mountain range lying along the Burma-Indian border.

The Government of India basically distanced itself from the refugee problem, although British and Indian officials and relief agencies in Manipur and Assam did what they could with the slender resources allocated to them. The officials constantly requested information from Burma as to Japanese movements and the numbers of refugees and the routes being used, but the Government of Burma had collapsed, and with that collapse any semblance of British authority vanished into the monsoon mud. In his book, *Burma: The Longest War*, Louis Allen wrote: 'The exodus of the Indian refugees reflected little credit on the foresight or compassion of the governments of India and Burma. Had it not been for the gallant and selfless work of volunteers, like the Assam tea planters, many thousands more refugees would have died' (90).

In the final estimate over 500,000 refugees reached India by various routes, and it is believed that up to 50,000 others died trying to walk there.

There was one group of people whose efforts certainly helped many refugees to stay alive, and that group was the hill tribes of Assam and eastern Manipur. Several refugee routes led through the territory of the Naga tribes and the Naga involvement in the survival of many refugees was substantial, but to date that involvement has not been well publicized.

THE HUKAWNG VALLEY – PANGSAU PASS ROUTE TO LEDO

Most refugees stranded at Myitkyina, plus some military units and groups of leaderless, demoralized and mutinous soldiers, marched to the Hukawng Valley and then through the jungle wilderness of the valley to the Pangsau Pass at 3,700 feet (1,136 metres) elevation, from where a mud track dropped steeply down to Ledo in Assam; this route was 268 miles (431 kilometres) long. There was no proper road, only a path that led over steep ridges and across rivers fiercely swollen by monsoon rain. The very few inhabitants near the route were tough Naga tribespeople.

When the Japanese invaders occupied Rangoon in March 1942, the land route used by the USA to move supplies to Nationalist China was cut. A new land route had been planned from Ledo in Assam over the Pangsau Pass into northern Burma, and although a road did not exist when the refugees arrived, some British officials were on the ground mobilizing local labour to prepare a route, starting with a jeep track. The bulk of this work was undertaken by the Indian Tea Association at the request of the Government of India. The Indian Tea Association mobilized hundreds of European tea estate managers and thousands of their Indian doctors, mechanics, vehicles and drivers, elephants and mahouts, camp managers, maintenance staff, cooks and labourers on two-month voluntary contracts. This injection of disciplined and well-managed labour into the situation saved the lives of thousands of refugees, and also built motorable roads that the British and USA forces did not have the engineering capacity to construct at that time.

In the wet swamps of the Hukawng Valley, isolated British officials and India Tea Association men attempted to cope with streams of malnourished and ill refugees, distributing what rations the Royal Air Force dropped on their route. One of the biggest problems was the banditry practised by some armed Indian deserters from Burma's military and police units; this lawlessness often happened under the eyes of British and Indian officers who abdicated responsibility for the recalcitrant sepoys. Rations were grabbed by the deserters and sold to refugees, and whatever else that could be seized from the miserable civilians, many of whom were dying, was extorted. Some of the refugees themselves stole extra rations and sold them to other refugees. Refugees, whose children were in dire medical condition, were tricked into paying for sometimes worthless injections by at least one refugee medical compounder who pretended to be a doctor.

In the middle of this epic and tragic situation, the Naga inhabitants of the Hukawng Valley could not avoid becoming involved. The European administrators hired Nagas to carry loads whilst refugee camps were established, and if a camp was near a village the headman might be paid for securing a ration dump that had been located there, or for maintaining a river crossing point or a section of trail. Nagas were paid to erect many overnight shelters for refugees at stages along the trail. Wealthy Indian refugees hired Nagas to carry their possessions, and sometimes frail or sick members of the refugee family were transported on litters by Nagas.

These services were not without risk to the Nagas as many infectious diseases were prevalent on the refugee trail, particularly when the monsoon rain pounded down and turned the trail into a vast expanse of mud. The corpses of dead refugees often lay abandoned near the trail suppurating into it, and many refugees defecated and urinated where they slept on the trail, adding to the incidences of disease threatening the bare-footed hill tribesmen.

The Indian Tea Association used an old opium trade path to develop a route for the refugees, starting it from the Assam end at Lekhapani. The route then ran through Tipong, Tirap, Kumlao, Fuffalo, Ngokpi, Namchick, Namky, Namgoi, Nampong, Pahari, the Pangsau Pass, Shamlung, Nawngyang Tagung Hka, Ngalang Ga, Namlip, Yangsung, Taikham Zup and then on to Shinbwiyang. The Royal Air Force dropped food at three locations south of the Pangsau Pass, which was the international border. Rampang Nagas supported the Indian Tea Association on the Assam side, with the headman's son from Yogli managing many of the porters that were hired.

Another route was developed to come in from the east, starting at Simon and joining the main trail at Nampong; this route passed through Namgoi Mukh and Yangman, and elephants were used from Simon to move food supplies as far as possible towards Nampong. During the monsoon, elephants could easily destroy the trail, and so their use had to be carefully planned so as not to interfere with foot movement.

NAGA SORES

One affliction that affected many refugees as they passed through Naga areas was what came to be known as the 'Naga sores'. In his book *Forgotten Frontier* Geoffrey Tyson describes the condition:

The Naga sore is an ulcer, peculiar to the part of the world from which it derives its name, which attacked those refugees who were badly undernourished, and whose food had been lacking in vitamins and calcium. A man trekking alone was apt to pay less attention to matters of food than a man travelling in a party, particularly a party containing a woman who could cook …. The Naga sore, or ulcer, starts as a small blister, usually on the leg or foot, in a place where there is not much flesh. It develops rapidly for four or five days and then stops. By this time, it may be five inches in diameter and half an inch deep, destroying all the upper layers of skin and often the tendons and muscles as well. Though it often has a clean appearance when washed, the underpart frequently stinks to high heaven, from the pus which rapidly accumulates in the cavity. The possession of a Naga sore or sores was a very considerable handicap to a refugee who was making his way on foot, and every camp doctor tried to find a cure, but without final success. One and all came to the conclusion that there was little hope until the refugee's general condition could be improved.

The most satisfactory ad hoc treatment on the road was to wash the Naga sore thoroughly with soap and water, followed by alcohol and a mixture of acriflavine in glycerine. In not a few cases, a Naga sore was complicated by the presence of hundreds of small maggots in the wound. On one occasion, kerosene oil was poured into a hole in a small boy's head, and three hundred and fifty half-inch maggots, of four different species, were removed. The boy survived and is now fit and well. Such are the powers of human survival (84–5).

THE CHINESE 5TH ARMY IN THE HUKAWNG VALLEY

The Chinese 5th Army, which had been fighting the Japanese in Burma alongside the British Army, marched out of Burma to India on the Pangsau Pass route, but its 7,500 men caused congestion and were inclined to seize all air-dropped supplies for themselves, ignoring the refugees and any Nagas who were guarding the food dumps. The bulk of the Chinese soldiers got lost, but aerial reconnaissance located them near Dalu on the Chindwin River, and special supply drops of food were made for them.

The Political Officer at Margherita in the Assam Valley, a police officer named Eric Lambert, volunteered to divert the Chinese troops away to the south-west of the Pangsau Pass, using footpaths through the Naga Hills. This remote area was Naga territory. Lambert achieved a successful diversion, working hard and sometimes violently to prevent the armed Chinese soldiers from looting food and livestock from Naga villages and from demolishing Naga houses for firewood. Lambert guided the Chinese into India from where they were transported to training bases near Ramgarh.

The American General J. W. 'Vinegar Joe' Stilwell was nominally the commander of Chinese forces in Burma, but as the Allied exodus from Burma gathered momentum no Chinese wanted to listen to him – they just kept marching towards either Yunnan in the east or India in the west. American planes flew into northern Burma to evacuate Stilwell and his staff, but to his credit he ordered his staff to fly out to India and set up training bases for the Chinese whilst he elected to march out into Manipur with a small party. Stilwell's group reached Homalin on the Chindwin River, and marched westwards on a gruelling journey through the Naga Hills to Imphal.

'V' FORCE IN THE NAGA HILLS

'V' Force was created by the British during the Japanese invasion of Burma. It was planned to be a 'stay behind' organization that would operate deep behind enemy lines, but it quickly concentrated on providing short-range reconnaissance and intelligence information from areas forward of the British front line. The Naga Hills region was titled No. 3 'V' Operations Area, and it reported to the Commander of Assam Zone 'V' Force. The 'V' Force personnel were drawn from the paramilitary regiment, the Assam Rifles, and from local villagers in the forward areas. Up to the end of 1944 the Assam Rifles sepoys operated into Burma up to and along the line of the Chindwin River, observing Japanese positions and reporting on the movements of enemy patrols.

Two Nagas received awards for service in 'V' Force. The headmaster of Ukhrul School, Ralengnao Khathing BA, received a commission as an officer in the 19th Hyderabad Regiment, Indian Army, and was attached to 'V' Force. Ralengao fitted into 'V' Force operations perfectly and after a year in the field he was appointed to be a Member of the Order of the British Empire (MBE) with this excellent citation that explains many of his duties:

This officer, the only NAGA Emergency Commissioned Officer, has for over a year without leave or rest, continued to do most excellent and valued work in a forward area of this Area of 'V' Force. The whole of last monsoon he remained forward, in most trying conditions, organizing his guerrillas, and gaining much valuable information at a time when no regular troops were operating permanently. He also gave invaluable help to the withdrawing Chinese Army. The information he gained has been confirmed. He has done very many useful, and daring, patrols and recces, including down to the MAWLAIK area, from whence he brought back information of the Japanese positions. This Indian Emergency Commissioned Officer, by his trustfulness, his hard work, his unbounding energy and enthusiasm, has done much for the defence of India, and is greatly deserving of recognition for his services to his country. (The British National Archives, TBNA)

From the citation, it is evident that Ralengnao was working with many Naga and Kuki villagers, organizing them into observation and reporting teams that kept a constant watch on Japanese movements. With the passage of time we now have no record of who those courageous villagers were, and what exactly they did in support of the Allied war effort, but we must remember and salute them.

Another Naga operated at a lower, nevertheless quite important, level and received a Mention in Despatches for his gallantry. He was referred to as No. 27131 Rifleman Amos Ao of the Assam

Rifles. As detachments of the Assam Rifles supported the activities of 'V' Force and other covert operations we can assume that
Amos spent some time in dangerous situations, along with other
Nagas in the same regiment, and his award would have been for
bravery displayed in the field. Sadly, his citation has not survived.

CHINDIT OPERATIONS THAT PASSED THROUGH NAGA TERRITORY

In 1943, and again in 1944, units of the British 'Special Force'
passed through Naga territory. A special Force, titled 3rd Indian
Division for deception purposes, was composed of several
British, Gorkha and West African units that had been trained to
operate behind enemy lines in northern Burma. The men were
nicknamed Chindits after the oft seen massive figures of myth-
ical Chinthe animals that stand outside the entrances to temples
in Burma. The role of the Chindits was classed as Long Range
Penetration and their task was to influence the battle fought by
conventional Allied forces by operating in the enemy rear and
disrupting Japanese logistical efforts and lines of communication.

During the 1943 operation, the Chindits had only a little con-
tact with the Nagas both on their march in, via the Tamu road,
and on their march out of Burma. In the 1944 operation, most
Chindits flew into Burma by glider or transport plane but one
brigade marched in from Ledo during February. The Brigade
Commander, Bernard Ferguson, wrote in his book *The Wild
Green Earth* of his arrival at the Chinese-garrisoned village of
Hkalak Ga in Naga territory:

> *Below on a crest no more than a mile away, lay the stockaded
> village of Hkalak. The crest was clear of jungle and neat houses
> circled it. Here was no straggling Naga village; it was a secure
> fort. A watch tower thirty feet high, built of logs and roofed
> with brown plantain leaves, dominated the countryside ...
> here was a company of Chinese under a Captain; there were
> three American officers: one a doctor, with an excellent little*

hospital; one a liaison officer with the Chinese; the third was the owner of the watch tower whose duty it was to report any aircraft seen ... The doctor at the hospital was a grand fellow, who accepted various sick men from us ... and also various men who had the ill luck to be wounded on Chinese booby-traps, which infested the area.

The local Nagas had been surprised at the size of the Chindit column – four thousand men, but they had had some measure of warning: unknown to us the bush telegraph had been in operation, even though the only Nagas we had seen had been a party of three on their way to the (Ledo) Road. The chief item of interest to the Nagas were our mules and ponies, the first they had seen.

I liked what little we saw of the Nagas. They were much more jungly and primitive than those other Nagas who live near the Manipur Road, a couple of hundred miles away to the south-west: although they looked much the same. They had frizzy hair not unlike Polynesians, and I swear you could smell them before they came around the corner. They would do nothing for money: opium was their only currency ... and without it the Nagas would neither work nor give us information ... The Nagas were the most parochial folk I have ever met with. In most of their villages there was someone who could speak Chingpaw, the tongue of the Kachins ... But the Nagas had not much information to give us, since between the areas where the Japs had been, and those where they had not, there was no coming and going.

Furthermore, the relations between the villages were strained; this and that village were allies against the other and the next; they would not band as a nation against us or against the Japs. We had amusing confirmation of this some months later, when we intercepted a runner carrying mail for the Japs south of the Chindwin. Among his despatches was one from a junior Jap officer to a senior, complaining for what appeared from the tone of the letter to be for the umpteenth time that the Nagas wouldn't help the Japs against us, but were continually asking the Japs for help against each other.

Naga veterans (including one Levy)

Chenchungba Ao
(3332559) 1st Assam, Naik, Fellowship Colony, Dimapur. Interpreter & Runner, Battle of Kohima (Kohima, Wokha, Tangkhul Area, Burma).

Keduchü Kupa
(564) 1st Assam, Kami Village. Battle of Kohima (Aradura, Pulie Badze, Burma).

Sovehu Nienu
(542) 1st Assam, Phek Village. Battle of Kohima (Jessami, Pulie Badze, Burma).

Penthungo Ezung
(4523) Sep, 1st Assam, Longsa Village.

Nyimchamo Lotha
(4332491) Sep,1st Assam, Wokha. Driver (Burma–Mandalay, accident in Mimeo).

Khakhu Khing
(3899) Sep,1st Assam Regiment (106 years), Tesophenyu Village. Fought at Zubza, Kohima, Jakhama, Burma.

Lemayanger Ao
(878) 3rd Assam, MT
Havildar. Half-Nagarjan,
Dimapur. Battle of Kohima

Tuochalie Rengma
(3159) 3rd Assam Regiment,
Tsemenyu. Demonstration
Platoon, Training Centre,
Shillong

Zhavise Angami
2nd Assam, Havildar
(Signals), Kohima, 97 years.
Trainer (Punjab Regiment)
Battle of Kohima (TCP Gate)

Khetozu Sema
(3417) 1st Assam, Sep.
Kuhuboto. Battle of Kohima,
Burma

Saisshe Sema
(2594) 1st and 2nd Assam
Regiment. Naik, Ighanumi,
Mandalay, Arakan

Shitozu Sema
(3435) 3rd Assam, Thilixu
Village, 92 years. Training,
Shillong

Veterans at an event in March 2016 in Kohima

Sosangtemba Longkumer
Sepoy, Naga Levies, Longsa
Village, Mokokchung

Nohol Natso
Jakhama Village, 97 years.
British Driver & Mechanic

Gallantry award winners

Subedar Imtisang Ao MM

Yambhamo Lotha
1st Assam Regiment, MID,
MM

Kumbho
MBE

Mhiesizolie Chasie
MID

Nikhalhu Makritsu
BEM

A. Kevichüsa
MBE

Chansao Lotha, MBE

Guardians of the cemetery

Samuel Mezhür
BEM

P. Atuo Mezhür

Lhouvi Mezhür

Three graves in Kohima

*I have heard, with what truth I don't know, that Naga re-
ligion tells them they have two lives to live: this one on earth,
and one more, of the same length, in the Village of the Dead.
The number of slaves that they will have in that second life
amounts to exactly the number of heads which they succeed in
bagging in this present one. Hence the jolly, old-world pastime
of head-hunting, which they still pursue with all the keenness
of Rugger players. I learned a few words of Naga from some
grinning children one day … but not enough to discuss higher
metaphysics such as these. And alas, I have long since forgotten
even those few words. (Ferguson 50–4)*

Bernard Ferguson's metaphysical musings may or may not have
any validity but his descriptions of Nagas are refreshing to read;
they were written 70 years ago before political correctness crept
in to stifle much of today's writing, and whilst his comments may
appear patronizing now, they are both amusing and informative.
No other Chindit commander has written so ably about the Nagas.

GENERAL STILWELL AND THE CHINESE ADVANCE FROM LEDO

After training his Chinese soldiers at Ramgarh, General Stilwell
moved them to the Ledo area, and arranged for reinforcements to
be flown in from Kunming in Nationalist China. American troops
also appeared as the Allies had decided that the planned supply
road from Ledo to Kunming must be built as it was important to
keep China in the war. Stilwell was given the task of advancing over
the Pangsau Pass and down the Hukawng and Mogaung Valleys to
Myitkyina where he was to capture the airfield. American engineers followed closely behind the Chinese troops and built a two-
lane road and laid a fuel pipeline beside the road. Concurrently,
the Nationalist Chinese in Yunnan were meant to advance from
China into Burma to meet up with Stilwell's troops.

Phase 1 of Stilwell's advance saw Chinese troops advancing
through the Naga Hills in October 1943. But now the Japanese

were also pushing forward in preparation for an invasion of India. Nagas in the area had to get out of the way as Japanese and Chinese troops fought each other at Sharaw Ga, Yupbang Ga and at Ngajatzup. Using air and artillery support, and a regiment of Chindit-trained Americans, Stilwell's Chinese pushed the Japanese down the Hukawng Valley to Shingbwiyang where they halted. An outpost was established at Hkalak Ga, as described by Bernard Ferguson above.

ALLIED AIRMEN PARACHUTING INTO NAGA TERRITORY

The description of 'Watch and Ward' operations in the north Cachar area (in the next chapter) gives an example of a rear-seat observer who bailed out and parachuted down into Naga territory. Closer to Kohima, another incident occurred that resulted in a Naga being awarded the Military Medal. No. L5 Sepoy Sare Angami served in the Naga Levies; he came from Chizami Village in Chakhesang area. Sare's citation describes his very brave actions:

Seeing one of our planes crash into the side of a mountain, Sepoy Sare took out a party of villagers and searched for the pilot. They located him alive but badly injured. They took him to Sepoy Sare's house, where Sare cared for him for nine days, completely disregarding the Japanese patrols searching for the pilot. The whole area was in enemy hands. Sepoy Sare then arranged and led a party of Levies who carried the wounded man three days' march through enemy territory to safety, handing him over to one of our columns. In addition to saving the life of this officer, Sepoy Sare took considerable intelligence to our columns, and entered enemy positions with a complete disregard for his own safety. (TBNA)

In his recently published book, *Among the Headhunters*, Robert Lyman tells the story of a group of Americans and Chinese who in 1943 parachuted to safety near the very remote Naga villages of Ponyo and Pangsha near the border. The group's aeroplane had developed mechanical failure and it crashed into a hillside after the passengers and crew had jumped out. When the authorities heard of the location of the survivors from the plane there was some concern as Pangsha warriors enjoyed a reputation as head-hunters. A rescue party left Mokokchung and marched via the villages of Helipong, Kuthurr, Chentang, Chingmei and Noklak to reach Pangsha where the Americans and Chinese were found still in possession of their heads as they had got on well with their Naga hosts. The rescue party marched back by the same route whilst the Pangsha villagers enjoyed the reward of a ton and a half of salt that was free-dropped from an aeroplane over their village.

WORKS CITED

Allen, L. *Burma. The Longest War 1941–45*. J. M. Dent & Sons Ltd, 1986.

Ferguson, B. 1946. *The Wild Green Earth*. London: Collins.

Lyman, R. 2016. *Among the Headhunters*. Boston: Da Capo Press.

Moser, D. 1978. *China-Burma-India*. USA: Time Life Books.

Pearn, B. R. 'Official Report on the Civil Evacuation of Burma 1942.' Courtesy of the Anglo-Burmese Library website.

Ramsay, Alasdair T. MBE, Major. '…and some fell by the wayside.' Orient Longmans, 1948.

The British National Archives (TBNA). TBNA: WO 373/79/416; WO 373/37/105.

Tuchman, B. W. *Stilwell and the American Experience in China, 1911–1945*. New York: The Macmillan Company, 1970.

Tyson, G. *Forgotten Frontier*. Calcutta: W. H. Targett & Co. Ltd, 1945.

Whitworth, D. MC, Brigadier. 'The Evacuation of Refugees and the Chinese Fifth Army from the Hukawng Valley into Assam, Summer 1942.' Lecture, 4 July 1943. (Courtesy of the Anglo-Burmese Library website.)

NINE

'WATCH AND WARD' IN THE NORTH CACHAR HILLS

Zemi Nagas patrol against Japanese threats, 1943–1945

Their active help to us was beyond value or praise.

Comment on the Naga tribe by General W. J. Slim,
Commander of the British 14th Army.

NORTH CACHAR IN 1942

The Japanese threat to Manipur and Assam became a reality in the second half of 1942 and Allied tacticians saw that the North Cachar Hills offered a possible enemy infiltration route. Japanese saboteurs approaching from the Imphal–Tiddim Road could descend on to the Bengal railway line from where they could move north into the Brahmaputra Valley or west into Bengal.

To counter this threat the British covert organization titled 'V' Force decided to install a 'Watch and Ward' scheme in the North Cachar Hills, as had been done in eastern Manipur and the Naga Hills of Assam. This scheme involved the employment of volunteer Zemi Naga and loyal Kuki scouts who would watch for enemy movement on the tracks leading into the hills, and once a threat had been identified tribal runners would move swiftly with reports to the nearest British military wireless station from where the military authorities in Bengal and Assam could be alerted.

The scouts would be armed for self-defence, but their priority would be the covert acquisition of sound information and its rapid delivery to a military signaller.

THE ZEMI NAGAS AND THE BRITISH

Unlike most other Naga tribes who had settled their military differences with the British in the nineteenth century, factions of the Zemis had been involved in an insurrection during the early 1930s. The religious Heraka movement had been started by a Rongmei Naga named Haipou Jadonang, a former Indian Army sepoy with First World War experience in Mesopotamia, and his very young female cousin Gaidinliu. Heraka practiced a return to basic tribal beliefs and customs and a rejection of the activities of Christian missionaries. A Naga Kingdom would be proclaimed and neighbouring Kuki tribe people, regarded as interlopers, would be massacred; the Cachar Naga area would be a better place, and this theme attracted many Naga villagers living lives of hardship in the hills.

When the British authorities woke up to what was happening, they apprehended Jadonang and hanged him in 1931 for the murder by human sacrifice of four Manipuri traders who had been travelling to Silchar. Jadonang's assistants in the murder were imprisoned. Gaidinliu, regarded as a goddess, now assumed the Heraka leadership role, and was a success as she inspired many of the North Cachar Hills Nagas into defiance of British rule including a refusal to pay taxes. Most Zemis supported Gaidinliu, and those who did not were too frightened to admit their lack of support. Her official entourage sold her 'holy water' and treated sick villagers with her 'magic spells', and of course money or tribute was required for this treatment and an accompanying 'blessing'.

The resident British paramilitary regiment, the Assam Rifles, sent detachments to scour the hills for Gaidinliu as she had now become a serious political embarrassment. She exhorted the men of Hangrum village to attack a local Assam Rifles post, explaining that her magic powers would turn the sepoys' bullets into water; tragically for them the attackers discovered that the bullets that hit their bodies continued to be metal that killed or wounded. Gaidinliu moved around the hills being concealed and protected by worshippers. But finally, her location was given to the authorities by the Kuki caretaker of a government guest house at Lakema, and the teenage goddess was captured by the Assam Rifles in October 1932; after trial she was sentenced to life imprisonment. Her colleagues strangled the family of the Kuki caretaker – he was absent from home collecting his reward.

Before she was arrested Gaidinliu told one of her henchmen named Masang that her possible capture or death would not matter as she would reappear in the future in such a shape that only the faithful would recognize her. This prophecy was to become extremely useful when 'V' Force started its 'Watch and Ward' operations in the North Cachar Hills.

THE 'NAGA QUEEN'

Living alone among the Zemi Nagas in 1942 was a single, young British female photographer who was recording the customs and culture of the tribe, and she had become a leading authority on the Zeliang Nagas. Her name was Ursula Violet Graham Bower, and because of the mutual trust and respect that had developed between herself and her tribal hosts she became known by her fellow Europeans as 'The Naga Queen'. One of the assistants in her initial work had been Gaidinliu's former accomplice Masang, who had served his time in a government prison for six months and then had been rehabilitated into Naga society. Masang was struck by a resemblance he noticed in Bower of Gaidinliu, and before his death he proclaimed Bower to be the reincarnation of Gaidinliu although Gaidinliu herself (in jail) was still alive! There was little that Bower could do about this and both she and the tribal members who fondly remembered the saga of Gaidinliu just accepted the situation, but Bower now received more respect and adulation from the Zeliang Nagas.

RAISING THE WATCH AND WARD SCOUTS

In August 1942, a 'V' Force Colonel visited Bower at her Laisong base. They agreed that she should raise and command the scout force for North Cachar. She was a civilian but she would be regarded as holding the rank of Captain in 'V' Force. With the assistance of the senior British administrative officer in the hills she commenced recruiting, deciding to tackle Hangrum village first. Bower knew that the Hangrum villagers influenced other Zemis, and that the village still remembered its dead from the Gaidinliu insurrection. The village had to be won over if 'Watch and Ward' was to be viable in the hills.

After heated debates with the villagers, and assisted by her Second-in-Command the Zemi Namkia Buing, 'Watch and Ward' was gradually accepted, and when other minor villages said 'Yes' the Hangrum elders had no arguments left and agreed to the scheme. Recruitment of fit young men went ahead without hindrance including men from the loyal elements of the Kuki tribe. 'V' Force slowly supplied finance and rations for Bower and ancient muzzle-loading rifles for the scouts, and when red blankets – the symbol of authority in the hills – were requested and then mislaid, a 'V' Force officer drove to Calcutta, and obtained nineteen scarlet blankets from British military hospitals. Although the rifles were ancient, they were very useful as villagers had been denied gunpowder for the previous two years due to wartime austerity measures. Now the scouts, who had spare powder and lead shot for shooting practice, were very popular in the villages as crop-security guards and their shooting skills increased. The scouts became a fact of life in the hills.

The area that Bower's scouts covered was shaped like a flattened triangle whose apex was Haflong on the railway line in the west, and whose base ran from Khuangmual south-west down the Jiri River to its confluence with the Jenam River. In every village on an entrance track into that triangle, a group of around five scouts and two runners was recruited. More runners were recruited in the interior villages along the main tracks, allowing for the non-stop progress of verbal or hand-held reports. The most critically important village in the Watch and Ward scheme was Haijaichak as all tracks led through it; the scout leader there was Hailkamsuong and his Second-in-Command was Gailuba, and both men were stalwart and professional in their duties.

Besides the immediate reporting of any enemy movement, the duties of the scouts were to escort all non-authorized travellers to Bower's Headquarters at Laisong, to report crashed aircraft and to be aware of everything that happened in the hills. A pass was devised that included a symbol recognizable to the illiterate scouts, and this was issued to government officials and other legitimate travellers.

A JAPANESE INCURSION

In mid-March 1944, the Japanese 15th Army, with support from the Indian National Army (INA), invaded the Indian Princely State of Manipur and the region of Assam just north of it. The Japanese intentions were to capture Imphal, the capital of Manipur, and Kohima, the Naga hill town that lay astride the route down into the Brahmaputra Valley. After replenishing themselves from captured British depots in Imphal and Kohima, the Japanese could then plan a descent into the Brahmaputra Valley, cause chaos by attacking the large Allied supply depots there, and cut off the supplies that USA pilots were flying into Nationalist China from eastern Assam. Meanwhile Indian National Army propagandists would attempt to trigger an anti-British revolt in Bengal.

The North Cachar Watch and Ward scheme, then eighteen months old, became aware of this crisis when two British sergeants from Silchar appeared at Laisong, and asked Bower if she knew the locations of any Japanese troops in her territory. Allied intelligence had reported that 50 Japanese soldiers had struck west from the Tiddim–Imphal Road, but their current location was not known. Bower and her 150 scouts, collectively armed with one service rifle, one single-barrelled shotgun, and 70 muzzle-loading rifles, were the only Allied defences between these Japanese and the railway line running past Haflong.

Bower's team was unaware of this Japanese threat but it immediately sent scouts forward to look for traces of the enemy. Meanwhile a company of the Indian Army Chamar Regiment moved up to Laisong to support the scouts, and 'V' Force

Headquarters rapidly supplied more service rifles, Thompson and Sten hand-held sub-machine guns, shotguns, grenades, ammunition and rations.

Interestingly one British officer had come close to the Japanese group. He was Lieutenant Colonel J. H. Williams who was known in Manipur and the adjacent Burmese areas as 'Elephant Bill'. Williams had been a pre-war specialist in the industrial use of elephants in the forests of northern Burma. During the British withdrawal into India in 1942, Williams had brought his elephants into Manipur where they were formed into Elephant Companies of the Indian Army, and employed in supporting military engineering projects.

'Elephant Bill' had been ordered to remove his 45 elephants from the battle zone to avoid the enemy killing or capturing and using them, and he marched on an extremely rugged cross-country route that started just south of Imphal and moved westwards to Silchar. Unknown to Williams, the Japanese were just behind his elephant party, and on the day that the beasts left the half-way village of Haochin, the Japanese arrived in the evening and killed a British Political Officer there. Next, the Japanese halted on the track at Haochin, and achieved their patrol mission for a time by blocking the route for groups of Indian Army non-combatants who had been ordered to march over the hills from Imphal to Silchar.

'Elephant Bill' carried on and finally reached Silchar, where the British troops had started using code words when communicating on public and railway telephone lines. 'One Elephant' meant ten Japanese, and so when the arrival of 45 elephants was notified great excitement was created until the elephants were known to be genuine beasts, and not 450 Japanese soldiers.

LOOTERS

While the Japanese threat receded, a more immediate problem was the chaos being caused in Naga and Kuki villages by undisciplined sepoys, mainly from the Indian Pioneer Corps, who had been ordered to march out westwards from Imphal through the Cachar

Hills to the railway. The reason for this was that with a siege of Imphal envisaged the British authorities attempted to remove as many non-combatants as possible from Imphal in order to conserve food stocks. But the military authorities did not provide sufficient rations for these men, nor did they arrange an adequate reception for them at the Cachar end of their journey. This was totally bad staff work by the Headquarters of the British 4th Corps in Imphal, and the probable cause was the ignorance of desk-bound men in Imphal offices about conditions on the tracks to Silchar.

'Elephant Bill' had come across this food problem on his route through Haochin, and had informed the authorities that rations needed to be dropped for these unfortunate sepoys, and they were. In the operational area of 'Bower Force' as the North Cachar Hills Watch and Ward Scheme was now called, the problems were compounded by the arrival of scores of armed stragglers from units such as the Ordnance Depot at Kanglatongbi, north of Imphal, that had been overrun and captured by the advancing Japanese. Some of these armed sepoys looted villages at their whim as they marched westwards, resulting in the villagers fleeing into the jungle with the consequence that the Watch and Ward duties were neglected.

Fortunately for Bower, Nepal, an ally of India and Britain, had sent some of its military units to fight in Assam and Manipur, including its Mahendra Dal infantry regiment. The Chamar Regiment sepoys had been sent to operate further south, but a platoon of Mahendra Dal sepoys arrived to assist Bower, and by using these Gorkhas offensively, a group of 32 armed looters in Haijaichak village was arrested whilst they were cooking a meal. With these looters marched off to face military justice, security was restored in the Bower Force area.

RECOVERY OF DOWNED AIRCREW

An important Watch and Ward responsibility was the observation of both enemy and Allied aircraft that got into trouble. If a plane was seen to crash in the hills, scouts would search for survivors, and escort any that they found back to Laisong. One such incident occurred when an American Vultee Vengeance plane with a British crew got into trouble over the Cachar Hills, and the observer in the rear seat, sensing an imminent crash, bailed out on his own initiative. The pilot regained control just before impacting the ground and flew off at low-level. The observer parachuted down safely and came across a group of Nagas who marched with him to Laisong, where he started a long road and rail journey back to his base. Meanwhile the pilot had landed at Imphal, and he turned around shouting 'Hi George, that was a near thing, wasn't it?' to find that George wasn't there!

THE WAR MOVES SOUTH AND THE SCOUTS DISBAND

In mid-1944, the defeated Japanese 15th Army started its disastrous retreat from Kohima and Imphal, and this led to small vulnerable groups of Japanese wandering southwards through the jungle to the east of the Cachar Hills. A platoon of the Maratha regiment replaced the Nepali Mahendra Dal sepoys, and Bower, armed with her Sten sub-machine gun, and her scouts moved east with the Marathas, hoping to hunt down enemy stragglers. The Maratha sepoys, some of them veterans of the Western Desert campaign, were keen to come to grips with the Japanese, but it appears that this aggressive outlook was not always shared by certain of the Maratha officers, and opportunities for offensive action were allowed to lapse. In the end, the Japanese and their remaining INA allies moved into Burma with the British 14th Army pursuing them.

The North Cachar Hills Watch and Ward scouts had had their day, and in November 1944, the order came for disbandment. The final parade was held at Laisong with all the scouts in attendance, along with some sepoys of the Assam Rifles, who had replaced the Marathas. The scouts, Zemi and Kuki, formed a three-sided hollow square and in turn each man marched forward to receive his discharge papers and an allocated prize – a rifle, or a knife, or an ivory armlet or cash. Those who received rifles immediately held a shooting competition in which the prizes were flasks of powder. Then feasting began and the Nagas and Kukis danced all night. It was a fitting finale for a 'V' Force unit out on a limb that had surmounted many difficulties, and had always performed most creditably in the field.

TRAINING ROYAL AIR FORCE AIRCREW IN JUNGLE SURVIVAL TECHNIQUES

In early 1945, although her scouts were disbanded and the fighting was raging many miles to the south in Burma, the military authorities still saw a useful role in Assam for Bower and some of her Zemi Nagas. She was appointed for six months as Chief Instructor in a jungle training camp located near Badarpur, north-west of Silchar. Here aircrew students were sent on two-week courses to learn techniques to help them survive if their planes came down in jungle.

The jungle campsite was sometimes visited by elephants and tigers to the amazement of the students, who were taught a variety of techniques designed to make them utilize jungle resources such as bamboo, edible plants, small animals and river fish. The aim was that each student would know how to survive whilst he avoided enemy contact on his way back to the nearest Allied position.

Naga instructors taught and demonstrated how to make overnight shelters, protect them with sharpened sticks, avoid elephants and tigers, make fires in monsoon conditions, boil water in bamboo sections, check the riverbanks for snakes and to have a sharp stick always ready to deal with them, to burn blood-sucking leeches off human flesh rather than to tug them off, to minimize risk when approaching villages and villagers, and to make spears and bows and arrows and use them for hunting food. The course finale was a 20-mile jungle trek back to base camp, utilizing the assimilated survival techniques. Not everyone liked the jungle, but those students who rose to the challenge, and learned how to deal with the realities of jungle survival, were unanimous in praising Bower and her Naga instructors for their man-management and instructional techniques.

RECOGNITION

At the end of her employment at Badarpur, Bower returned to her anthropological studies with the Zemi Nagas. During the war, Indian Army military offices in the rear areas had housed far too many capable men who should have been fighting in forward areas rather than attending club social engagements most evenings of the week; but that was how it was in the dying days of the British Raj. Ursula Violet Graham Bower by her personality, bravery, leadership skills and achievements in the field had risen above such shiny-shoed office workers, and had attracted recognition from General W. J. 'Bill' Slim, Commander of the 14th Army. Bower was appointed to be a Member of The Most Excellent Order of the British Empire (MBE). Her faithful Ward and Watch Assistant, Namkia Buing, was awarded the British Empire Medal (BEM). Both awards were made in the Civil Division of that Order.

WORKS CITED

Bower, U. G. MBE. *Naga Path*. London: John Murray, 1952.

Glancey, J. *Nagaland. A Journey to India's Forgotten Frontier*. London: Faber and Faber, 2011.

Thomas, V. *The Naga Queen. Ursula Graham Bower and Her Jungle Warriors, 1939–45*. Stroud: The History Press, 2012.

Thompson, J. *The Imperial War Museum Book of War Behind Enemy Lines*. London: Sidgwick & Jackson, 1998.

Williams, J. H. OBE, Lieutenant Colonel. *'Watch And Ward' in the North Cachar Hills: Elephant Bill*. London: Rupert Hart-Davis, 1950.

TEN

THE JAPANESE ADVANCE TOWARDS KOHIMA IN 1944, AND THE HEROIC STAND OF THE 1ST BATTALION THE ASSAM REGIMENT AT JESSAMI AND KHARASOM

The main weight of the enemy advance fell on this battalion, in the first battle of its career. Fighting in its own country, it put up a magnificent resistance, held doggedly to one position after another against overwhelming odds, and, in spite of heavy casualties, its companies although separated never lost cohesion. The delay the Assam Regiment imposed on the 31st Japanese Division at this stage was invaluable.

Field Marshall Viscount Slim, *Defeat into Victory*

THE JAPANESE PLAN

The 1942 Japanese invasion of Burma, now Myanmar, did not cover the entire country. In the north-west, the Chin Hills were not occupied, although Japanese troops did demonstrate their ability to perform such an occupation should they wish to do so. In the north, Fort Hertz, now Putao, was never occupied and it remained as an Allied bastion where guerrillas from the Kachin tribe were trained and deployed southwards. The northern end of the Hukawng Valley was also unoccupied by the Japanese, but they did control much of the upper Chindwin River.

In March 1944, a Japanese invasion of the Princely State of Manipur and the Naga tribal lands north of it was mounted across the Chindwin River with the title of Operation U-Go. The aim of this invasion was the capture of Imphal, the capital of Manipur, and the occupation of Kohima to the north, which would block the route that the Allies would have to take to recapture Manipur. The Japanese 15th Army was responsible for the invasion and its commander, Lieutenant General Renya Mutaguchi, wished to continue his advance beyond Kohima down into the Brahmaputra Valley, a main Allied transport artery where there were many large Allied supply bases, and from where the USA was flying weapons and supplies to Nationalist China. But Mutaguchi's superiors did not immediately endorse such a continuation of the invasion.

Mutaguchi's divisions, the 15th, 31st and 33rd, were to travel light over very inhospitable terrain relying on the capture of British supply dumps for their future food, vehicle and fuel requirements. This practice had worked during the Japanese invasions of Malaya and Burma. Once the Imphal Plain and its surrounding heights had been seized, truck convoys carrying artillery, mortar and small-arms ammunition would move up from Burma using a road kindly built by the British from Imphal into the Chin Hills. This route was called the Tiddim Road and it was easily linked into the Burmese system. The Japanese tanks were eventually able to use this road to travel into Manipur.

Mutagachi had been encouraged to 'think big' by contact with Indian National Army (INA) officers in Burma who stated that their troops, recruited from Japanese prisoner of war camps, would be greeted as liberators inside India, and that they would easily induce Indian Army sepoys in Manipur to desert to the INA. Eventually the equivalent of an INA division operated in the 15th Army rear areas with some detachments deployed forward for patrolling and propaganda tasks, but the INA soldiers were never well-equipped, maintained or supplied by their Japanese sponsors.

To support U-Go, another operation named Ha-Go was mounted

on Burma's west coast in the Arakan in early February 1944. This was designed to draw British troops away from Assam, and to pretend that the Japanese would enter India through the Arakan. Assumptions were made by the Japanese based on their victories in Malaya and Burma that once British supply lines were cut, the forward troops would retreat or surrender. But this was not the case as by 1944 Allied aircraft were well-practised in resupplying forward locations, either by landing cargo aircraft on speedily constructed airstrips, or by parachuting or free-dropping supplies. Operation Ha-Go failed, and the Japanese 55th Division units involved in the operation had to retreat without supplies. Some Japanese formation commanders reasoned that U-Go was just as likely to fail as Ha-Go had, but these prescient generals were quietened by Mutaguchi.

THE JAPANESE ADVANCE ON KOHIMA

In the south of his invasion front, Mutaguchi launched his 33rd Division against the British 17th Indian Light Division that operated around Tiddim. After destroying the 17th Division, the 33rd was to attack Imphal from the south. Further north, the 15th Division with some help from the 33rd Division advanced to destroy the British 20th Indian Division in the Kabaw Valley and Shenam Pass, and was then to attack Imphal from the east. In the north, the 31st Division under Lieutenant General Kotoku Sato advanced to seize Kohima and isolate Manipur, then if permission was granted to attack the British supply bases in the Brahmaputra Valley; the 31st Division would lead the way. This account deals only with 31st Division's thrust on Mutaguchi's invasion front, and the gallant resistance that the Japanese met from the Indian Army 1st Battalion, The Assam Regiment.

Sato's 31st Division crossed the Chindwin River on the night of 15/16 March 1944, moving quickly onwards across the Kabaw Valley. The South Raiding Column moved on a southern axis, fighting a severe battle in the Naga Hills against 50th Indian Parachute Brigade at Sangshak which lasted until 26 March, when the remaining paratroopers were ordered to break out of their defended perimeter and withdraw to Imphal. In fact, Sangshak was not a tactical problem for 31st Division to resolve, as it was in

15th Division's area of responsibility, but Major-General Miyazaki commanding the southern 31st Division Left Raiding Column felt himself obliged to destroy 50th Indian Parachute Brigade so that it could not threaten his rear.

The sacrificial delaying action fought by 50th Indian Parachute Brigade against very heavy odds was of real value, as it bought time for the British 5th Indian Division to fly in to reinforce IV Corps in Imphal and slowed 31st Division's advance on Kohima. Regrettably IV Corps Headquarters had been caught off-guard, not imagining that a Japanese attack of this speed and scale was possible. After fighting for Ukhrul and Sangshak, the South Raiding Column of 31st Division moved west and cut the Imphal–Kohima Road south of Kohima.

Sato's Central Raiding Column split and headed for Kharasom and Jessami whilst the North Raiding Column also headed for Jessami, striking through the very difficult terrain of the Somra Tracts where there were no roads, only occasional bridle paths and goat tracks. The Japanese had planned their routes well, making their own covert reconnaissance, as well as utilizing some Kuki tribesmen who had been discontented since Britain firmly put down a Kuki uprising during the Great War. Thanks to Kukis showing the Japanese where many British 'V Force' advanced observation posts were concealed, the British early warning system in the Kuki and Naga Hills did not work as planned. As a result, the Japanese took out several posts and achieved surprise by moving rapidly westwards. (But it must be emphasized that, as this Chapter shows, there were also many Kukis who fought bravely and loyally for British India.) On 27 March, the first serious contacts occurred between elements of the 138th Regiment and the 1st Assam Regiment that was defending Jessami and Kharasom. (Further details on the Japanese 31st Division are given below.)

THE 1ST ASSAM REGIMENT

The Assam Regiment was a new regiment in the Indian Army, having been formed in Shillong in 1941. Men from the Ahom, Naga, Mizo, Kuki, Khasi, Garo, Lushai and Manipur tribes of India's north-east were at first recruited, and these were followed by Adis,

Nishis, Monpas and domiciled Gorkhas and Sikkimese. Roman Urdu became the common military language. The cap badge depicted a rhinoceros and the regimental colours were black and orange, those of the state of Assam. Pith hats were offered to the regiment, but were rejected as being unsuitable and tailors made side hats; later when Gorkha hats became available they were issued. A determined group of Indian and European regimental officers drove the training forward despite an initially inadequate provision of clothing, accommodation, equipment, vehicles and weapons due to the rapid expansion of the Indian Army.

Six months after its formation, the first operational deployment was to Digboi and Ledo in north-eastern Assam, where the oil field installations were secured and exploratory patrols were made into the Hukawng Valley in Burma, to survey a new road planned by the USA to run from Ledo to Kunming in Nationalist-held China. The second deployment was into Burma again, to the Tamu area of the unhealthy Kabaw Valley and onwards to the Chindwin River, both to report on the refugee situation from Burma and to reconnoitre for signs of Japanese activity. Here the battalion suffered its first fatal casualty when No. 566 Sepoy Thesie Angami of Zame Village died of cerebral malaria.

The patrolling activities in this wild country provided a good grounding in the military skills that the unit was soon required to use on the battlefield, and the battalion's contribution to the defence of India's north-eastern borders was recognized by the Commanding Officer, the tough no-nonsense, energetic and inspirational Lieutenant Colonel William Felix 'Bruno' Brown. He was appointed to be an Officer of the Order of the British Empire (OBE) with this citation:

For the first 3 months after the Burma Army withdrew from Burma, Lt. Col. Brown with his Battalion was holding the Outpost Line along the Burma Frontier North and South of TAMU with patrols operating as far forward as the Chindwin. It was a most trying time – Morale was at a low ebb as a result of the withdrawal from Burma, refugees in the last stages of exhaustion were coming through in hundreds, communications were precarious, rations were short and difficult to get out to forward troops and weather conditions could hardly have been worse. In spite of all these difficulties Col. Brown by his resourcefulness, determination and unfailing cheerfulness inspired his men to carry on and thereby enabled a constant watch to be kept on the KABAW Valley. On more than one occasion Lt. Col. Brown personally led successful raiding parties to round up villages harbouring enemy agents. His initiative, determination and devotion to duty was of a high order. (TBNA)

The battalion then returned to Digboi where it was located from March 1943 to 19 February 1944, when it moved to the 57th Reinforcement Camp at Kohima. Almost immediately from there, the battalion made a three-day march over the sixty-mile route through the Naga Hills to Jessami.

Many Nagas served in the 1st Assam Regiment and, as a matter of fact, the four Military Medals awarded to the Regiment were all won by Naga sepoys who demonstrated bravery on the battlefield. It is worth our looking in detail at the actions of the 1st Assam Regiment as it fought against the Japanese advance on Kohima, because the fighting was on Naga soil and, for the first time, modern warfare was arriving on the ground in the Naga Hills. Some of the soldiers' names mentioned in this chapter are not Naga names, but they are the names of brave soldiers and their story needs to be told for us to appreciate exactly how well the 1st Assam Regiment fought at Jessami and Kharasom.

THE BRITISH SITUATION AT JESSAMI

By February 1944, IV Corps had reconsidered its earlier plans for a British advance south along the Tiddim Road into Burma, as ominous indications from the upper Chindwin River signalled that the Japanese were preparing to invade Manipur. In early March, the Corps Commander ordered the concentration of his divisions in a rather languid fashion, 17th Indian Light Division having to fight its way through Japanese blocks as it withdrew up the Tiddim Road to the Imphal Plain. The 20th Indian Division saw action in the Kabaw Valley as it withdrew up on to the Shenam Pass, which was to be held to the last. The 23rd Indian Infantry Division was held in reserve while giving depth in defence to the Ukhrul region. These moves were all part of Army Commander General Slim's plan for IV Corps to fight on the Imphal Plain, where British supply lines were short and anchored on two all-weather airfields, but where the Japanese supply lines would be dangerously over-extended.

The 50th Indian Parachute Brigade was in the Ukhrul area because its commander had requested that his brigade be deployed into the north-east of India to gain experience of jungle and mountain conditions. The brigade was without one of its three battalions, but the 1st Assam Regiment was allocated to the brigade order of battle, tasked with the defence of the villages of Jessami and Kharasom. One company of 1st Burma Regiment was attached to 1st Assam Regiment and deployed to defend Phekekedzumi (Phek) village. Thus 1st Assam Regiment found itself on its own at the northern tip of the British defence plan in what had been considered to be a quiet location, as British staff appreciations had ruled out any possibility of the advance of more than a Japanese regiment through the remote and rugged Somra Tracts. Colonel 'Bruno' Brown located his 'A' Company at Kharasom, and sound defensive positions were constructed there, and also for the remainder of the battalion in Jessami. The Mechanical Transport Platoon was back at Kohima as trucks could not move on the few rough recently constructed jeep tracks and the narrow bridle paths in the Naga Hills.

A jeep track came from Kohima to the Thetsiru River just east of Jessami, and another jeep track meandered from Jessami to Ukhrul via Kharasom. The centre of the Jessami defence was the junction of the two jeep tracks, and a network of interconnecting bunkers and trenches was laid out. A low barbed wire entanglement surrounded the outer bunkers and foxholes, and fields of fire were cleared in all directions. Towards the centre an inner line contained the command post, the bunker of Medical Officer 2nd Lieutenant Abdul Wahid, mortar base plates and supply dumps. The inhabitants of Jessami were Angami Nagas (now called Chakhesang), and they began to move off with their possessions into the surrounding jungle.

At Kharasom, the 'A' Company Commander Captain John

McCulloch 'Jock' Young, Argyll and Sutherland Highlanders attached to 1st Assam Regiment constructed similar but smaller defences and stocked ammunition, water and food. Here the inhabitants were Tangkhul Nagas and they also made arrangements to hide their livestock and possessions. Reconnaissance patrols moved into the Somra Tracts and Burma, discovering recent activity by Japanese patrols. Up until then, the 'V' Force tripwire had not been reporting enemy activity on the border.

CONTACT IS MADE WITH THE JAPANESE

All battalion officers took out patrols and on 16 March the Quartermaster, Lieutenant David Elwyn Lloyd Jones, led a lightly armed reconnaissance patrol of two rifle sections from 'C' Company through the Somra Hills via Kanjang to Molhe, a 'V' Force stockade post near the Burma border. The patrol's task was to reconnoitre tracks, camping sites and water points, and it took two days of hard hill climbing to reach Molhe. There an officer of the Burma Regiment reported that many agitated groups of Nagas were leaving their villages in Burma and crossing into India via Kanjang, a Kuki village, east of and not far from Kharasom. The villagers stated that 300 Japanese troops were advancing towards Molhe. This movement of Nagas continued throughout the night and the villagers used flammable wood torches to light their way in the dark along the narrow footpaths.

During the next day, the Burma Administration Deputy Commissioner of the Naga Hills arrived to report that the 'V' Force Headquarters at Kanjang Kuki village had been captured, and that groups of Japanese troops were moving westwards. Lieutenant Lloyd Jones immediately used Naga runners to take this news down the jungle tracks back to Jessami. It was very fortunate that the Quartermaster's patrol was in that area as the British intelligence organization had failed, and but for the presence of the patrol the Japanese would have surprised Jessami and Kharasom. Lloyd Jones then covertly observed Japanese movement around Molhe. The two Naga Naiks commanding the sections, Sentimenba Ao and Tekasashi Ao, were particularly useful to Lloyd Jones during this period.

At Jessami, Colonel Brown reacted to the news brought by the Naga runners by ordering Major Sidhiman Rai to advance towards Molhe with the remainder of his 'C' Company with the task of delaying the enemy, but he was to keep his company intact. Lieutenant Peter Steyn with one platoon of 'D' Company was dispatched east of Kanjang to protect the rear of 'C' Company. Major Geoffrey Blake Thurgood, 9th Battalion the King's Own Scottish Borderers attached to 1st Assam Regiment, was sent with five 'V' Force sepoys to establish an information centre at Kanjang.

Two patrols were operating north of Jessami under Major Albert Irwin Calistan and Lieutenant John Narbrough Corlett; on arrival at Yisi both patrols were informed by villagers of Japanese movement, and they sent this information back to Jessami using the radio of a US Air Force aircraft observer post there. Major Calistan was ordered to return to Jessami whilst Lieutenant Corlett was told to take the combined strength of both patrols to the Naga village of Meluri, nine miles north-east of Jessami. Corlett's task was to watch the Laruri–Phekekedzumi track and to prevent a surprise attack on the Burma Regiment garrison at the latter village.

At Jessami, final preparations for a battle were made and a five-day supply of water was brought from the stream that was half a mile outside the defensive position; tubes of bamboo were used as containers. A final jeep convoy of ammunition arrived from Kohima but after the empty jeeps had departed, it was found that 250,000 rounds of .300-inch aircraft machine gun ammunition, which was of no use to the battalion, had been delivered; precious time was spent in burying this ammunition.

THE FIGHTING WEST OF MOLHE

Major Sidhiman Rai moved quickly forward towards Molhe and linked up with Lloyd Jones' reconnaissance patrol. Contacts with the Japanese started almost immediately and Sidhiman Rai fought a series of delaying actions, constantly taking a toll on the advancing enemy. One of his Platoon Commanders, Subedar

Sarbeswar Rajbongshi, was isolated during heavy fighting and later received a Military Cross:

On the 25 March 44 in the MOLHE area Subedar Sarbeswar's platoon was very heavily attacked from three sides and cut off from the remainder of the Company. Due to his excellent control and outstanding leadership, his platoon inflicted very heavy casualties on the attacking Jap forces. This Viceroy's Commissioned Officer finally extricated his platoon with great skill, although hard pressed on all sides. Throughout the fight this Viceroy's Commissioned Officer displayed coolness and leadership worthy of the highest praise. (TBNA)

Sidhiman Rai was also awarded a Military Cross for his prowess as a company commander, and his citation describes his grasp of tactics and his leadership ability:

This officer was in command of a company sent out to reinforce a small recce patrol which had made contact with the enemy at MOLHE. His task was to delay the enemy advance as much as possible thus giving the garrisons at JESSAMI and KHARASOM time in which to complete their defences as far as possible. He made contact with Lieutenant D. E. L. Jones' patrol on the 22 Mar 44 and handling his company with great skill time and time again repulsed heavy enemy attacks. On several occasions, he laid ambushes which resulted in heavy Jap casualties. He continued to delay the advance until 25 Mar 44 when a particularly heavy attack from three sides caused his company to be dispersed. Collecting them again at a previously detailed rendezvous some 5 miles to the rear, he laid several more ambushes causing severe losses to the enemy and delaying them for a further day and a half, after which he skilfully withdrew his company to JESSAMI. Throughout the period 22–27 March '44, this officer displayed calm courage, leadership, determination and devotion to duty, of the highest order which was an inspiration to all who served with him. (TBNA)

During Sidhiman Rai's various actions, Peter Steyn and his 'D'

Company platoon marched to the sound of the guns and joined up with 'C' Company. But groups of Japanese were moving quickly towards Jessami and heavy firing was heard at Kanjang, where Major Thurgood was captured. He died soon afterwards having been observed receiving a hard time as a prisoner. 'C' Company began to fragment due to constant enemy attacks, and the northern part of the company moved to Meluri and met up with John Corlett's group. The survivors of 'V' Force were moving back to Phekekedzumi (Phek) through Meluri and its commander, Lieutenant Colonel N. A. Stanley, ordered Corlett's group and this fragment of 'C' Company to move with him. This move of John Corlett to Phekekedzumi was to prove fortuitous for the Jessami Garrison. Sidhiman Rai and Peter Steyn got the rest of their men back to Jessami in time to join the main battle there.

'B' COMPANY'S DEFENCE OF KHARASOM

Captain Young's 'A' Company at Kharasom had been deploying men on patrols whilst others worked on the defences, and a smaller but similar perimeter to the one at Jessami had been constructed. Also, and importantly, Captain Young had received the same order as had Colonel Brown at Jessami – to fight to the last round and the last man in order to give the Kohima garrison time to organize itself. But unfortunately the Kohima defence plan was being subjected to order, counter-order and confusion. The reports from Molhe of Japanese movements had been passed to Kharasom and a platoon of 'D' Company was sent there to strengthen 'A' Company. Groups of 'V' Force personnel and the paramilitary Assam Rifles moved into Kharasom from the Upper Chindwin, but some of them were in bad shape and Young sent them back to Kohima on 26 March.

During the following morning 'Stand To' at 0600 hours, Young telephoned Jessami to report that at least a battalion of Japanese infantry with pack-mules, plus elephants carrying and pulling guns and mortars was approaching his position. That was the last time that anybody outside Kharasom spoke to 'Jock' Young, as the telephone line was then cut by the enemy. These Japanese troops were advancing from Ukhrul, and they appeared not to know that Kharasom was garrisoned by the Assam Regiment. When the enemy column was abreast of the defences, a company fire order was given, and many hits were made on Japanese personnel before they got into effective cover and reorganized themselves.

After being initially surprised, the Japanese reacted by making a series of attacks on 'A' Company's trenches and bunkers. Regrettably, the Company 2nd in Command, Subedar Karindra Rajbongshi, was killed by an enemy mortar bomb during the first attack; Havildar Zachhinga Lushai was also killed as he attempted to destroy an enemy radio post facing his platoon sector. The Japanese pulled back at noon but attacked at dusk, again failing to penetrate the defensive perimeter. This pattern was repeated for the next three days, with the Japanese making fanatical frontal attacks but always being repulsed by the defenders. To vent their spleen the Japanese burnt down Kharasom Village, the Naga inhabitants looking on with anger and despair from the surrounding jungle they took cover in.

On 31 March, a new battalion column of Japanese with mules and elephants was seen approaching Kharasom from Chakyang. 'Jock' Young knew that his men were too exhausted to effectively resist these fresh troops, and his water supply was almost finished. An Orders Group was held where the company was instructed to break out with the walking wounded and fight its way to Kohima, but one man was to remain in the perimeter with the seriously wounded to carry out the 'last man last round' instruction – this man was to be John McCulloch Young.

Once the orders had been issued to platoons and sections, several of the sepoys became restive and some discipline was lost as men pulled out too soon, but three separate groups of sepoys made it back to Kohima. 'Jock' Young's exact fate is not known, but reports from villagers stated that explosions came from within the perimeter as Young presumably demolished ammunition stocks. The following morning, a Japanese attack entered the perimeter to be met with grenades thrown from a bunker; Japanese machine gunners engaged the bunker at close range until 'Jock'

Young was dead. He had obeyed his orders, and he had also saved the fit men in his company and the attached platoon from 'D' Company, as most of those made it back to Kohima, but he and the severely wounded were dead. Ironically, the order to defend Kharasom to the last had been rescinded, but communications in the Kohima area were so chaotic that the new order to withdraw never got through. 'A' Company officers who made it back to Kohima found that the military authorities there were unable to comprehend that Kohima was being threatened by large numbers of Japanese troops, as they preferred to believe their own staff appreciations and so considered that the Japanese in the area were just small groups there to raid British lines of communication.

Peter Steyn's *The History of the Assam Regiment* states that to assist in the disengagement of the Kharasom Garrison from its attackers, and to provide transport in the withdrawal, 23 jeeps were sent out under an escort from 1st Battalion 1st Punjab Regiment, but that the jeep column was ambushed and captured intact by the enemy. The jeeps were then used by the Japanese to move supplies along the Imphal-Kohima road (78). In *The First Punjabis: History of the First Punjab Regiment*, Ibrahim Qureshi describes the ambush at a road block, followed by heavy and confused fighting that resulted in the Punjabis losing 2 men, and 13 wounded, but does not mention the loss of the jeeps. However, the citation for a Military Cross award to Subedar Abdul Ghani MBE of 1st Punjabis mentions the 'Battle of the Jeeps' on 30 March 1944 on a track east of Tuophema that led to Kharasom (295–6).

THE DEFENCE OF JESSAMI

Details of the contact were telephoned back to Kohima, and a request for unit identification was received in reply. Naik Jamkishei Kuki of 'B' Company and Paokhodang, a 'V' Force scout, volunteered to crawl forward over the open ground to the nearest body. Naik Jamkishei was killed, but Scout Paokhodang persevered until he was forced back by accurate fire from enemy reinforcements. Major Sidhiman Rai then took a platoon out but he also was forced back by heavy enemy fire. For the remainder of the day, the Japanese tried to draw fire from the garrison's mortars and machine guns, so that the locations could be engaged by their mortars and regimental guns.

That night, to the shouts of 'Banzai!' complemented by cracker-bombs and attacking mortar and machine gun fire, several Japanese charges were made against the perimeter, but none of them managed to break into it. The Japanese tactics did not vary and were defeated by the defensive fire of the Assam Regiment sepoys. Individual Japanese infiltrators were more successful, and a few covertly crawled through the outer defences only to be killed by sepoys in the inner ring of bunkers. During this first night, the defenders did not lose any men, killed or wounded.

The dead Japanese infiltrators were, in fact, a bonus as some of their corpses carried documents, equipment and a unit flag. Volunteers were called for to take these items back to Kohima, and Lance Naik Jogendra Nath and a sepoy slipped out of the perimeter and successfully delivered the items to Kohima Garrison Headquarters. During the second day of the siege, the Japanese and INA soldiers called out both in English and Hindustani for the surrounded sepoys to surrender. Sovehu Angami, a 3-inch mortar Havildar fighting with 1st Assam Regiment at Jessami, later recalled: 'The INA soldiers would ask our soldiers to go and join them in Hindi. Sometimes, our soldiers would invite them in Hindi and fire at them when they appeared!' (Chasie, Interview). Sovehu was injured by shrapnel from mortar fire.

The high ground to the south overlooked the perimeter, and the second day's fighting saw most of the Assam Regiment mortar baseplate positions being targeted by Japanese fire. These defensive mortars, which could not be protected by overhead cover because of the high trajectory of the weapon, were hit by Japanese fire and became unserviceable. The sepoys manning the mortars could take cover in bunkers during the enemy counter-battery fire, but the mortars had to stay assembled in their open pits ready for action. No. 356 Naik Imtisang Ao commanded a mortar at Jessami and he later received a Military Medal after the Kohima fighting, for bravery commanding mortars there, the citation mentioning his 'conspicuous success in the Jessami action'. Imtisang Ao was later commissioned as an officer in the regiment.

Another NCO whose gallantry was recognized at Jessami received an Indian Distinguished Service Medal. He was No. 202 Havildar Khandarpa Rajbongshi:

This platoon havildar commanded a sector of the JESSAMI box between 28th March and 1st April 44. He was a constant inspiration to his men, cheering them on and steadying them as wave after wave of attacks were put in on his front. Time and again he filled the breach when casualties caused gaps in his sector, and often at great hazard to his life he fetched up ammunition to his forward posts. His untiring efforts at JESSAMI and again at KOHIMA between 5th and 20th April displayed superb leadership, devotion to duty of a high order and complete disregard of personal danger. (TBNA)

The second night's fighting replicated the first night – waves of attackers shouting 'Banzai!' surged towards the perimeter after having wound themselves up into a frenzy. The attacks were repulsed but it was much harder work as the loss of the mortars meant that the hordes of Japanese were not being broken up before they reached the wire. Infiltrators again crawled through but as before were killed by the defenders' inner ring. Many sepoys were showing signs of great strain and fatigue but their battle drills continued to be performed professionally: red-hot Bren gun barrels being stripped off the weapons and immediately replaced with cooled and clean barrels; Japanese grenades and cracker bombs that landed in trenches were immediately seized and thrown back.

Havildar Seikham commanded an isolated bunker outside the perimeter and when he ran short of food and ammunition the Jemadar Adjutant, Jemadar Tonghen Kuki and Sepoy Thangtinjam took their chances against enemy fire to take supplies to Seikham, Thangtinjam getting across to the bunker first. Tonghen Kuki received a Military Cross for his gallantry:

After three days of hard fighting between 28th and 30th March 44 at JESSAMI, it was known that our men in a forward and isolated bunker position were short of food. Jemadar TONGHEN KUKI volunteered to get the food to them although aware that the ground was covered by Japanese machine guns at very short range. Despite the fact that he was clearly visible to the enemy he again and again crossed the open space to the bunker carrying food, water and ammunition, under constant enemy fire from which he was eventually badly wounded in the head. The magnificent courage of this Viceroy's Commissioned Officer undoubtedly saved the lives of the men in the bunker as well as enabling them to continue the fight. His complete disregard of personal safety and determination were in the finest traditions of the service. (TBNA)

Back at Kohima, it was decided to rescind the 'fight to the death' instructions given to 'Bruno' Brown and his men but the telephone line had been cut, and the one radio at Jessami had been damaged and was unserviceable. An uncoded message telling the Jessami Garrison to break out and return to Kohima was dropped from an aircraft, but it landed outside the perimeter and the Japanese got to it first. The enemy then knew more than 1st Assam Regiment knew, and Japanese plans were made to ambush the tracks to Kohima.

At Phekekedzumi (Phek), John Corlett knew of the withdrawal order and soon realized that 'Bruno' Brown did not, so Corlett decided to deliver the message to Jessami himself. Later after the Kohima fighting John Corlett received a Military Cross, and the first part of his citation reads:

When this officer's battalion had been invested at JESSAMI with no other orders than to hold on it became necessary to send orders for it to withdraw. The battalion wireless had been damaged and various attempts by runner and by air had failed to get the message through. Lieutenant CORLETT, who had previously come with a patrol from JESSAMI to PHAKEKEDZUMI, volunteered to deliver the message although he knew not only that this would entail passing through the enemy's lines but also that any movement at night near his own box would be fired on. The battalion dispositions had been changed since he had left JESSAMI, and in the old battalion position he found himself among the enemy. He however continued in his attempts and succeeded in locating the Garrison and delivering his message. He thereby saved the Garrison from destruction and brought a much-needed accession of strength to the KOHIMA Garrison. On the day after his arrival in JESSAMI (1 Apr 44) and before the evacuation he behaved with great gallantry manning a Light Machine Gun himself when all the men of the Sub-Section had become casualties, and going himself for more ammunition under heavy and continuous fire. (TBNA)

In fact, John Corlett was fired upon by the Jessami defenders as he approached them at night, but by strenuously and positively using his voice he was safely admitted within the perimeter. Meanwhile the Phekekedzumi troops withdrew in good order to Kohima. 'Bruno' Brown considered that it was too late that night to effect an orderly withdrawal from Jessami so the garrison remained fighting during the following day whilst plans were made and orders issued. Knowing that the Jessami Garrison intended to withdraw, the Japanese decided to destroy it, and attacked repeatedly, getting inside the perimeter where some bunkers changed hands more than once in very savage fighting. In the end, the 1st Assam Regiment regained control of its ground but there were large gaps in the defences, so once darkness fell the withdrawal plan started.

Back at Kohima, the 1st Assam Regiment was written off by the senior military authorities who interpreted orders to defend the Dimapur supplies bases as meaning that Kohima should not be garrisoned and all troops should be moved to Dimapur. Fortunately, 'Bruno' Brown and his sepoys were unaware of this. The Jessami defenders moved in groups in different directions according to the sector that they had been defending, but some groups walked into Japanese ambushes, and sepoys were killed, wounded, captured and missing. The Medical Officer, Lieutenant

Abdul Wahid, was one of those captured as was the Head Clerk, Jemadar Phukon, but Phukon managed to escape later during the Japanese retreat. A recently commissioned Jemadar, Lalhuliana Lushai, was one of those killed in action.

Major Calistan was successful in getting most of his sepoys back to Kohima, and later he was awarded a Military Cross, the Jessami part of his citation being:

> *Between 28th March 44 and 2 April at Jessami this Officer's Company was heavily attacked by the enemy. In spite of wave after wave of Japanese attacks, this officer by his magnificent example of cool courage and confidence and constant inspiration to his men succeeded in maintaining intact his perimeter. On 2nd April 44 when this perimeter was evacuated, this officer succeeded by his skilful leadership and determination in extricating the majority of his company and leading them safely to Kohima. (TBNA)*

But one of the last words on the defenders of Jessami should go to 'battalion bad boy' No. 1778 Sepoy Wellington Massar, a man of the Khasi tribe. Later at Kohima Wellington was to repeat the acts of bravery that he displayed at Jessami, for which he received an Indian Distinguished Service Medal. The first portion of the citation reads:

> *Throughout the battle at JESSAMI between 28th March and 1st April this sepoy, a Number 1 on a Light Machine Gun, showed courage and determination of the highest order. In spite of repeated attacks on his post by ever increasing numbers of the enemy supported by mortar fire and infantry gun, he remained cool and steady, maintaining a very accurate fire which took a heavy toll of the attackers. When his Light Machine Gun had stoppages, he continued to hold the attackers at bay with rifle and grenades. When the withdrawal was ordered on the night of 1st/2nd April he was the last man to leave his sector. (TBNA)*

Wellington was to die of wounds at Kohima after losing a leg. Another 'bad boy' in a British regiment was to show the same contempt for danger and the same prowess on the Kohima battle-field. He too was to die at Kohima and he was to receive the posthumous award of the Victoria Cross. It is a fact that men who do not fit in barracks, and are the despair of Adjutants and Havildar Majors, sometimes find their spiritual home on the battlefield and they thrive there until they are killed; so it was with Sepoy Wellington Massar.

KOHIMA

Colonel 'Bruno' Brown and his main party from Jessami arrived at Kohima on the afternoon of 3 April. Small groups straggled in also, having been helped considerably by Naga villagers they met on the way who invariably welcomed, sheltered and fed them. The captured sepoys had different experiences, from those who were ritually beheaded, as was No. 524 Sepoy Ngulkhothang Sanchou of Chahsat, Manipur, who was taunted so much by his captors that he kicked a Japanese officer down, to those like Company Havildar Major Satkhosei who planned and executed escapes. Whilst 12 men of 1st Assam Regiment were recorded as being killed in action or dying of wounds at Kharasom and Jessami, the exact number of sepoys who died in ambushes or in captivity on the trails back to Kohima will never be known. Some sepoys who knew the local terrain, such as No. 542 Havildar Sovehu Angami of Phekekedzumi Village, avoided enemy ambushes by striking northwards into the Brahmaputra Valley, from where he returned to Dimapur, rejoined his battalion, and later fought in the Kohima Battle.

At Kohima, the decision to abandon the town had been reversed and key features were to be defended. 1st Assam Regiment was quickly allocated ground to occupy and hold, the Assam Rifles barracks at Kohima providing food, boots, clothing, blankets, equipment and weapons and ammunition. On 4 April, the 1st Assam Regiment numbering just over 260, and all ranks and unwounded sepoys, prepared for their next round with the Japanese 31st Division, strengthened by the experiences of the past fortnight which had shown that Japanese attacks could be defeated.

The British XXXIII Corps was now responsible for Kohima and it reported in its despatches:

> *161st Brigade arrived at Kohima on 29 March. Orders were given to the Jessami and Kharasom garrisons to withdraw on the night of 31 March/1 April – the former via Milestone 44 Phekekedzumi track, the latter via Gaziphema. A message in clear was dropped on Jessami by air but, unfortunately, not on the garrison. The consequence of this was that, when 1st Assam Regiment withdrawal took place, all roads and tracks leaving from Jessami were heavily ambushed by the enemy. The withdrawal of 1st Assam Regiment completed a brilliant operation by a comparatively new battalion in their baptism of fire. Not only had it held the enemy attacks and inflicted more casualties than it suffered, but it had successfully delayed the enemy's advance and thus given valuable time for preparation to the Kohima Garrison. The spirit of the battalion was magnificent throughout, and in the end, it had extricated itself without any of the help it had been led to expect. (Steyn 79)*

Lieutenant Colonel William Felix Brown OBE, who sadly was later to be killed in action in Burma, was awarded a Distinguished Service Order with the citation:

> *Lieutenant Colonel BROWN's battalion occupied positions at the villages of JESSAMI and KHARASOM, some sixty miles East of KOHIMA, in order to prevent the enemy's advance from that direction. On 28 March, the enemy attacked in force; these attacks continued daily and though unsupported, Lt-Col BROWN continued to fight his battalion with no thought of withdrawal, thereby imposing many valuable days of delay on Japanese forces advancing against KOHIMA. Many attempts by air and runner to order Lt-Col BROWN's battalion to withdraw failed; eventually an officer of the Assam Regt. succeeded in getting through the Japanese lines with orders to withdraw. Lt-Col BROWN by his resourcefulness, succeeded in extricating his battalion and in leading a large portion of it through successive*

Japanese ambushes to concentrate at KOHIMA and continue to fight. Throughout the whole of these operations this officer's leadership, initiative, courage and unfailing cheerfulness in adversity instilled in all ranks under his command a high spirit and devotion to duty for which no praise can be too great. (TBNA)

NOTES ON THE JAPANESE 31ST DIVISION

Leslie Edwards' book *Kohima: The Furthest Battle* is the best source for plotting Japanese movements and dates during Operation U-Go. He writes:

The third of the three Japanese divisions, 31 Division (containing 15,000 men), the one ordered to take Kohima, advanced in three columns being split into further sub-columns taking different routes towards their interim and final objectives. The first across the Chindwin River was the northern column, or Right Raiding Column, at Pinma, near Tamanthi. In it was the 3rd Battalion, 138 Regiment, with various ancillary units, which, after engaging in some minor skirmishes with defensive units on the west bank of the river, entered the Somra Hills intending to approach Jessami from the north and then head towards Kohima.

The southern column, the Left Raiding Column, crossed the Chindwin south of Homalin on 15 March at Monkali, Hpanaing and Letpantha, crossed the Burma/India border on 18 March and headed towards Ukhrul intending to turn north to approach Kohima from the south. In it were all of 58 Regiment, the 2nd Battalion 31st Mountain Artillery Regiment, the Headquarters of the 31st Infantry Group (comprising the three infantry regiments under Miyazaki) and ancillary units.

In the middle column, the Central Raiding Column, was the main body of 31 Division, which over several days crossed the Chindwin at Maungkan and Kawya, roughly midway between Tamanthi and Homalin. It included 124 Regiment, the rest of 138 Regiment, the rest of the 31st Mountain Artillery

Regiment, the Headquarters of 31st Division, and other units. It headed south towards Somra where it split, the 1st Battalion of 138 Regiment going to Kharasom, the rest going north to Jessami. (63)

The Divisional resupply plan was to secure food from British dumps at Kohima once that town had been captured. The Division acquired oxen and horses from villagers in Burma, and in the Naga Hills loaded these with supplies, but this logistical tactic on the whole failed as the beasts kept falling down the steep hillsides in the Somra Tracts. Elephants acquired in Burma were useful to the Japanese for pulling regimental guns and carrying ammunition, but the Japanese gunners' advance was limited to the speed of the elephants.

WORKS CITED

Edwards, L. *Kohima, The Furthest Battle*. Stroud: The History Press, 2009.

Keane, F. *Road of Bones: The Siege of Kohima 1944*. London: Harper Collins, 2010.

Kirby, S. W. Major General. *British Official History. The War Against Japan. Vol. III. 'The Decisive Battles'*. Naval & Military Press, Reprint 2004.

Prasad, B. Gen. Ed. *Official History of the Indian Armed Forces in the Second World War, 1939–45. 'The Reconquest of Burma'*, Vol.1. India: Orient Longmans, 1958.

Qureshi, M. I. Major. *The First Punjabis. History of the First Punjab Regiment*. Aldershot: Gale & Polden, 1958.

Slim, W. *Defeat into Victory*. Pan Military Classics, 2009.

Steyn, P. MC, Captain. T*he History of the Assam Regiment*. India: Orient Longmans, 1959.

The British National Archives. TBNA: WO 32/11; WO 33/13; WO 33/75; WO 33/213; WO 34/54; WO 34/266; WO 34/267; WO 373/35/260; WO 373/79/354.

ELEVEN

23 LONG RANGE PENETRATION BRIGADE IN THE NAGA HILLS

Supporting the Kohima and Imphal Battles, April–July 1944

To sum up, therefore Deep Penetration means the operation of regular columns of high calibre in the heart of the enemy's war machine, engaging targets he is unable adequately to protect, and thus compelling him to alter his plans, thus causing a situation of which our own main forces are able to take advantage.

Major-General Orde Wingate DSO (and two Bars),
General Rules for the Forces of Deep Penetration

23 LONG RANGE PENETRATION (LRP) BRIGADE

The brigade had originally been the 23rd Brigade of the British 70th Division, but in November 1943 70th Division was broken up and its brigades transferred to the 3rd Indian Division; that divisional title was in fact a cover for the British Special Force that was created by Brigadier Orde Charles Wingate to operate behind the Japanese lines in Burma. Special Force had mounted an operation named Longcloth into Burma in 1943 between February and April, and although casualties were high the exploit was well publicized, and attracted positive Allied public attention and imagination. As mentioned previously, the men in Special Force became known by the adopted name of Chindits, a word derived from the Chinthe statues that guard Burmese temples.

The brigade trained near Jhansi in India, learning skills that would allow both survival and competent operational practices when deep behind enemy lines. The battalions learned how to cross rivers on rafts and personal temporary flotation devices, demolish enemy bridges, tactics to attack enemy-held villages, jungle marching with pack-mules followed by speedy bivouacking, the reception of air-dropped supplies, and how to evade destruction by dispersing and meeting up again at predetermined rendezvous. None of the Chindit formations had artillery and their light weaponry and tactics were designed for them to swiftly strike and withdraw as raiders, rather than to stand and fight as normally equipped infantry.

Special Force mounted a second operation named Thursday into Burma on 5 March 1944, selected brigades being flown in by glider apart from one brigade that had marched in from Ledo in Assam, in February. The aim of Operation Thursday was to operate in the Japanese rear so that the Allied main forces, who were General Stilwell's USA and Chinese troops operating in north Burma, could continue advancing, whilst behind them USA engineers constructed a road from Ledo to Kunming in Nationalist China.

23 Long Range Penetration Brigade had expected to fly into Burma with the other airborne brigades of Special Force, but it was suddenly withdrawn from the Special Force order of battle and despatched into north-eastern Assam to operate under the direction of the British 33rd Corps; initially for a few days it guarded the strategic Bengal–Assam railway line up which USA supplies were brought before they were flown over the intermediary mountains known as 'The Hump' to Kunming. The reason for this sudden redeployment was that Allied intelligence agencies had been alerted to a planned Japanese invasion of the Indian Princely State of Manipur, and the adjacent Naga Hills area of Assam to Manipur's north.

The three divisions of the Japanese 15th Army, supported by elements of the Indian National Army, did invade Manipur and the Naga Hills in the second half of March 1944, with the northernmost division, the 31st, advancing through the Hills to attack Kohima.

23 Long Range Penetration Brigade was soon relieved of its railway defence duties and despatched into the Naga Hills in nine columns. Each of the four British infantry battalions in the brigade produced two columns and Brigade Headquarters was the ninth column. Each pair of columns was controlled by its battalion commanding officer who commanded one of his battalion columns, the Battalion 2IC commanding the other one. Brigade HQ directed the operation, acting on orders received from the British 33rd Corps.

The brigade tasks were to disrupt the enemy lines of communication so that the Japanese 31st Division would not receive its supplies, and so be compelled to withdraw from Kohima. The brigade had the other task of protecting the left flank of the British 33rd Division. These tasks were important for should the enemy attacks on Kohima and Manipur prove successful, the Japanese would be able to descend into the Brahmaputra Valley and cause havoc amongst all the Allied supply bases located there. There was also the likelihood that the Indian National Army elements would create civil disturbance problems amongst sympathetic sections of the Indian population.

Initially all ranks in 23 Brigade were disappointed at not being in Burma with their fellow Chindits. The remote and steep mountainous terrain of the Naga Hills and the dense jungle that covered it were extremely physically challenging. Whilst the brigade mission might have been more aptly described as 'short range penetration' it was a real Chindit task that complemented the activities of the British main forces that were battling to defend and relieve Kohima and Imphal, the capital of Manipur. The brigade moved on foot with its mules and a few ponies during the monsoon period for three months, being resupplied by air drops. Column commanders received regular drops of silver rupees (in coins) to pay Nagas who had laboured or otherwise provided assistance and information. Casualties were flown out by light plane when a suitable airstrip could be constructed in the wild terrain. Messages and captured documents were suspended in pouches between poles for light planes to 'snatch' them up with hooks and retrieve them.

At the end of the operation, columns surrounded the town of Ukhrul whilst 20th Indian Brigade attacked the town, dislocating the withdrawal of the Japanese 31st Division. 23 Long Range Penetration Brigade succeeded in the tasks given to it, killing or capturing hundreds of Japanese and Indian National Army stragglers and foragers; the brigade itself suffered nearly 160 battle casualties. The risks had been high, particularly for wounded men who could not be evacuated. In one incident, the Japanese tied ten wounded British soldiers to trees and bayoneted them to death, but that incident only strengthened the resolve of the Chindits.

The brigade's success would not have been possible without the positive and unflinching support provided by the former head-hunting Naga tribes people whose land the British and Japanese were fighting over. The Nagas carried food and casualties for the brigade, sheltered wounded and lost soldiers and bailed-out airmen, recovered supplies dropped into dense jungle, constructed landing strips, formed Home Guards to protect villages used by the brigade, and enlisted as sepoys in a Levy force that scouted, and whenever possible, fought against and killed Japanese and Indian National Army stragglers.

Sections of one other tribe in the area, the Kukis, did declare themselves for the Japanese, but apart from a few dissident Nagas the bulk of the Nagas offered active support to the British. 23 Brigade's operational tasks would have been much harder if not impossible to achieve if the Nagas had fought against the brigade, and had laid the ambushes that the Naga Levies used against the Japanese. But the Nagas selflessly supported the brigade, despite the casualties that they sometimes suffered in the process.

The Composition of 23 Long Range Penetration Brigade

- Brigade Headquarters commanded by Brigadier Lancelot E. C. M. Perowne (32 Column).
- 60th Field Regiment, Royal Artillery operating as infantry (60 and 80 Columns).
- 2nd Battalion Duke of Wellington's Regiment (33 and 76 Columns).

- 4th Battalion Border Regiment (34 and 55 Columns).
- 1st Battalion Essex Regiment (44 and 56 Columns).
- 12th Field Company, Royal Engineers supporting all columns.
- Medical detachments supporting all columns.
- The brigade administrative echelon was located at Agartala airfield in the Indian Princely State of Tripura; RAF squadrons flew from that base to support the brigade.

The Composition of a Column

The column strength was around 400 men with over 50 mules and a few ponies.

Column Headquarters

- One rifle company of four platoons armed with rifles and light machine guns.
- One reconnaissance platoon supported by a section of Burma Rifles (later changed to Assam Rifles).
- One commando platoon, Royal Engineers (demolition specialists).
- One mortar platoon containing two 3-inch mortars.
- One machine gun platoon containing two Vickers .303-inch guns.

Royal Air Force (RAF), signals, medical and veterinary detachments. The RAF detachment commander was an active pilot who directed air support and casualty evacuation, and he communicated on a radio that needed 10 mules to transport the radio set, batteries, generator and fuel. Other mules carried the mortars, machine guns, ammunition and supplies.

THE NAGA LEVIES

23 Long Range Penetration Brigade was configured to fight in Burma, and its attached intelligence specialists were from the Burma Intelligence Corps, and its attached reconnaissance men were from the Burma Rifles. As most of these specialist troops were unfamiliar with the topography and languages used in the

Naga Hills, they were withdrawn from the brigade before deployment began. The Burma Rifles sepoys were replaced by men from the Assam Rifles. A new military unit, the Naga Levies, was authorized to be raised to support the British and Indian formations fighting in the defence of Kohima, including 23 Long Range Penetration Brigade.

Whilst British 33rd Corps was the authority for the raising of the Naga Levies, the prime mover in reassuring and motivating the Naga communities was the Chief Intelligence Officer in Assam, a very experienced police officer named Eric T. D. Lambert, who supervised an organization named the Frontier Intelligence Staff. Lambert also arranged for the provision of British political and administrative officers with deep knowledge of the Nagas to march with columns, or to be advisors with 33rd Corps. Three of these officers were P. F. Adams, J. H. F. Williams, and Charles Pawsey MC; they were commissioned into the Indian Army to provide them with military status should they be captured by the enemy.

A ceiling figure of 2,310 Nagas was authorized for the Levies and the basic unit was a platoon of 35 men consisting of one Jemadar, one Havildar, three Naiks and 30 sepoys. Platoons of Levies were raised in any Naga area that was threatened by the Japanese. Nagas could enlist under the category of active Levies who scouted and fought where required, or as Home Guards who were responsible for village defence and general local tasks. An active Levy sepoy earned ₹25 per month whilst a Home Guard earned only ₹5. Naiks, havildars, jemadars and officers acting as advisors to column commanders earned enhanced salaries. A system of financial rewards remunerated Levy sepoys and Naga villagers who captured Japanese or INA personnel, or who brought in proof of having killed enemy soldiers in combat.

All Levies were armed with government-issued rifles or shotguns in addition to their personal tribal weapons, and the Levies were entitled to appropriate death and disability benefits. In order to swiftly provide professional military training to Levy recruits, the Shillong Depot of the Indian Army Assam Regiment loaned an officer, a havildar and 30 Naga sepoys who quickly taught modern rifle and grenade skills and relevant infantry tactics to their very willing students.

As the Levies were Indian Army sepoys, they were entitled to receive gallantry awards and campaign medals. This resulted in Naga Levies receiving three Military Crosses, one Indian Distinguished Service Medal and eight Military Medals – an impressive total for a levy force that was only in action for a few months. Some other Nagas who as civilians had significantly assisted in resistance to the Japanese threat received appointments to become Members of the Order of the British Empire (MBE), whilst others were awarded British Empire Medals.

INTERPRETERS

Each column in 23 LRP Brigade needed a few interpreters who could speak both English and relevant Naga dialects/languages. By having more than one interpreter a column could continually send out patrols knowing that they would be able to communicate with Naga villagers, who more often than not had news of Japanese troop movements. Interpreters were not required to fight the enemy and their pay was ₹60 per month. They were also entitled to death, disablement and wound compensation, and to a final gratuity payment when their employment ceased.

But good interpreters were hard to find and this letter from Eric Lambert to Brigadier Lance Perowne, Commander of 23 LRP Brigade, shows the lengths to which Lambert and the British Administration went to locate and produce suitable men:

SECRET

No. 21/Police(5)T-255C, Dated the 17th June 1944.

To. Brig Perowne, 23 Bde.

My dear Perowne,

It is proposed to send you interpreters from anywhere we can get them. For the time being we are sending you two

English speaking Tangkhuls from Ukhrul. English speaking Tangkhuls are very few and far between but any we can find are being sent. The balance will be made up of loyal Kukis and Manipuris. Arrangements have been laid on with the High School in Jorhat for three, with the Shillong High School for three more. Tangkhuls and Manipur State have been asked to supply 30 interpreters, Tangkhuls for preference, and number to be made up from proved loyal Kukis and Manipuris.

Yours sincerely, (signed) E. Lambert.

Lambert also wrote personal letters to Nagas whom he knew well, and asked the Royal Air Force to drop the letters on designated villages. This encouraged several of the recipients of the letters to come out of the hills and join Chindit columns as interpreters.

Flight Lieutenant W. A. Wilcox, a RAF detachment commander who later wrote the very descriptive book *Chindit Column 76*, was very enthusiastic about one of his column's interpreters, 'Mr, Kumbho'. This Naga gentleman, Kumbho Angami, was a teacher from the Government School in Kohima who had volunteered to be an interpreter with a Chindit column. In July 1945, Kumbho Angami was appointed to be a Member of the Civil Division of the Order of the British Empire (MBE) for his stout work and the fortitude that he displayed whilst marching with the Chindits.

At the same time, eight other interpreters were awarded British Empire Medals. They were: Chohozhu Sema, Khakhu Sema, Kohoto Sema, Lhouvisielie Angami, Nikhalhu Angami and Zhuikhu Sema, all from the Office of the Deputy Commissioner, Naga Hills, and Hezekhu Sema, Sub-Divisional Office, Mokokchung and Hoshekhe Sema from the Naga Hills.

Other Nagas receiving the British Empire Medal for assisting the Chindits were Hetoi Sema, a Forest Chowkidar; Virialie Angami, described in the London Gazette as a Cultivator and Artisan; Pfuzielhu Angami, described as Headman of Jotsoma and Viliezhu Rengma, Headman of Tseminyu Village. Flight Lieutenant Wilcox described Viliezhu Rengma as: 'The community's Christian Pastor, an efficient little man. Whenever porters were needed, his was the voice that brought them scurrying to the school-house. Stern but kindly, he was the undisputed King of Tseminyu; his word was law' (*Chindit Column 76*, 56).

SCOUTING JAPANESE POSITIONS

The Active Naga Levies were extremely useful to the Chindit columns when operations were conducted on the Levies' home ground. Sepoy Zashei Angami was awarded a Military Medal for his gallantry as a scout, and his citation describes both the significance of his actions and the danger that he exposed himself to:

5th May 1944. At PHEKEKEDZUMI. Sepoy Zashei Angami was serving with a Long Range Penetration Column. When they approached his native village, he volunteered to go on ahead, and find out the enemy dispositions. With a complete disregard for his own safety he made a very close reconnaissance single handed. He then returned and led our troops by a cleverly chosen covered line of approach into an advantageous position near the enemy. Complete surprise was achieved. In the attack Sepoy Zashei Angami's courage was exemplary. Thirty enemy were killed, ten wounded for practically no casualties. Throughout his scouting was of the greatest value, and he worked untiringly, and showed himself fearless. (TBNA)

Another Military Medal recipient was Sepoy Nihoshe Angami who scouted for a column at Phekerkriema on 28 April 1944. An extract from his citation describes his bravery:

When our troops approached Phekerkrima (Phekerkriema – on the old Bokajan Track) it was believed that the enemy had an ambush in the village. Sepoy Nihoshe Angami (name is wrong and I drew a blank when I went to Nerhema, his village) volunteered to enter the village alone, dressed as a villager and unarmed. He went forward at dusk, and searched the whole village, and reported it clear. It was a very brave act. (TBNA)

NAGA LEVIES OFFICERS

Two Levy officers were awarded the prestigious Military Cross for gallantry and the leadership that they displayed whilst patrolling in support of Chindit columns. Extracts from their citations follow:

> Jemadar Prembahadur Lama commanded a Platoon of Naga Levies all through the campaign. His Platoon accompanied a Long Range Penetration Column. The work in scouting out forward of the column, carried out brilliantly by his Levies, resulted in the Column never once being ambushed or surprised. His work contributed in no small measure to the cutting of the Enemy Line of Communication, and the clearing of the Naga Hills. (TBNA)

Jemadar Visai Angami was another Platoon Commander in the Naga Levies and he very literally made a name for himself:

> He patrolled many miles forward of our troops, through country strongly held by the enemy, and enabled us to surprise an enemy force of about 200. He did very valuable service in encouraging the villagers in areas isolated by the Enemy, and arranging for intelligence to be taken to the nearest troops. As a result of his coolness under fire, the British Troops called him 'THE BRAVEST OF ALL THE SCOUTS'. (TBNA)

SPRINGING A BRITISH AMBUSH

One Naga Levy, Sepoy Pungoi Angami, was awarded a Military Medal for very courageously using deception to lure enemy troops into a British ambush at Sakrabami. The relevant part of his citation reads:

> Sepoy Pungoi Angami whilst patrolling forward, located an enemy patrol approaching our troops. An ambush was laid. Sepoy Pungoi Angami went out unarmed and dressed up as a villager. He went straight up to the enemy patrol leader, and by signs and the use of the word 'British' caused the patrol to

change its direction, and he led it straight into the ambush. The (enemy) patrol was twelve strong, and only two escaped, seven being killed and three wounded. (TBNA)

A MAGNIFICENT SOLO EFFORT

Perhaps one of the most remarkable acts of ruthless bravery occurred near Rükhroma (now Rüsoma) when a one-man Naga Levy ambush killed at least three Japanese and wounded others. Sepoy Lozelie Angami (of Kohima Village) received a Military Medal for his actions, and part of his citation reads:

He waited until a single Jap came along, and sprang out and killed him with his dao. A little later two Japs came, both armed; with a complete disregard for his own safety, he attacked them. He killed the first and the second fled, dropping his rifle. An enemy patrol came to investigate, and Sepoy Lozelie Angami threw one of the grenades he had captured into the middle of them killing at least a further one, and wounding several. (TBNA)

Lozelie Angami returned to base with proof of his first two Japanese dead, for which he received a well-earned total financial reward of ₹100.

THE ROLE OF THE CIVIL POLICE IN SUPPORTING 23 LRP BRIGADE

As the columns of 23 LRP Brigade moved into the Naga Hills, Eric Lambert organized Naga civil policemen to move with them. John Colvin's book *Not Ordinary Men: The Battle of Kohima Reassessed* provides details of these policemen that are not found easily elsewhere. Around a dozen Constables worked out of Wokha once the Chindits had secured it, serving under the Honorary Magistrate, Chansao Lotha. The policemen ran intelligence groups, acted as guides and escorted groups of captured enemies back to Mokokchung. An Ao policeman, first name unknown, was awarded the Indian Police Medal for intelligence duties that he performed. In the same area Constable No. 34 Kholese Angami and a friend who had been a sepoy, Merenungba Ao, were captured by the Japanese but escaped by killing one of their captors.

Constables No. 29 Ngurohie and No. 18 Dolhucha obtained useful information from the southern Angamis on the south side of the Patkai Hills; these two policemen helped to kill three Japanese and to capture another. Two other Constables, No. 3 Khrulhel Angami and No. 26 Menguzelie Angami, worked well for the columns they were with, and both men received the Indian Police Medal. Constable No. 4 Kelhikhrie Angami was sent to his village, Tuophema, on 2 April, where he hid for over a fortnight before reporting to the Wokha Honorary Magistrate on 18 April with valuable information; he then returned to the enemy area to guide a column until the end of May. But the risks were high for these courageous policemen, and Constables No. 55 Bishnudhoj Angami and No. 1 Veheyi Angami were both captured and shot by the Japanese.

The small domestic Naga Hills Police Force had nearly 100 per cent of its personnel working at the sharp end of the battlefield with British troops. Two of these policemen were killed, two were wounded and one was missing, presumed killed. Three Indian Police Medals were awarded to this Force, but regrettably the names of the recipients are not known.

The Wokha Honorary Magistrate, Chansao Lotha, was later appointed to be a Member of the Order of the British Empire, Civil Division (MBE), and he received a certificate from the Governor of Assam that described the reasons for the honour he received:

From Governor's Camp, Assam

MBE CHANSAO LOTHA

You have done invaluable service in the Lotha country. You served Government for 30 years in various capacities, finally as Acting Head Clerk in the Deputy Commissioner's Office, Kohima. On your retirement, you were made Honorary Magistrate at Wokha where you were mainly responsible for the Civil Administration of the Lotha Country. At the time of the Japanese invasion you stayed on in Wokha organising forward intelligence. You only left Wokha an hour or so before the Japanese entered the place and returned immediately the Japanese retired. You continued to render assistance of the utmost value to the columns passing through your area during the whole period. (Lambert Papers)

EXAMPLES OF ROUTES IN THE NAGA HILLS TAKEN BY CHINDIT COLUMNS

76 Column marched on the route: Merapani, Bhandari, Sanis, Yekhum, Wokha, Kontsenyu, Tseminyu, Chiechama, Nerhema, Tuophema, Gariphema, Kidzumetuma, Khesomi, Chosumi, Runguzumi, Khulazu Basa, Khulazu Bawe, Therepasemi, Phesachaduma, and finally to Kohima.

34 and 55 Columns passed through Mariani, Mokokchung, Longsamtang, Chongliyimsen, Chungtha, Longkum, Longsa, Sakhalo, Lakhuni, Chungtia, Moko, Sukomi, Satakha, Sathazumi, and on to Ukhrul.

AN ORDER OF THE DAY BY THE COMMANDER OF THE BRITISH 33RD DIVISION

Probably the best way to judge the performance of 23 Long Range Penetration Brigade in the Naga Hills is to read extracts from a couple of descriptions written by senior commanders. General Sir M. G. N. Stopford KBE CB DSO MC, the Divisional Commander, wrote in an Order of the Day:

The task given you ... necessitated traversing many hundreds of miles of the most difficult country imaginable, in parts of which malaria and disease were rife, under severely trying

*climatic conditions, and against a cunning, ruthless enemy.
I doubt if such a feat, demanding superb physical fitness, in-
exhaustible endurance and unlimited determination has ever
been carried out by British troops in the history of the Army
... These operations have ended in the biggest defeat that the
Japanese Army has yet suffered and I wish to thank you for the
magnificent part which you have played in it (Stopford).*

After the death of Orde Wingate, Major General W. D. A.
Lentaigne DSO was appointed to command Special Force, and he
wrote of the men of 23 Long Range Penetration Brigade:

*They made new, and widened existing, tracks over appalling
country at the height of the monsoon, and thereby evacuated
their sick and wounded; they carved out light plane strips on
6,000 feet high knife-edged ridges; they bridged swollen rivers by cables, and hauled their mules completely under water
across raging torrents. Their columns passed where no troops
had been before and are unlikely ever to go again (Lentaigne).*

But hopefully now with the passage of time and a reappraisal of
what the brigade did, along with who did much of the hard work
– digging jeep tracks, flattening airstrips, carrying casualties and
supplies for scores of miles, recovering air drops from deep jungle, assisting in river crossings, taking high risks by scouting into
Japanese locations, and by fighting side by side with the Chindits
– the contribution of the Nagas can be seen as a most vital factor
in the brigade's success.

WORKS CITED

Chindits: Special Force Burma 1942–44. www.chindits.info/html
Colvin, J. *Not Ordinary Men. The Battle of Kohima Re-assessed.*
London: Leo Cooper, 1994.
Good, H. W. W. Captain, Royal Army Medical Corps (MO with
4 Border). 'Some Medical Aspects of Long Range Penetration'.
www.jramc.bmj.com/content/132/2/85.long/html

Lambert, E. Papers in the Kohima World War II Museum, York, UK.

Ltu, Khrienuo. 'Nagas Role in World War II'. *Journal of North-East India Studies*, Vol. 3(2) (Jul.–Dec. 2013), 57–69.

Lyman, R. *Japan's Last Bid for Victory. The Invasion of India, 1944.* Barnsley, UK: Praetorian Press, 2011.

'Operations of the 23rd British Infantry Brigade. Naga Hills, April-July 1944.' UK National Archives: WO 203/6389.

'Organisation Naga Levies and Home Guard.' UK National Archives: WO 203/4652.

Shears, P. J. *The Story of the Border Regiment, 1939–1945.* London: Nisbet & Co. Ltd, 1948.

The British National Archives, TBNA: WO 203/6389; WO 373/37/102; WO 373/37/103; WO 373/37/104; WO 373/37/105; WO 373/41/330; WO 373/41/332.

Weiler, Terence G. Recorded interview by Imperial War Museum on experiences with Column 60 of 23 LRP Brigade in the Naga Hills. www.iwm.org.uk/collections/item/object/80018329.html

Wilcox. W. A. *Chindit Column 76* (of 23 LRP Brigade in the Naga Hills). Calcutta: Longmans, Green & Co. Ltd, 1945.

TWELVE

THE 1ST BATTALION THE ASSAM REGIMENT AND THE 3RD (NAGA HILLS) BATTALION THE ASSAM RIFLES AT THE SIEGE OF KOHIMA

3–20 April 1944

THE SITUATION IN KOHIMA IN EARLY APRIL 1944

The resident security battalion in Kohima was the paramilitary 3rd (Naga Hills) Battalion, The Assam Rifles. In peacetime, the Assam Rifles provided military support to the civil police and it sometimes went into frontier or trans-frontier areas where the civil police did not go. Basically, the Assam Rifles was a light infantry regiment that was not equipped up to the same scale as a conventional infantry battalion. Most of the sepoys were Nepalese Gorkhas who had settled in Assam after service in a Gorkha battalion, but after the outbreak of war in 1939 the regiment started recruiting from the north-eastern hill tribes and many Nagas had joined.

In April 1944, there was a very limited Assam Rifles presence in Kohima because most of the sepoys had been deployed into forward areas with 'V' Force in response to Japanese movements across the Chindwin River in north-western Burma. However, the 3rd Battalion Depot was functioning, and as sepoys of the regular Indian Army 1st Assam Regiment trickled into Kohima after the epic fighting at Kharasom and Jessami, the depot re-equipped them. Many of the 'V' Force actions had been betrayed by disloyal eastern Kuki riflemen who went over to the Japanese, and as the survivors of these actions (which included many loyal western Kukis) arrived in Kohima, the riflemen were placed alongside the 1st Assam Regiment for operations. From then on, the sepoys of the Assam Regiment and the Assam Rifles fought and sometimes died together as comrades-in-arms.

Due to command inadequacies, the manning of Kohima by Indian and British Army units had been in shambles. A succession of orders and counter-orders ensued in the last week of March. Units were even removed by higher authorities from the garrison strength without the Garrison Commander, Colonel Hugh Richards, being informed. The nub of the problem lay in the strategic priority of defending the Dimapur supply bases in the plains below Kohima. Generals who were located at the plains looked only at the plains, and could not see Kohima's tactical importance as a blocking position that could stop enemy vehicles and tanks from descending on to the plains. The other big problem was the military assessment of the higher authorities which assumed that the Japanese could only move two battalions on foot through the Naga Hills from the Upper Chindwin and therefore the threat to Kohima could not be a strong one. Even when survivors from 'V' Force at Jessami and Kharasom appeared in Kohima, the military staff did not want to believe that the Japanese 31st Division was rapidly approaching.

The final command debacle occurred when as the British 161st Brigade was moving up from Dimapur to garrison Kohima it was ordered back to Dimapur. This last move was a shock to the Naga inhabitants of Kohima, who had believed that the British would defend Kohima strongly. The Deputy Commissioner for the Naga Hills, Charles Pawsey, was resident in Kohima and he was given a military rank and appointed as the civil liaison officer to the garrison. Many Nagas had been digging fortifications in Kohima at the request of Pawsey, but when 161st Brigade withdrew, the Naga population also withdrew into the surrounding villages. Then 161st Brigade was reordered to occupy Kohima, but only one infantry battalion, the 4th Royal West Kents, managed to get up from Dimapur before the Japanese blocked the road.

1ST ASSAM REGIMENT AND 3RD (NAGA HILLS) ASSAM RIFLES IN THE SIEGE OF KOHIMA

Some accounts of the siege of Kohima correctly emphasize the vital work of the Royal West Kents but pay little attention to the work of Indian troops during the Kohima fighting. The truth is, many Indian troops were present plus a battalion from the Nepalese Army, and whilst some of these troops were non-combatants, and many others were not trained to fight as infantrymen, many were professional soldiers who fought well and hard. We will now take a look at the experiences of the Assam Regiment and Assam Rifles soldiers during the siege, as there were more than a few Nagas serving in both the forces at Kohima.

3 APRIL

An Assam Rifles patrol encountered Japanese soldiers south of GPT ridge on the Aradura Spur and killed 15 of them.

4 APRIL

Nagas scouting for the British reported the advance of a column of Japanese from Viswema/Jakhama. Eighty men of the Assam Regiment from 'A', 'D' and Headquarters (HQ) Companies, with two 3-inch mortars, occupied part of Jail Hill. The transport platoon of the Assam Regiment plus one platoon from 'D' Company occupied a section of GPT Ridge. 'B' and 'C' Companies of the Assam Regiment and HQ Company of the Assam Rifles occupied a section of the spur above the Garrison Hospital (known as IGH Spur), where they stayed throughout the battle. Assam Regiment companies were very weak as only 260 men had so far arrived back from Jessami and Kharasom, and HQ Company was the only company formed that the Assam Rifles had in Kohima, but 'V' Force detachment men were added to it as they trickled in from the Chindwin. Colonel 'Bruno' Brown, the Commanding Officer of the Assam Regiment, worked in the Garrison Battle HQ with Colonel Richards.

5 APRIL

Undisciplined and pointless firing by some Indian non-combatant troops took place and many were later disarmed by their officers. The Japanese quietly occupied Naga Village, and in the morning, captured Indian drivers and their trucks coming into the village.

The two Assam Regiment platoons on GPT Ridge discovered that the other Indian troops on the ridge had abandoned their weapons and run away. The Nepalese troops sent to reinforce GPT Ridge vanished after coming under Japanese fire. By dawn the following day, all the Assam Regiment troops had been pulled back off GPT Ridge on to Jail Hill. Meanwhile the Royal West Kents arrived from Dimapur and occupied key defensive positions, but their Commanding Officer, Colonel John Laverty, did not wish to fully cooperate with the Garrison Commander, Colonel Richards. This unnecessary friction led to Colonel Brown receiving permission to leave the Garrison Battle HQ and return to the Assam Regiment on IGH Spur. A company of Rajput soldiers managed to get into the perimeter and join the defenders. A Japanese 75-mm gun and a machine gun in Naga Village fired effectively on the defenders across the valley. But one Naga sepoy, No. 356 Naik Imtisang Ao, 1st Assam Regiment, responded very calmly and professionally to the enemy threat and for his actions he received a Military Medal with the citation:

Naik Emtisang Ao, having commanded a mortar section with considerable success in the JESSAMI action on 25 March 1944 to 1st April 1944, marched the 56 miles to KOHIMA through enemy lines, arriving there in time for the fighting. On the afternoon of 5 April 1944, he assisted in the firing of a 3-inch mortar from an exposed position on a hillside, engaging an enemy 75-mm gun at 800 yards. When ammunition in the position was exhausted, he assisted in carrying the mortar up a fire-swept hillside to a new position. Later in the evening, having organised ammunition carrying parties, he put down heavy fire in front of our last remaining position on GPT Ridge, broke up a Jap attack and enabled the position to be held for a further 12 hours, quite regardless of Jap counter-barrage. The following morning, returning to his mortar position at first light he was wounded. This Naik showed a capability in handling his weapon, keen devotion to duty, and a calm disregard of danger that was exemplary. (TBNA)

During this day, 80 of the Kohima Garrison were killed and 100 were wounded as the Japanese stepped up pressure on them. The Japanese infantry commander made a massive mistake by sending his strongest unit to occupy Cheswema Village instead of using it to overwhelm the defenders on Garrison Hill.

6 APRIL

The Japanese brought artillery forward on elephants. Heavy enemy fire caused many Indian sepoys to desert but on Supply Hill (known as F. S. D. Hill) a good commander kept his troops in place. At Jotsoma, the British occupied and defended a piece of land called a box and placed 12 artillery guns in it. During the battle, these guns were to fire around 400 shells per day from each gun. Their fire saved the defenders on Kohima Ridge from being overrun. The Japanese moved into Pulomi Village from Maram. Jail Hill was strongly attacked by the Japanese and eventually the defenders withdrew to Detail Hill (known as D.I.S.); Assam Regiment sepoys counter-attacked Jail Hill and safely covered the withdrawal of their Transport Platoon. The Royal West Kents attacked Jail Hill, guided by sepoys from the Assam Regiment, but the attack failed. However, the two Assam Regiment 3-inch mortars that had been left on Jail Hill when many of their operators had been killed or wounded by enemy fire were recovered by brave men who went back to get them. During this fighting on Jail Hill the Assam Regiment casualties were 2 officers and 20 sepoys killed or wounded. Hot food in the Kohima trenches became a thing of the past as the Japanese used their weapons against fires or smoke coming from trenches, so the sepoys lived on biscuits and tinned rations. Cheswema village became a Japanese collection point for pigs that were obtained from Nagas in the area. The Japanese occupied Wokha, and patrolled along the Mokokchung track to Chukiya and Sakhalu.

7 APRIL

A group of brave Indian sappers (engineers) attacked and blew up the garrison bakery and its stores in Kohima to prevent the Japanese occupiers from using it. The Japanese isolated Jotsoma by blocking the Dimapur Road below the village. Japanese artillery fired at the Kohima defenders from GPT Ridge and Meriema Ridge. The Japanese also cut the water supplies that the garrison had been using; from now on the defenders had to use small springs, and patrols had to spend all night collecting water. The Assam Rifles guarded the springs; washing and shaving was forbidden and water for drinking was rationed. An ADS (medical Advanced Dressing Station) was dug into the ground near the top of IGH Spur, and trenches were dug for the wounded soldiers. But this became a target for Japanese artillery, mortars, machine guns and snipers, killing many of the wounded men and re-wounding others two or three times. Gallant Indian non-combatant troops dug the ADS bunkers and trenches and acted as stretcher-bearers, medical orderlies, water carriers and gravediggers. That night 98 walking wounded, led by a Naga guide provided by Charles Pawsey, walked through the jungle to an area below the Japanese block on the Dimapur Road, and were taken by truck to Dimapur. An Assam Rifles flank guard protecting the wounded was fired on but the enemy withdrew after the Assam Rifles returned fire.

8 APRIL

A British patrol discovered a Japanese block at Milestone 36 on the Dimapur Road. The Japanese brought back most of their Cheswema troops to join in the fighting at Kohima.

9 APRIL

The Japanese attacked from the Treasury Hill and captured the District Commissioner's bungalow. A mixed group of Burma Regiment and Assam Regiment sepoys counter-attacked, and whilst the Assam Regiment soldiers got back into the bungalow the Burma Regiment men were held up by effective enemy fire, and the sepoys had to withdraw after four of them had been wounded, leaving the Japanese to capture the bungalow again. The Royal West Kents then dug in on a new higher defence line that included the Club House and the south-western end of the tennis court. On IGH Spur, the Japanese attacked before dawn and took ground, but an Assam Rifles counter-attack drove them back down the hill.

10 APRIL

The Royal West Kents were forced off Detail Hill by continuous Japanese attacks; this left the defenders of Supply Hill at a disadvantage as they were then fired on from Detail Hill. The Japanese in Naga Village, and on Meriema Ridge fired accurately into the DC's bungalow area. Many of the Kohima defenders were now very stressed and some were trembling from the effects of shell-shock. Seventy wounded men were re-wounded by Japanese fire in the ADS, and a shell hitting their operating theatre dugout killed a surgeon, an orderly and a patient. On Kohima Ridge, the total of Assam Regiment and Assam Rifles sepoys fit to fight was 150. The Royal Air Force delivered some successful attacks on Japanese positions on Jail Hill and GPT Ridge. Around the Kohima battlefield, the fit British and Indian defenders numbered only 600 men now, a drop from around 1,000 at the start of the siege.

11 APRIL

In the area around the DC's bungalow, Japanese snipers, some of them tied to trees, continued to cause casualties. British troops moving up from Dimapur had to fight a Japanese patrol in Kiruphema Village. Secüma Village was captured by the British, and a feature named Punjab Ridge near Jotsoma was also captured.

12 APRIL

Thirteen wounded men were killed by Japanese fire in the ADS, and 60 wounded men were re-wounded. From a location near Supply Hill, Urdu-speaking voices called to the Indian defenders to surrender; the call was ignored and it may well have come from Indian National Army troops serving with the Japanese. The enemy attacked IGH Spur again but the defenders managed to beat off the attack. In Meriema Village, the Japanese ordered 200 Naga porters to march to Piphema with loads of supplies. The British Chindit 23rd Long Range Penetration Brigade started moving from the railway north-east of Dimapur into the Naga Hills up the Bokajan Track.

13 APRIL

The Royal Air Force commenced dropping supplies by parachute on to the Kohima defenders, but the first planes made a mistake and dropped 3-inch mortar ammunition on to the Treasury, which the Japanese occupiers collected and started firing at the defenders. Some loads broke free from their parachutes over the defenders' positions, killing or injuring men below. In the early morning, the Japanese fired on the ADS and killed 21 men including two doctors, and re-wounded 30 other men; more casualties were sustained in the afternoon. On Supply Hill, the Rajput Regiment defenders lost so many men that they could not prevent Japanese infiltration. Subedar Utham Singh Chettri and No. 9 Platoon of the Assam Rifles were sent to clear the enemy out, which they did successfully; Subedar Chettri was awarded the Military Cross. Colonel Laverty's attitude of limited cooperation with Colonel Richards was adopted by some of his men who ignored liaising with flanking Indian units. The bodies of many defenders who had been killed needed burying, as did the Japanese attackers who had fallen, but some of the Royal West Kents would not lend their picks and shovels to other units who did not have them, so the decomposing bodies added to the stench of excrement and urine in the defenders' trenches, as latrine pits could not be safely dug and used because of enemy machine gun and sniper fire. Flies proliferated and settled everywhere. Many men of the Assam Regiment were now showing signs of fatigue and mental strain, and the officers had to maintain tight control. In Secüma Village, a British patrol killed 19 Japanese. The Japanese sent a unit from Chakhabama to Cheswema, and also placed an outpost at Phekerkriema.

14 APRIL

During an air drop, one Royal Air Force plane crashed into GPT Ridge, it had probably been hit by enemy fire. Some supply loads broke away from parachutes again, causing casualties to the defenders below. In the bungalow area, two platoons of Assam Regiment and Assam Rifles sepoys took over from the Royal West Kents who needed relieving; these soldiers were to stay in this location for the next five days until the siege of Kohima was lifted by the British troops slowly advancing from Dimapur. Nine Indian sepoys were killed or wounded as they ran in to take over the defending trenches. The Japanese tried infiltrating their positions at night, but 2-inch mortar bombs fired at 200 yards range, plus gunfire from the artillery at Jotsoma, stopped their movement. During the rest of the night the sentries responded aggressively with grenades and rifle fire whenever they heard Japanese movement. In the ADS, 13 wounded men were killed in the operating theatre dugout; over 20 wounded men were re-wounded. At Zubza, a dug-in Japanese company of soldiers was annihilated by British tanks using their guns; however, the Japanese had killed several British tank crews in ambushes before the tank crews learned how to operate in jungle conditions. The Jotsoma box was surrounded by the corpses of Japanese who had been killed whilst attacking it.

15 APRIL

Japanese artillery fire from Meriema Ridge was effective against the defenders of the Bungalow area, as were the captured British mortars in use by them. The Japanese sniped at water points during daytime hours; they also sniped at the ADS with deadly results. The Japanese attacked Jotsoma again and failed. This proved to be their last serious attack against the Jotsoma box. In the bungalow area, a Naga hero of the Assam Regiment, No. 555 Naik Dilhu Angami, was awarded a Military Medal for raiding a Japanese bunker. His citation tells the story:

> *At KOHIMA on 5th April 44, this naik led a small grenade raid on a Japanese bunker position, which had a light machine gun on a fixed line firing direct on Battle Headquarters. His party had advanced to within 15 yards of the Jap bunker when the light machine gun covering their advance had a stoppage thus bringing his party under heavy Jap fire from two sides. Undaunted the naik gallantly rushed the bunker shouting 'Charge, Charge!' using his CMT (short rifle) for giving covering fire. Inspired by his action and leadership, his four grenadiers followed, completed their task and withdrew with 7 Jap rifles, 2 grenades and a Warrant Officer's sword, under cover of the light machine gun which by then had been got into action again. (TBNA)*

The four sepoys with Dilhu Angami had run across the tennis court with grenades in their hands, and with the safety pins removed from the grenades; they were indeed brave men. The sepoy firing the light machine gun was the Khasi Wellington Massar; he was severely wounded during this attack and later died of his wounds, but not before he received the Indian Distinguished Service Medal for bravery displayed in this action and previously at Jessami.

16 APRIL

On Kohima Ridge, the Royal Air Force delivered a good supply drop. The surrounding trees were festooned with coloured parachutes that had snagged there. The troops advancing from Dimapur edged closer to Kohima Ridge when a Punjabi battalion occupied Piquet Hill. A British battalion attacked Japanese troops entrenched near Khabvuma Village, but the attack failed.

17 APRIL

By early morning, the Japanese had overrun several of the forward trenches on Supply Hill which allowed them to move up the southern slope. At the request of Colonel Laverty, Colonel Rodgers sent Colonel Brown with a mixed company of Assam Regiment and Assam Rifles to relieve the Royal West Kent soldiers on Supply Hill. Unfortunately the Assam Regiment sepoys suffered casualties from enemy mortars as they approached the hill, and even further casualties from two Japanese machine guns firing from GPT Ridge. Nevertheless, the relief was made and the Royal West Kents moved back over Kuki Piquet on to the south side of Garrison Hill. But Japanese troops fired very accurately on to Supply Hill from Jail Hill, and when a heavy enemy barrage fell on Supply Hill in the evening, all the defenders on Supply Hill withdrew rapidly to Kuki Piquet. Some of the weaker troops snapped and their nerves broke, but their units kept their cohesion and continued fighting. A Japanese attack moved on to Supply Hill and occupied it. Assam Regiment troops were now in three defensive locations – the bungalow area, IGH Spur and Kuki Piquet. The Japanese withdrew from Khabvuma leaving behind 40 dead; most of the Japanese casualties had been caused by British mortar fire hitting their bunkers.

18 APRIL

The heavy Japanese firing on Kuki Piquet demoralized the defenders, many of whom were at the end of their tether as they had been fighting Japanese advances in 'V' Force or at Jessami and Kharasom, well before the siege of Kohima began. At 0230 hours with the support of machine guns and mortars the Japanese attacked Kuki Piquet, screaming fiercely and using phosphorous grenades to set alight the defenders' shelters. The defenders, particularly the Rajputs and the Royal West Kents who were less battle-weary than the Assam Regiment, held their ground for a time with the support of artillery fire from Jotsoma; but the Japanese attack prevailed and the surviving defenders retreated on to Garrison Hill, where some men fixed bayonets and prepared for the next Japanese move, believing that the end was near. But the Japanese halted their advance perhaps to regroup their troops, and later in the day the siege of Kohima was lifted as troops from Dimapur moved into the defended perimeter. It was at 1600 hours that the Assam Regiment soldiers in the bungalow area were relieved by the Punjab Regiment. The Japanese gave the Punjab boys a hard time, causing 22 casualties and taking some ground that the Assam Regiment had never surrendered. But the next day the Punjab soldiers retook the lost ground. The walking wounded were sent down the Dimapur Road, but the Japanese could see them and several of the men were hit again by machine guns, artillery, mortars and sniper fire. The Assam Regiment soldiers on IGH Spur maintained their defensive positions, commanded by Colonel Brown and joined by Naik Dilhu Angami and the other men from the bungalow area. Captain Albert Calistan, Assam Regiment, who had commanded the troops in the bungalow area later received a Military Cross.

19 APRIL

More British troops came into the perimeter and tried to expand it, but the Japanese kept them under pressure, killing and wounding several new officers and men who had inadvertently been exposed.

20 APRIL

The survivors of the 1st Assam Regiment and 3rd Assam Rifles were transported by trucks down to Dimapur. The Assam Rifles casualty figure for the siege of Kohima is not known, but the Assam Regiment lost 36 officers and men killed and wounded out of a force that started the siege 260 strong. It is probable that many more men were lightly wounded but opted for treatment from their own unit medical orderlies, as life expectancy in and around the ADS was often painfully short.

The Commanding Officer of the 1st Assam Regiment, Lieutenant Colonel W. F. 'Bruno' Brown OBE, was awarded a Distinguished Service Order, and his citation has been displayed above as a tribute also to the determined and brave Assam Regiment troops who fought under him during the siege of Kohima. But the Japanese had no intention of surrendering ground at Kohima, and the 1st Assam Regiment was soon to be back in action.

WORKS CITED

Edwards, L. *Kohima, The Furthest Battle*. Stroud: The History Press, 2009.

Lambert, E. Papers in the Kohima World War II Museum.

Steyn, P. MC, Captain. *The History of the Assam Regiment*. India: Orient Longmans, 1959.

The British National Archives (TBNA). London, UK.

THIRTEEN

THE 1ST ASSAM REGIMENT AND NAGA VILLAGERS ON PULIE BADZE MOUNTAIN, KOHIMA

7 May to 7 June 1944

THE 1ST ASSAM REGIMENT AFTER THE SIEGE OF KOHIMA

After leaving Kohima Ridge on 20 April 1944 the battalion was allowed three days in Dimapur to collect itself together, and reorganize before it was once again deployed operationally at Piphema at Milestone 28 on the Dimapur–Kohima Road. The new operational role was to secure Piphema as a strong point in the rear of the operations now being conducted to drive the Japanese out of the Kohima area. But despite the massive amount of supplies in the Dimapur area the battalion was not re-equipped properly or speedily, and some men did not receive a change of clothing; nor were groundsheets or capes issued despite the very wet weather. This resulted in a high sickness rate at Piphema, with many sepoys needing to be sent back to Dimapur to recover. In time, these problems were resolved and by 4 May, all the sepoys received an issue of new olive-green coloured uniforms.

At Piphema, four pieces of high ground needed securing and as reinforcements had not yet arrived for the battalion, sentry duties were constant. Within the perimeter there were also some non-combatant troops whose ideas of deportment and discipline differed from those of the battalion. The sepoys probably enjoyed going out patrolling to ensure that the Japanese did not infiltrate into their area; there was no contact made with the enemy on these patrols. Later the task of patrolling was voluntarily taken over by Naga villagers so that all the British infantry units could be used in the extremely fierce fighting to clear Kohima of well dug-in Japanese troops.

Interestingly, the Japanese troops encountered in the Dimapur area were small patrols of the Indian National Army (INA) who were on reconnaissance, sabotage, mine-laying and propaganda missions. One INA propaganda patrol entered a Naga village and explained the benefits of joining the Japanese side and expelling the British from India; however, their arguments made no impact on those villagers although a few Nagas further to the east had joined the Japanese side. A few of these INA patrols were effective, but others either deserted or avoided contact with British troops.

Whilst the 1st Assam Regiment was in Piphema, some local Angami Nagas stepped forward and offered to fight the Japanese. These men were armed with rather old firearms from the Dimapur base and the warriors were enlisted in the Naga Levies whose head-quarters was near Kohima. Some of these Nagas performed well as evidenced by a sack containing heads that was brought back by patrols that had penetrated Japanese areas. There was an agreed rate of rupees to be paid for bringing back proof of an enemy kill and that is listed in an Appendix at the end of this book.

Two Naga interpreters to the DC, Zhuikhu Sema and Nikhalu Angami of Tsiepama village from the area, later received the BEM for their roles in helping the British troops.

Although the siege of Kohima had ended, and the Dimapur road was free for use, the Japanese had not gone away; they grimly held on to and defended their well-constructed positions in Kohima and most of them chose to fight to the death. The British units fighting them began to lose many men who were both killed and wounded. Meanwhile the monsoon rain pounded down, making the forward movement of ammunition and supplies and the evacuation of casualties extremely difficult.

The Japanese defensive plan at Kohima used two natural features to secure its flanks. At one end were the defended villages of Meriema and Cheswema, and at the other end were strong bunkers built high on the Aradura Spur that ran up to Pulie Badze Peak. The Aradura Spur positions denied the British freedom to use the Kohima–Imphal Road, and it was very important that this road was opened as the American aircraft supplying the surrounded British garrison in the Imphal area were soon to be deployed to other tasks.

The British commanders were concentrating on killing the Japanese on Aradura Spur or forcing them to withdraw, and several attacks were launched but all failed. In some cases, torrential rain made it impossible for heavily laden men to climb the almost vertical, slippery, jungle-covered slopes; in other instances, British troops made successful preliminary attacks and then ran into effective enemy fire coming from other extremely well concealed bunkers that they had not known about. The troops doing the attacking were mainly from the British Army 2nd Division, a formation that had been destined for the North African desert before it was diverted to India, and the soldiers and their officers and commanders were still learning how to fight efficiently in the Asian jungle during the monsoon period.

But one infantry unit did know how to fight effectively on this ground and in this weather – it was the 1st Battalion of the Assam Regiment.

PULIE BADZE MOUNTAIN

During the fighting for Aradura Spur, the British Army, through Eric Lambert the Chief Intelligence Officer in Assam, and through Charles Pawsey the Civil Liaison Officer at Kohima, asked for support from Naga villagers in carrying supplies forward and in carrying casualties off the mountain. The response was magnificent and part of the citation for the Military Cross awarded to Jemadar Ünilhu Angami, Naga Levies, of Khonoma is very relevant:

When our troops made their right hook to ARADURA, he raised three thousand Naga tribesmen to act as porters, and he

was responsible for providing local men as guides for the march.
He showed the greatest skill and initiative on this operation
and it was largely due to his efforts that complete surprise was
achieved. In addition, he has served for two years as headman of
the Naga Porter Corps, giving devoted service. (TBNA)

At first Naga women joined in the portering work, but as the
risks increased and casualties occurred the job was done by men
alone, and in some cases, the Naga men understandably declined
to go to certain locations where they knew that the Japanese were
waiting to target them. But on the whole, the Nagas accepted the
tasks that their headmen agreed to perform, and many British
soldiers owed their lives to speedy casualty evacuations down
treacherous mountain slopes; groups of Nagas would form relays of porters so that stretchers could be taken down hills swiftly
without the need for the stretcher-bearers to stop to rest.

On 7 May, the 1st Assam Regiment was holding its firm base
at Piphema, with an additional base at Milestone 32.5, when
Colonel Brown was requested, but not ordered, to move his battalion forward into the fighting area; he agreed immediately and
was given the independent task of capturing a Japanese bunker
on the lower slopes of Pulie Badze Mountain.

Two British attacks on the bunker had already failed and it was
being observed by a battalion of Punjab Regiment. The Assam
Regiment, only two companies strong, took over from the Punjab
Regiment on 8 May. One Assam Regiment company acted as porters and mule drivers while the other immediately moved to de-
fine the extent of the bunker. This was done by patrols drawing
enemy fire, and although four sepoys were wounded, the size of
the oval-shaped bunker was determined. The bunker was large
enough to hold two Japanese companies but it was believed that
only one company with four machine guns was holding it.

As it was getting dark, the forward Assam Regiment company formed a perimeter, dug trenches and laid trip wires ahead
of the trenches; the artillery at Jotsoma registered targets around
the bunker. At around 2200 hours the perimeter was strongly attacked by the Japanese who shouted cries of 'Banzai' and threw

many grenades. But the sepoys in their trenches repulsed the enemy who withdrew when artillery fire was called down on the bunker. Enemy 'jitter patrols' then wandered around the perimeter in order to keep the sepoys awake and nervous, but by 0430 hours the Japanese had quietened down. Two Assam Regiment soldiers had been killed and ten others were lightly wounded. At first light, patrols discovered that the bunker was empty and the sepoys occupied it. Nearby in the undergrowth, were several bodies of Japanese soldiers with the right hands cut off; this was a Japanese ritual as part of a dead soldier's body was repatriated back to Japan to be cremated, and the ashes placed in the family shrine.

An Assam Regiment patrol proceeding to advise the nearest British battalion that the bunker was secure encountered a Japanese patrol. The sepoys had fired first and killed three of the enemy while the remainder ran away. Tragically, the British battalion had thought that the bunker could not be captured and had withdrawn, leaving the Japanese to occupy the old British battalion's trenches which had a commanding view of the mountainside, and the bunker that the Assam Regiment had secured (it was the 1st Assam's job to capture the bunker and the British battalion's job to occupy or destroy it). These trenches became the pivot of the Japanese defence line when they later fought to keep Aradura Spur in their hands.

The 1st Assam Regiment then occupied a position named Ring Contour that was at the 6,000 feet high point on the mountain. Patrols were daily sent up Pulie Badze to find and occupy other enemy positions. A dug-out was found but the patrol leader was killed as he was entering the dug-out. Then another bunker was found that gave supporting fire on to the first bunker.

Meanwhile down below in Kohima, GPT Ridge, Jail Hill and FSD Hill were successfully recaptured by the British, but the Japanese held out in Naga Village and on Aradura Spur. The 1st Assam's daily patrolling caused casualties to both sides and began to wear out the nerves of the sepoys, who seemed to have been forgotten while the main events in the Battle for Kohima were happening below them.

Meanwhile half the battalion, supported, when requested, by Naga villagers, were occupied in bringing supplies up to Ring

Contour and in escorting walking wounded or carrying the wounded in stretchers back down the hill. Through Charles Pawsey, villagers were remunerated in cash or commodities for the labour they expended in supporting the British troops.

Finally, some 3-inch mortars were brought up the mountain and the Japanese bunker complex was given a good blasting with mortar fire before a British brigade attack was mounted. Although the attack failed, an Assam Regiment patrol the following day found the first bunker to be empty. A second brigade attack was launched and met only half-hearted resistance in other locations. The 1st Assam Regiment then mopped up the remaining old enemy positions and by 7 June, there were no living Japanese left on Pulie Badze, the survivors having moved south-eastwards in an attempt to return to Burma.

The Commander of the British 2nd Division, Major General John Grover, sent a message to Colonel Brown that included the comments:

> *For over a month your battalion has had the task of protecting the right flank of the Division on the spurs below Pulebadze. This was a most important task since it was essential to the success of my operation that the Japanese should not be permitted to work round that flank again and threaten our positions above Jotsoma. Your position on the now famous Ring Contour was also essential to the flank protection of the operations of 6 Infantry Brigade.*
>
> *I should be glad if you will tell all ranks of your battalion that I appreciate the keen way in which they have carried out their constant patrolling in thick and difficult country, and their success in ultimately clearing the small but strong enemy position located on the spur above them.*
>
> *I congratulate your battalion for voluntarily undertaking further operations at a critical time when our resources were much stretched, although your battalion had suffered such heavy casualties and was badly in need of a rest and refit. (Steyn 252)*

CASUALTIES ON PULIE BADZE AND A TRIBUTE TO NAGA VILLAGERS

But the 1st Assam Regiment had paid a great price in blood on Pulie Badze as a dozen men had been killed in action, or died of wounds or illness during that month, and many others had been wounded. On 13 June, the battalion marched down from Pulie Badze and was finally taken to Shillong to rest weary limbs and frayed nerves.

A fitting tribute to the Naga villagers who supported the British was later given by Field Marshall Sir William Slim who wrote in his book *Defeat into Victory*:

> ... the gallant Nagas whose loyalty ... had never faltered ... they guided our columns, collected information, ambushed enemy patrols, carried our supplies, and brought in our wounded under the heaviest fire ... Many a British and Indian soldier owes his life to the naked, head-hunting Naga, and no soldier of the Fourteenth Army who met them will ever think of them but with admiration and affection. (341–2)

WORKS CITED

Colvin, J. *Not Ordinary Men. The Battle of Kohima Re-assessed*. London: Leo Cooper, 1994.

Edwards, L. *Kohima. The Furthest Battle*. Stroud: The History Press, 2009.

Prasad, B. Gen. Ed. *Official History of the Indian Armed Forces in the Second World War, 1939–45. 'The Reconquest of Burma'*, Vol.1. India: Orient Longmans, 1958.

Slim, Sir W. Field Marshall. *Defeat into Victory*. London: Cassell & Co. Ltd, 1956.

Steyn, P. MC, Captain. *The History of the Assam Regiment*. India: Orient Longmans, 1959.

The British National Archives (TBNA). London, UK.

FOURTEEN
NAGA LEVIES AND VILLAGERS DURING THE BATTLE FOR KOHIMA

Without the invaluable intelligence system and the splendid band of porters we should indeed have been sunk.

Major General John Grover, Lambert Papers 13

Without the intelligence provided by the tribesmen of the country we should not have achieved the success we have.

Lieutenant General Montagu Stopford, Lambert Papers 13

THE NAGA LEVIES

Once the Japanese commenced their advances on Kohima and Imphal in March 1944 the British started to think about raising local Levies in Naga areas. There were successful precedents in Burma, where the Western Chin Levies and the North Kachin Levies had been raised and were operating successfully against Japanese and Indian National Army units. It did take time before the British reluctantly accepted that a Japanese threat against Kohima did exist, but men like Chief Intelligence Officer for Assam, Eric Lambert, a friend of the Nagas who had been a former occupant of the Deputy Commissioner's bungalow in Kohima, could see what was happening and they prepared plans. Details of how Naga Levies were recruited, trained, employed and remunerated are detailed above and are also in an Appendix at the end of this book.

NAGA LEVY OPERATIONS DURING THE FIGHTING FOR KOHIMA

During the fighting around Kohima, a Naga Levies Headquarters was established near the town and commanded by Captain J. G. Ruther of the British Army. From the headquarters, Levy Patrol Commanders or individuals were tasked to go on reconnaissance missions. These brave men did not often carry weapons and they dressed as villagers. Report Centres were also set up in villages secured by 2nd Division or 23rd Long Range Penetration Brigade. The village headmen living in enemy-occupied territory would send trusted men to a Report Centre with information on whether the Japanese and Indian National Army troops were living in or near their villages. Often British planes or artillery guns would then attack these positions, which sometimes resulted in villagers being killed or wounded. However, the flow of information continued as the Nagas in general were on the side of the British. The Japanese were, for the most, just taking what food and goods they wanted from villages whereas the Indian National Army troops would often behave ignobly. Nagas felt no affinity with plains Indians. In contrast, the British troops behaved themselves and paid for what they took with silver rupees or with commodities such as salt or rice.

AN INDIVIDUAL PATROL RESULTING IN A SUCCESSFUL AIRSTRIKE

A good example of a very brave individual effort was the patrol of No. L.57 Havildar Neibotha (Mekro) Angami, of Kezoma Village, that resulted in the award of the highly regarded Indian Distinguished Service Medal. His was the only such medal awarded to a Naga Levy, with the following citation:

> At PFUTSERO on 4th May 1944 and days following. Learning that the enemy was concentrating at the 24th mile on the KOHIMA-JESSAMI track near Pfutsero, Havildar Neibotha Angami set out alone from his report centre at KHEZOMA, and on reaching the enemy position he allowed himself to be captured. He well knew of recent atrocities on Nagas, and this was a very

brave act. He worked for four days as a porter, then escaped. He thus pinpointed enemy food and ammunition dumps. He then did a patrol of 115 miles into Naga Levies HQ near Kohima. He confirmed our knowledge of dispositions in five villages. A very successful air strike resulted. During the enemy retreat, he located their concentration area near CHAKHABAMA, and enabled a second air strike to go in. His organisation of intelligence and leadership were of the highest order. (TBNA)

AN EXAMPLE OF TWO NAGA LEVIES SCOUTS WORKING TOGETHER

In another incident two brave scouts worked together to achieve a good result, with each of them receiving the Military Medal. They were No. L.230 Sepoy Malo-o Angami and No. L.245 Sepoy Zetseilie Angami, both of Chedema Village. Their citations were identical:

CHEDEMA Area. 2nd May and days following. Accompanied by one other Levy he patrolled from Naga Levy HQ near KOHIMA through the enemy positions in CHEDEMA. He then watched the enemy traffic on the Jeep Track for 36 hours, and then pushed on to the CHAKHABAMA area, where he investigated the enemy HQ. The intelligence brought in allowed a highly successful air strike to go in. He patrolled this area consistently. The enemy were fully aware that these two men were working as scouts, and they were continually fired on. They were quite undeterred and they were successful on account of their superior jungle craft. They did valuable and devoted work for our troops. (TBNA)

EXCELLENT PATROL WORK BY A NAGA LEVIES COMPANY COMMANDER

In the previous chapter about operations on Pulie Badze Mountain we saw that No. L.90. Jemadar Ünilhu (Chasie) Angami of Khonoma Village received a Military Cross, and part of the citation was for his raising of 3,000 volunteer Naga villagers to act as porters during the British attacks on Aradura Spur. The other part of his citation reflected his brave and very professional work as a Patrol Leader:

> *APRIL/MAY/JUNE 1944. KOHIMA. Throughout the campaign ünilhu Angami commanded a company of Naga Levies. His conduct at all times was exemplary, and he showed the greatest courage in contact with the enemy. His leadership was of a very high order, and he inspired great confidence in his men. He led five patrols which penetrated many miles behind the enemy lines, and which came under heavy fire. (TBNA)*

A TURNING POINT IN THE BATTLE TO CLEAR THE JAPANESE OUT OF KOHIMA

One individual patrol by No. L.87 Sepoy Ziecha-o (Whuorie) Angami of Kohima Village resulted in the British troops making a big tactical move forward, and a Military Medal being awarded. Ziechao's citation tells the story:

> *20th April 1944 at KOHIMA. In order to secure intelligence urgently needed by our troops Sepoy Ziechao Angami went alone from JOTSOMA report centre across the ZUBZA River to MEREMA, where he daringly investigated enemy positions. He continued until driven off by machine gun fire. He then continued through Kohima Village and on to Jail Hill. He returned through the Bazaar area and down the ZUBZA River, bringing in the most valuable intelligence from the above areas. This intelligence assisted greatly in the decision to move a Brigade into Kohima Village. On a second occasion, he brought intelligence from REKROMA through the enemy lines at great risk. He was absolutely unafraid of the enemy. (TBNA)*

At the time of his patrol Ziecha-o was not a sepoy, and in his papers in the Kohima World War II Museum at York, Eric Lambert described what he did when Ziecha-o's information reached him at 0200 hours in the morning:

Considering this information sufficiently valuable to wake the Divisional Commander, I personally called on him in his dug-out. An excellent example of the reliance placed on Naga information was John Grover's decision, after only a few questions, to move a brigade across the valley and straight into the Village.

This required a considerable number of porters, but my messenger sped out during the night and the brigade was on the move by dawn with Joseph, the track overseer from the Bokajan Road as guide with scouts provided by Setsware.

Mongosisu [Megosieso Savino] of Khonoma, a Naga evangelist and English speaker from the Baptist Mission, led the porters drawn from the villages of Mezoma, Sachema [Secüma], Kizuphema [Kiruphema], Piphima [Piphema], and other hamlets.

When the Japanese came to take up their positions in the village in the morning they found it occupied by a complete brigade of British troops.

The problem of rewarding Ziecha-o, a civilian, for his remarkable bravery, was successfully overcome by recruiting him then and there into the Assam Regiment (he was later transferred to the Naga Levies) and obtaining for him the distinction of the Military Medal.

After the move had taken place, the Japanese surrounded the village and the difficulty of evacuating the wounded became severe. Efforts were made to approach the village with an armoured ambulance through the bazaar but this ended in failure, and the only alternative left was to transport them by stretcher across the Zubza Valley, by a Naga path, to a convenient location on the main road below Jotsoma, a long tedious and hazardous journey and an extremely painful one for the wounded.

After some discussion, the village of Jotsoma, near divisional headquarters, agreed to undertake this risky task providing up to 200 men and women for the purpose.

Led by a British doctor, the porters crossed the valley to a point in the jungle below the village. They waited here until the

Corps artillery put down a heavy artillery barrage above their heads and a sortie was made with the wounded from the village to meet the advancing porters. In this way, several successful journeys were made until one day the timing went wrong and the porters walked into the barrage. Some of the Nagas were killed and wounded and a few others turned and fled, but the majority retreated below and when all was quiet returned to where the wounded troops had been left and picked them up and carried them back with their own dead and wounded. After this event, it was decided that women would in future not take part, but there were moments of worry whether the village would in fact continue this risky task.

They continued as before and when they learned that the officer concerned in the (artillery) error was to be court-martialled, the elders came in a body to the Divisional Commander and requested that he should be forgiven. One of the casualties, later evacuated, was Mongosisu [Megosieso] who had stayed on in the village till he was wounded in the leg by a mortar fragment.

Jotsoma was most ably led throughout by the senior headman, Pfuzilhu [Pfüzielhu Nakhro], who in the opinion of the divisional commander should have received a knighthood in recognition of his work. The best I could get for him was the British Empire Medal.

Scouts, guides, messengers, porters, stretcher bearers, interpreters, accommodation and food were all provided by this village which set a splendid example eagerly to be followed by the rest of the Angamis. (Lambert Papers)

Whilst Charles Pawsey was involved in local activities during the fighting for Kohima, Eric Lambert was at Jotsoma organizing intelligence efforts, and advising senior generals on support that could be obtained from the whole of the Naga community.

Eric Lambert's description quoted above of what both Naga individuals and complete villages did cannot be bettered as a testament to the loyalty given, the hard labour performed, the risks taken, and the blood shed by Nagas during the battle for Kohima.

WORKS CITED

Colvin, J. *Not Ordinary Men. The Battle of Kohima Re-assessed.* London: Leo Cooper, 1994.

Lambert, E. Papers in the Kohima World War II Museum, York, UK.

The British National Archives (TBNA): WO 373/37/107; WO 373/37/117; WO 373/41/331; WO 373/41/375.

FIFTEEN

SANCOL 153 GORKHA PARACHUTE BATTALION DEPLOYS A RIFLE COMPANY INTO THE NAGA HILLS

June–July 1944

> *But little of this could have been achieved without the assistance of the Nagas.*
>
> Eric Neild, Medical Officer of 153 Gorkha Parachute Battalion

50TH INDIAN PARACHUTE BRIGADE AFTER THE BATTLE OF SANGSHAK

50th Indian Parachute Brigade defended the Sangshak area for six days and nights of heavy fighting against strong elements of the invading Japanese 15th and 31st Divisions. The brigade lost 40 officers and 585 men during this period. The night of 26–27 March 1944, the remaining defenders of the Naga village of Sangshak, if they were physically capable, obeyed orders and withdrew in small groups from their perimeter towards Imphal. Men trickled in over the following weeks, often telling stories of assistance provided by Naga villagers that allowed the sepoys to survive and continue their trek through the jungle towards Imphal and the British IV Corps Headquarters located there.

In his book *With Pegasus in India*, Eric Neild, the Medical Officer of 153 Gorkha Parachute Battalion states: 'Some weeks later a wounded British soldier was brought in by Naga stretcher-bearers. They had found him, nursed him and at length carried him to safety. It was our first personal experience of Nagas, and it was not by a long chalk the last of the valuable assistance which we were to receive from these tribesmen' (68).

50th Indian Parachute Brigade had problems in re-equipping as the Japanese had seized the large ordnance base at Kanglatongbi, and Imphal was besieged, but soon sufficient equipment and rein-forcements were provided for operations to resume. The brigade was then used as 'Corps Troops' and elements were allocated to various tasks around the Imphal Plain, such as manning positions on Nungshigum Hill, patrolling in the Iril Valley, and fighting to repulse enemy attacks north of Bishenpur. Because of the heavy officer attrition in Gorkha infantry regiments around Imphal 153 Gorkha Parachute Battalion loaned officers to these units until replacement regimental officers had been flown in from India.

SANCOL

In early June, 153 Gorkha Parachute Battalion was located on the south-west slopes of a hill named Mung Ching west of Litan on the Imphal Road; its job was protecting the left flank of the British 20th Division. Divisional Headquarters decided to mount a company-strength covert reconnaissance into the Naga Hills south-east of Mung Ching. The duration was expected to be only two or three weeks, and the aim was to assist Allied aircraft in targeting elements of the Japanese 15th and 31st Divisions that were withdrawing from the Imphal and Kohima battlefields into northern Burma. When targets had been chosen, radio messages would bring down air strikes on to them, the communications going back through 20th Division. A company of 120 men from the 153rd Battalion was formed for the mission which was com-manded by Major J. V. Sanders and named SANCOL. A section of Assam Rifles speaking Naga languages, and some Naga Levies who knew the ground were attached to the column; Eric Neild accompanied it as the Medical Officer.

The column could not receive air drops as that would alert the Japanese to its presence, so rations for 48 hours were carried including cash to purchase further food supplies from the Naga villages in the area. The former Naga headmaster of Ukhrul school, Captain Ralengnao Khathing MBE BA, was provided as the Column Intelligence Officer. Ralengnao Khathing had been awarded his BA in Economics at Calcutta University, and his MBE had been awarded for his military intelligence duties in 'V' Force, a covert reconnaissance organization, during the Japanese invasion of Burma.

It was known that Japanese foraging parties were active in the area, operating southwards from Litan where the enemy 15th Divisional Headquarters was, and also from Sangshak where the same Division's Rear Headquarters was located. Further east in the Kabaw Valley, enemy troops from the 31st Division and the Indian National Army were on the move having passed through Ukhrul on their retreat from Kohima. The Japanese plan to feed units from captured British supply dumps had failed, and the Japanese soldiers were starving, wet-through from the monsoon downpours, and dispirited.

THE MAPHITE RANGE OF HILLS

SANCOL left Mung Ching on 22 June with mules carrying the reserve ammunition, extra tea, sugar and milk, and rock salt for restoring the Gorkhas' salt levels after climbing up and down the hills. After crossing a ridge 4,400 feet high, the column dropped down to the Toubal River and crossed it in waist-deep water to reach Tumoukhong Village, the last Manipuri village before entering Naga territory. The mules had been left at the Toubal River, and Naga porters carried the loads from that point. The route then went through the first Naga village, Nungdam, and over the 6,000-foot high Maphite Range of hills, but first a detour had to be made to avoid a Kuki village as some Kukis were actively assisting the Japanese. Eventually the column crossed the range and dropped down to Tangkhul Hundung Village where a base was made.

Here Eric Neild started treating Nagas with a variety of medical ailments and he realized that his stock of medical supplies, which was initially intended only for the column's use, was soon going to be exhausted. They found out that insufficient rock salt had been brought as the Nagas preferred payment in that commodity rather than in Indian currency notes. From this village, radio contact was made with the British 100th Brigade who were the link back to Divisional Headquarters, and messages were sent by Morse Code using a Codex system that avoided plain language.

Patrols went out every day assisted by Naga guides. Usually they returned with INA prisoners who had to be interrogated and classified as White (usually Indian prisoners of war claiming to have escaped from Japanese captivity), or Black (die-hard INA politically motivated Japanese allies), or Grey (in the middle and often opportunists). The prisoners were then sent back to Divisional Headquarters. However, the column's main problem was not the prisoners but the interrogation and classification details which, written on paper, tended to disintegrate in the monsoon rain.

ADVANCING TOWARDS THE KABAW VALLEY

As the Imphal–Kohima Road had been opened by British troops on the same day that SANCOL crossed the Toubal River, the pressure on the Imphal garrison was reduced significantly, and 152 Indian Parachute Battalion was sent forward to take over the Tangkhul Hundung base. Meanwhile SANCOL pushed on to reconnoitre the jeep track that ran from Ukhrul to Humine in the Kabaw Valley. Two unarmed Nagas moved ahead on the track to scout for Japanese troops whilst the column dropped down to cross another river, and then to climb a 4,000-foot-high ridge before descending to Loushing Village. As Ralengnao Khathing's men knew that the Japanese were in Loushing, the march was off-track and through thick jungle.

Just before they reached the village, all the inhabitants were found sheltering along a stream, and they reported that a dozen Japanese were in the village manning a medical relay station, where casualties could recover before marching onwards. A guide took a Gorkha attack group to the village, but an overenthusiastic light machine gunner tripped and fired a burst just before the attack went in. The Japanese responded immediately, jumping up from their beds and sprinting into the jungle in their underwear. The Gorkhas piled up all the abandoned Japanese equipment and clothing in a hut and set it alight to destroy it, but regrettably this led to the fire spreading to the rest of the huts which were all burned down.

The column marched on to Khonjan village where another unfortunate incident occurred. Ten village men, thinking that the Gorkhas were in a nearby ambush position, led a Japanese party into the ambush killing ground, but nothing happened as the ambush party had been disturbed by another large group of Japanese, and the Gorkhas had withdrawn. The Japanese realized what had happened and shot the ten Nagas dead. After that incident, a more reflective SANCOL marched on to Tusom where a column base was established.

A CHANGE OF ROLE TO OFFENSIVE ACTION

Divisional Headquarters then changed SANCOL's role from covert observation to raiding, and ordered an attack on the Humine–Ukhrul track. Ralengnao Khathing and Major Sanders had reconnoitred the area for an attack whilst SANCOL was advancing, and the chosen targets were the villages of Mungba, Bongba Khunou and Bongba Khulen, which were large staging posts for the Japanese on the track. The company concentrated at Tusom from its patrolling activities and moved east to cross the Makiong Khong River. It then made a silent off-track approach until dusk approached. After a meal-break the company moved forward in three groups led by Naga guides.

The guides led the Gorkhas straight on to the huts in each village where the Japanese were resting, and each attack party waited until dawn. One Japanese sentry was found dozing and he was swiftly and silently killed. At first light, when the enemy started to leave their huts, the Gorkhas opened fire and riddled the bamboo structures with Light Machine Gun and Thompson (hand-held) machine gun fire. A total of over 55 Japanese troops were killed in all three villages for the loss of one Gorkha killed when he ran forward to obtain identification documents. SANCOL then beat a hasty retreat back down to the Makiong Khong River to find that it had risen dramatically and could not be waded across. Luckily a three-strand 'V' shaped rope bridge was found downstream and the column gingerly, one by one, stepped along the rope above the by-now raging torrent. Then the steep hill up to Tusom had to be climbed by the exhausted Gorkhas.

As covert observation had been replaced by offensive action, 20th Division arranged air drops on Tangkhul Hundung and Tusom villages, where there were suitable areas of ground with open spaces. Eric Neild wrote:

> *Our problem was the five hundred-odd women and children who thought the dropping had been put on for their entertainment. We had already been warned that at the supply drop at Tangkhul Hundung two had been killed and several injured. We managed to chase most of them up to the top end of the village, but a number insisted on sitting under some of the huts in the middle. As it chanced, a box of grenades tore itself from its parachute and hit one of those huts with a tremendous thud – the Nagas left like scalded cats. After that the Dropping Zone was clear. (86)*

The remainder of 153rd Gorkha Parachute Battalion moved forward towards Tusom, ambushing and killing scores of the enemy who were now decisively beaten and retreating rapidly. Suddenly, Divisional Headquarters signalled that the Gorkhas were to march back to Imphal from where they would fly into India to regroup and retrain in the parachute role. One Gorkha had pneumonia and had to be carried back by Naga stretcher-bearers who worked in relays of eight men from one village to the next, where another eight men would be ready and waiting. Eric Neild commented: 'It was a wonderful sight to watch them manipulating the stretcher across the swollen streams.'

The last word on SANCOL also comes from Eric Neild:

It is impossible to estimate factually SANCOL's exact contribution in the disruption of the Japanese retreat, but materially, in ambushes, against one killed and two wounded of our own, over a hundred Jap bodies were counted; but little of this could have been achieved without the assistance of the Nagas. They provided much information and maintained us entirely. These primitive people, who were head-hunters only a few decades ago, had never lost faith in the British, even during the darkest days at Kohima, so that they too are proud of the memorial stone there which says: HERE WAS THE INVASION OF INDIA STOPPED. (88)

Award of the Military Cross to Captain Ralengnao Khathing MBE

Ralengnao Khathing, 'V' Force, was awarded a Military Cross with the citation:

For highly distinguished service and gallantry in action.

In June, a force known as SANCOL was organised to harass the Japanese and report their movements in an area to the EAST of IMPHAL. Captain KHATHING was appointed as adviser to the commander SANCOL. SANCOL operated without Lines of Communication and lived entirely off the country. The period of the operations was 23 JUN 44 to 28 JUL 44. The operations were most successful. Japanese sources of supply were cut, their Line of Communication was most successfully harassed, and information of the greatest value was obtained. It is estimated that 150 Japanese were killed and 43 Jiff (INA) Prisoners of War were captured. The operations of SANCOL were a great embarrassment to the enemy's 15th Division and assisted to a large extent in its final defeat.

As adviser to the commander Captain KHATHING was of the greatest assistance in the success of the operations. He is known and respected by the NAGA population from KOHIMA to HUMINE. He organised and controlled a most efficient system of obtaining information from villagers. He imbued them with the spirit to fight against the Japanese and to give the troops every assistance. He organised the collection of supplies for the column. Without him it would NOT have been possible for the column to live on the country and so carry out its task. Not only was Captain KHATHING tireless in his duties as adviser to the commander, but he also took part in several most successful ambushes. In these he showed leadership of a very high order and great personal bravery. During the period of the operations he gained the admiration and respect of all ranks of SANCOL, British and Gorkha, and proved himself to be a leader and commander of the highest order. (TBNA)

WORKS CITED

Neild, E. *With Pegasus in India. The Story of 153 Gorkha Parachute Battalion.* Singapore: Private publication. Printed by Jay Birch & Co. Ltd, 1970.

Khera, P. N. and Prasad, S. N. *Official History of the Indian Armed Forces in the Second World War. The Reconquest of Burma*, Vol. II, June 1944–August 1945. Delhi: Pentagon Press, 2014.

The British National Archives (TBNA). WO 373/39/132. London, UK.

SIXTEEN

THE ASSAM MILITARY UNITS AFTER THE KOHIMA FIGHTING

June 1944 to August 1945

Raised six years ago at a time when Assam was gravely men-
aced, you were entrusted along with other units of the Indian
Army with the Defence of India's North-Eastern Frontier. This
trust you have loyally discharged; the Province is proud of you
… you will now have rest and recreation amidst these green
and pleasant hills.

Speech by His Excellency the Governor of Assam to the
Assam Regiment on 30 May 1947

THE FIGHTING IN MANIPUR

Once the Japanese started to withdraw back to the Upper Chindwin
River from the Kohima battlefield, the priority for the British 2nd
Division was to open the road from Kohima to Imphal. The Allied
aeroplanes used to supply Imphal during the Japanese encircle-
ment of that town were urgently needed elsewhere, and the Kohima
Road had to be used for future delivery of supplies into Manipur.

The Naga Levies continued in its task of supporting the British
23rd Long Range Penetration Brigade and SANCOL that were destroying retreating elements of the Japanese 31st Division and the
Indian National Army. It appears that the Naga Levies were retained

as a military unit until there were no enemy troops remaining in Naga territory anywhere in Assam, Manipur and Burma.

The 3rd (Naga Hills) Battalion of the Assam Rifles continued its task as a 'V' Force forward reconnaissance unit and closely followed up the retreating enemy into Burma. A Naga from Changki Village serving with the battalion, No. 32120 Lance Naik Yangra Songba Ao, Assam Rifles attached to 'V' Force, was awarded a Military Medal with the citation:

> *During the period under review, August 16th to November 15th, 1944, this Non-commissioned officer has performed his duty in an outstanding manner, being a perfect example to his men and leading them on many strenuous patrols and keeping up their morale in spite of the trials of the monsoon during an advance of 200 miles from Kohima to the Zibaw Taung dam. He has now served for many months with 'V' Force on the Chindwin during 3 monsoons. (TBNA)*

Although this is a short citation it is a good example of the trials and tribulations, especially imposed by the climate, that the Assam Rifles had to contend with. It also shows the distance that the Riflemen covered on foot, and it highlights the importance of the very effective leadership and example displayed by Yangra Songba Ao.

In mid-June 1944, the 1st Battalion the Assam Regiment marched off Pulie Badze Mountain and was transported by truck to Dimapur, where once again the Assam Rifles generously opened its stores to reclothe and re-equip the Assam Regiment sepoys. A period of rest and retraining in Shillong followed for the 1st Assam Regiment.

THE ASSAM REGIMENT IN SHILLONG, MADRAS AND MYSORE

In Shillong, the Assam Regiment had raised two new battalions. A Training Battalion trained new recruits and prepared them for both battlefield routines, basic first-aid medical skills and the very necessary administrative practices of health and hygiene discipline in the field, without which military units can quickly deteriorate through disease because of the large numbers of men concentrated into small areas. A 2nd Battalion the Assam Regiment had also been raised. Both units received much assistance from the Gorkha Training Centre near Shillong.

The 2nd Battalion the Assam Regiment contained several Nagas and the unit had hoped to join the 1st Battalion in Assam on operations against the Japanese, but India's domestic turmoil intervened. To counter Congress rioters and potential saboteurs, the 2nd Battalion was sent to Ranipet to perform security duties on the railway lines around Madras (now Chenai). These duties were not particularly popular but were well performed. After a few months patrolling railway lines the battalion marched 200 miles in full marching order down to the Kolar Gold Mines near Bangalore, and not one sepoy fell out on the march.

In its new location, the 2nd Battalion was part of a Training Brigade that trained British and Indian units in jungle warfare. The Brigade Commander soon realized that the Assam Regiment sepoys were at home in the jungle, and he then used the unit as his Demonstration Battalion. The Assamese sepoys would demonstrate military skills to the other units that passed through the brigade. When news of the Kohima fighting was received many sepoys in the 2nd Battalion were openly angry that they were stuck in Mysore on training duties while their homeland was being overrun by the enemy. But the military authorities were inflexible and a great opportunity was missed to move local soldiers into a war zone that they knew well and wanted to fight over. The 2nd Battalion was to stay-put in Mysore.

THE 1ST BATTALION ASSAM REGIMENT MOVES FORWARD INTO BURMA

Elephant Falls Tented Camp, Shillong, was the home of 1st Assam Regiment between 18 June and 15 September 1944. All ranks had hoped for more time to rest and retrain and see their families where possible, hoping that the 2nd Assam Regiment would move forward from Mysore to Assam to take over the front-line duties. But as previously noted that did not happen. In mid-September, the 1st Battalion was deployed forward to a location west of Tamu in the Kabaw Valley, where it again practised jungle tactics and patrolling. All around lay wrecked Japanese vehicles and many enemy corpses, testifying to the effectiveness of Allied airstrikes that had hit the enemy as it retreated from Kohima; many of these airstrikes had been called by fellow sepoys in the Assam Rifles 'V' Force units. The retreating Japanese had been without transport, petrol, food, medical and ammunition supplies as they had failed to capture these in significant quantities during their attacks on Kohima and Imphal. Many hundreds of wounded or sick Japanese soldiers had been abandoned on their withdrawal routes, and often they had chosen to kill themselves to avoid the dishonour of being taken prisoner.

In early October, the battalion advanced into Burma and because the British were determined to pursue the enemy through the months of the monsoon, road traffic in the torrential rain became a massive problem. The answer was to drop supplies from aeroplanes on to advancing units; sacks of rice would simply be thrown out of the plane, but less robust items would descend under parachutes.

In November, the battalion supported the operations of the East African Brigade by crossing the Chindwin River at Kindat north of Mawlaik. This crossing, including swimming mules across, was accomplished successfully and the battalion became the first complete Allied unit across the Chindwin. After advancing on the east bank of the river, the 1st Assam handed over the job to an East African unit, and recrossed the Chindwin to Mawlaik where they became the reconnaissance battalion for the 19th Indian Division. However, this new assignment did not last long because of a shortage of necessary supplies. For example, the 1st Assam Regiment had a mortar platoon containing, on paper, six 3-inch mortars, but only two mortar barrels were in the hands of the platoon. The 19th Division was in a hurry to move south and was disinclined to rectify an equipment situation that higher authorities should have resolved, and the battalion reverted to ordinary infantry duties.

The battalion advanced southwards into Burma, skirmishing with enemy foraging parties, but detailed military operations were hampered by a lack of suitable radio sets. On 4 January 1945, one such operation went wrong when the enemy were found in possession of a village that the British Division should have been holding. The Commander and the three Section Commanders of the leading Assam Regiment platoon were cut down by enemy fire, and then the Commanding Officer of the Battalion, Lieutenant Colonel William Felix Brown OBE DSO, was shot dead by a Japanese sniper. This was a tragic loss as Colonel Brown had been an inspirational leader who had total confidence in the ability of his sepoys. A new Battalion Commander took over and the advance continued, but the Divisional Commander changed the role of the battalion to that of the Divisional Defence Battalion, and companies were distributed amongst the brigades in the Division.

On 28 January 1945, a Naga from Kohima Village with only around six months' military service behind him, No. 2587 Sepoy Dunio (Pienyü) Angami, 1st Assam Regiment, performed a very brave act that led to his being awarded the Military Medal but also to being severely wounded. His citation read:

At KABWET on the 28th January 1945 No. 2587 Sepoy DUNIO ANGAMI, when 'B' Company less one Platoon, 1st Assam Regiment and 'A' Company 2nd Royal Berkshires in attacking enemy strong point at Point 280 were pinned to the ground approximately 30 yards from a number of bunkers, stalked forward alone and cleared two of them with grenades. This allowed one Platoon of the Assam Regiment and one Platoon of the 2nd Royal Berkshires to get to the flank of the remaining enemy position. Shortly afterwards having obtained more grenades No. 2587 Sepoy DUNIO ANGAMI went forward again and on getting to within one yard of another enemy bunker he rose to his knees and flung all his grenades into the bunker. Whilst doing so his arm was smashed by enemy fire from the bunker. Sepoy Dunio Angami's determination under very heavy enemy fire, his devotion to duty and complete disregard of personal safety were an inspiration to all. His valour in tackling enemy bunkers alone was of the highest order and in the full traditions of the service. (TBNA)

MANDALAY AND FURTHER SOUTH

In early March, the 19th Division reached Mandalay and fought hard and successfully for that famous Burmese city. The battalion was involved in the fighting and it also provided the bodyguard for the Divisional Commander, taking casualties during a Japanese ambush of the Divisional Commander's vehicle. After the capture of Mandalay, the 1st Assam Regiment was moved to Meiktila where it mopped-up Japanese stragglers, capturing from the enemy both a 75-mm gun and a bullock; the bullock was adopted as a regimental mascot and named George. The mascot George stayed with the battalion until 1947 when the battalion finally left Burma.

The next large town that the battalion fought over was Toungoo, and here a Naga from Bhuo Village made a name for himself. No. 504 Lance Naik Yambhamo Lotha, 1st Assam Regiment, was commanding a light machine gun group when his bravery resulted in him receiving a Mention in Despatches, the citation reading:

On 8th May 1945 at PEINNEBIN near TOUNGOO, BURMA No. 504 Sepoy (Lance Naik) YAMBHAMO LOTHA was moving with the leading group when in command of the forward section of No. 7 Platoon which was patrolling in the jungle with orders to locate and destroy an enemy party reported in the vicinity. The section by its silent approach completely surprised a party of 18 Japanese. On seeing them Sepoy (Lance Naik) YAMBHAMO LOTHA personally crept with the light machine gun to a flank position within 25 yards of the still unsuspecting enemy and opened fire, killing three. The remainder took up positions in bunkers and returned his fire, whereupon he moved further to their rear, and now some 200 yards from our nearest troops, continued to fire on this and another party, thus acting as stop gun and preventing any attempt to outflank his Section until the remainder of the Platoon was in action. By his good leadership in the approach and by his prompt initiative and offensive action he enabled the patrol to inflict several casualties on the enemy without loss to themselves. His skill and dash in the face of an enemy superior in numbers was an inspiration to the men under his command. (TBNA)

Twelve weeks later, Yambhamo displayed bravery again, and this time he received a Military Medal:

On the 29th July 1945 at AUNGGYANTHA, near TOUNGOO, BURMA, No. 504 Sepoy (Lance Naik) YAMBHAMO LOTHA was second in command of a Section forming part of a fighting patrol ordered to destroy any enemy found WEST of the SITTANG river in this area. The patrol was engaged by light machine gun fire from a position dug in on the river bank and the leading Section having been pinned down the remainder of the Platoon executed a flanking attack. In this attack, a three-man post was first encountered by YAMBHAMO's section, and was charged at the bayonet point. In this charge, the Section Commander and another man were wounded by grenades but Sepoy (Lance Naik) YAMBHAMO undeterred rushed ahead and killed the enemy in the post with a grenade and his sten gun. The enemy light machine gun then opened up on the section at about 40 yards range and mortally wounded the already hit Section Commander. YAMBHAMO in the face of this fire immediately charged across the open ground and firing from the hip killed the light machine gunner. His dash and skill undoubtedly saved his comrades from suffering a considerable number of casualties, and his courage and leadership in twice charging across open ground in the face of close range fire was an inspiration to all. This Non-commissioned officer has already been awarded an Immediate Mention in Despatches for gallantry in the face of the enemy in May. (TBNA)

Yambhamo's action above was part of the heavy fighting that went on in late July and early August to stop the Japanese troops in Central Burma from escaping into Thailand. The war itself officially ended when, after being bombed twice by devastating

US atom bombs, Japan ceased fighting and surrendered on 14 August 1945. But many Japanese in Burma either did not get the news or did not believe it, and the British forces were involved in skirmishes with Japanese troops for the next few weeks.

The 1st Assam Regiment next involved itself in aiding civilian communities to get their towns and villages working again, and in hunting down Burmese bandits known as dacoits who were looting and murdering civilians. One highlight for the division was its tattoo in November when all the battalions put on a display. The 1st Assam Regiment had Kukis, Lushai, Assamese and Nagas in tribal dress performing dances. But the emphasis now was on getting sepoys home on leave. Meanwhile a 3rd Battalion of the Assam Regiment had been formed in Shillong. The 1st Battalion moved to the hill station of Maymyo, north-east of Mandalay, and built a new camp there. From Maymyo, companies were deployed on internal security operations wherever needed in the country, and this continued until the battalion departed from Burma in 1947.

The 1st Battalion the Assam Regiment could be proud of its fine record in the Burma Campaign of the Second World War. The following Naga sepoys were awarded a Mention in Despatches for gallantry displayed during the Burma Campaign, but their citations are not available:

No. 635 Naik Tekasashi Ao (Killed in Action 20 January 1945).
No. 563 Lance Naik Kemvü Angami.

WORKS CITED

Steyn, P. MC, Captain. *The History of the Assam Regiment*. India: Orient Longmans, 1959.
Interviews of Naga veterans collected by Charles Chasie.
The British National Archives (TBNA). London, UK.

APPENDIX 1

NAGA SECOND WORLD WAR GALLANTRY AWARDS IN DATE ORDER

UNIT	NAME	No	RANK	LOCATION	ACTIVITY DATE	LG DATE	AWARD
19th Hyderabad Regiment attached 'V' Force	RALENGAO KHATING		Lieutenant	'V' Force area & route of Chinese 5th Army withdrawal	mid 1942 – mid '43	16 Dec '43 p 5472	MBE
Assam Regiment	EMTISANG AO	356	Naik	Kohima	5 Apr '44	08 Feb '45 p 803	MM
1st Assam Regiment	DILHU ANGAMI	555	Naik	KOHIMA	15 Apr '44	5 Oct '44 p 4571	MM
Naga Levies	ZIECHAO ANGAMI	L87	Sepoy	KOHIMA	20 Apr '44	3 May '45 p 2336	MM
Naga Levies	NIHOSHE ANGAMI	L206	Sepoy	PHEKER-KRIMA	28 Apr '44	3 May '45 p 2336	MM
Naga Levies	PREMBAHA-DUR LAMA	L36	Jemadar	23 LRP Bde area	Apr – Jun '44	13 Sep '45 p 4559	MC
Naga Levies	ÜNILHU ANGAMI	L90	Jemadar	KOHIMA & ARADURA	Apr – Jun '44	13 Sep '45 p 4559	MC
Naga Levies	VISAI ANGAMI	L7	Jemadar	Naga Hills	Apr – Jun '44	13 Sep '45 p 4559	MC
Naga Levies	MALOO ANGAMI	L230	Sepoy	Chedema	2 May '44 onwards	13 Sep '45 p 4559	MM
Naga Levies	ZETSEILIE ANGAMI	L245	Sepoy	CHEDEMA – CHAKHA-BAMA areas	2 May '44 onwards	3 May '45 p 2336	MM

UNIT	NAME	No	RANK	LOCATION	ACTIVITY DATE	LG DATE	AWARD
19th Hyderabad Regiment attached 'V' Force	RALENGAO KHATING MBE	1577	Capt	SANCOL area		8 Feb '45	MiD
Naga Levies	MEIBOTHA ANGAMI	L57	Havildar	KOHIMA-JESSAMI track	4 May '44 onwards	3 May '45 p 2336	IDSM
Naga Levies	ZASHEI ANGAMI	L146	Sepoy	PHEKEKED-ZUMI 23 LRP Bde	5 May '44	3 May '45 p 2336	MM
Naga Levies	LOZELIE ANGAMI	L60	Sepoy	Dihoma/ Rekrema	8 May '44	3 May '45 p 2336	MM
Naga Levies	PUNGOI ANGAMI	L190	Sepoy	SAKRABAMI	18 May '44	3 May '45 p 2336	MM
19th Hyderabad Regiment attached 'V' Force	RALENGAO KHATING MBE	1577	Capt	SANCOL area	Jun – Jul '44	28 Jun '45 p 3382	MC
Assam Regiment	TEKASASHI AO	635	Naik	Burma	Late 1944 – Early '45	5 Apr '45 p 1823	MiD
Naga Levies	SARE ANGAMI	L5	Sepoy	NAGA HILLS	Mid '44	3 May '45 p 2336	MM
Assam Rifles attached 'V' Force	YANGRA SONGBA AO	32120	Lance Naik	Chindwin area	Aug – Nov '44	13 Sep '45 p 4559	MM
1st Assam Regiment	DUNIO ANGAMI	2587	Sepoy	Kabwet	28 Jan '45	24 May '45 p 2652	MM
1st Assam Regiment	YAMBHAMO LOTHA	504	Lance Naik	Pein-nebin near Toungoo	8 May '45	20 Sep '45 p 4681	MiD
North Cachar	URSULA VIO-LET GRAHAM BOWER		Watch & Ward North Cachar	Laisong	October 1942 onwards	24 April '45 p 2166	MBE
North Cachar	NAMKIA BUING		Watch & Ward North Cachar	Laisong	October 1942 onwards	24 April '45 p 2166	BEM
Civilian	MHIA-SIZOLIE ANGAMI		Interpreter for Charles Pawsey	Kohima		19 July '45 p 3759	MiD
Civilian	KAWATO SEMA					19 July '45 p 3759	MiD
Civilian	KRUHI ANGAMI					19 July '45 p 3759	MiD

UNIT	NAME	No	RANK	LOCATION	ACTIVITY DATE	LG DATE	AWARD
Civilian	LIBEMO					19 July '45 p 3759	MiD
Civilian	THEP-FOORYA HARALU			Kohima		19 July '45 p 3759	MiD
Assam Rifles	AMOS AO	27131	Rifleman			19 July '45 p 3759	MiD
1st Assam Regiment	YAMBHAMO LOTHA	504	Lance Naik	Aunggyan-tha near Toungoo	29 July 45	1 Nov '45 p 5314	MM
Civilian	CHANSAO LOTHA		Honorary Magistrate	Wokha	April 1944 onwards	17 Jul '45 p 3679	MBE
Civilian	KEVICHÜSA ANGAMI		Honorary Captain	Kohima	April 1944 onwards	17 Jul '45 p 3679	MBE
Civilian	KUMBHO ANGAMI		Interpreter	Kohima	April 1944 onwards	17 Jul '45 p 3679	MBE
Civilian	CHOHOZHU SEMA		Interpreter		April 1944 onwards	17 Jul '45 p 3679	BEM
Civilian	KHAKHU SEMA		Interpreter		April 1944 onwards	17 Jul '45 p 3679	BEM
Civilian	HETOI SEMA		Forest Chowkidar		April 1944 onwards	17 Jul '45 p 3679	BEM
Civilian	HEZEKHU SEMA		Interpreter	Mokokchung	April 1944 onwards	17 Jul '45 p 3679	BEM
Civilian	HOSHEKHE SEMA		Interpreter		April 1944 onwards	17 Jul '45 p 3679	BEM
Civilian	KOHOTO SEMA		Interpreter		April 1944 onwards	17 Jul '45 p 3679	BEM
Civilian	LHOU-VISIELE ANGAMI		Interpreter		April 1944 onwards	17 Jul '45 p 3679	BEM
Civilian	NIKHALHU ANGAMI		Interpreter		April 1944 onwards	17 Jul '45 p 3679	BEM
Civilian	PFÜZIELHU ANGAMI		Headman of Jotsoma	Jotsoma	April 1944 onwards	17 Jul '45 p 3679	BEM
Civilian	VILIEZHÜ ANGAMI (Rengma)		Headman of Tseminyu Village, Kohima	Tseminyu	April 1944 onwards	17 Jul '45 p 3679	BEM
Civilian	VIRIALIE ANGAMI		Cultivator and Artisan		April 1944 onwards	17 Jul '45 p 3679	BEM
Civilian	ZHUIKHU SEMA		Interpreter		April 1944 onwards	17 Jul '45 p 3679	BEM

UNIT	NAME	No	RANK	LOCATION	ACTIVITY DATE	LG DATE	AWARD
Assam Regiment	KEMVÜ ANGAMI	563	Lance Naik	Burma	1945	19 Sep '46 p 4715	MiD
N. Levies	Megosiesu SAVINO	L86	Jemadar	Naga Hills	1944	27 Sep '45	MiD
N. Levies	PHU HOTO SEMA	L37	Havildar	Naga Hills	1944	27 Sep '45	MiD
N. Levies	RUDAI ANGAMI	L8	Havildar	Naga Hills	1944	27 Sep '45	MiD
N. Levies	TOLOPU SEMA	L253	Havildar	Naga Hills	1944	27 Sep '45	MiD
N. Levies	Zaputsolie ANGAMI	L94	Havildar	Naga Hills	1944	27 Sep '45	MiD
N. Levies.	INAGHU ANGAMI	L158	Sepoy	Naga Hills	1944	27 Sep '45	MiD
N. Levies	KHEHOYI SEMA	L145	Sepoy	Naga Hills	1944	27 Sep '45	MiD
N. Levies	Kuzukha ANGAMI	L287	Sepoy	Naga Hills	1944	27 Sep '45	MiD
N. Levies	Lhoujou ANGAMI	L68	Sepoy	Naga Hills	1944	27 Sep '45	MiD
N. Levies	Lhoukuo ANGAMI	L69	Sepoy	Naga Hills	1944	27 Sep '45	MiD
N. Levies	Melhuzu ANGAMI	L83	Sepoy	Naga Hills	1944	27 Sep '45	MiD
N. Levies	PUKHATO SEMA	L33	Sepoy	Naga Hills	1944	27 Sep '45	MiD
N. Levies	PUKHEHO MAO	L203	Sepoy	Naga Hills	1944	27 Sep '45	MiD
N. Levies	THEPFUSI ANGAMI	L3	Sepoy	Naga Hills	1944	27 Sep '45	MiD
N. Levies	TOKIHIE ANGAMI	L50	Sepoy	Naga Hills	1944	27 Sep '45	MiD
N. Levies	VISIEZO ANGAMI	L56	Sepoy	Naga Hills	1944	27 Sep '45	MiD

APPENDIX 2

AWARD LIST WITH CITATIONS TO NAGAS

(All awards except those for the Indian Police Medal can be found in the online archives of the London Gazette. Citations, where available, can be found in The British National Archives, London, and Supplement to The London Gazette, 27 September 1945).

Lieutenant Ralengnao Khathing BA, 19th Hyderabad Regiment attached to 'V' Force (Ukhrul Village).

This officer, the only NAGA Emergency Commissioned Officer, has served for over a year without leave or rest, continued to do most excellent and valued work in a forward area of this Area of 'V' Force. The whole of last monsoon he remained forward, in most trying conditions, organising his guerrillas, and gaining much valuable information at a time when no regular troops were operating permanently. He also gave invaluable help to the withdrawing Chinese Army. The information he gained has been confirmed. He has done very many useful, and daring, patrols and recces, including down to the MAWLAIK area, from whence he brought back information of the Japanese positions. This Indian Emergency Commissioned

Officer, by his trustfulness, his hard work, his unbounding energy and enthusiasm, has done much for the defence of India, and is greatly deserving of recognition for his services to his country. (TBNA)

APPOINTMENT TO BE A MEMBER OF THE CIVIL DIVISION OF THE MOST EXCELLENT ORDER OF THE BRITISH EMPIRE (MBE)

Chansao Lotha, Honorary Magistrate Wokha.
Chansao's certificate:

You have done invaluable service in the Lotha country. You served Government for 30 years in various capacities, finally as Acting Head Clerk in the Deputy Commissioner's Office, Kohima. On your retirement you were made Honorary Magistrate at Wokha where you were mainly responsible for the Civil Administration of the Lotha Country. At the time of the Japanese invasion you stayed on in Wokha organising forward intelligence. You only left Wokha an hour or so before the Japanese entered the place and returned immediately the Japanese retired. You continued to render assistance of the utmost value to the columns passing through your area during the whole period. (TBNA)

Honorary Captain KEVICHUSA ANGAMI,
Assistant to District Commissioner, Kohima. (Citation not found.)

KUMBHO ANGAMI, Teacher
Government School, Kohima and Interpreter with 23 LRP Brigade. (Citation not found.)

URSULA VIOLET GRAHAM BOWER,
'Watch & Ward', North Cachar Hills. (Citation not found.)

BRITISH EMPIRE MEDAL, (CIVIL DIVISION) (CITATIONS NOT FOUND)

CHOHOZHU SEMA, Interpreter,
Office of the Deputy Commissioner, Naga Hills.

HETOI SEMA, Forest Chowkidar.

HEZEKHU SEMA, Interpreter,
Sub-Divisional Office, Mokokchung.

HOSHEKHE SEMA, Interpreter, Naga Hills.

KHAKHU SEMA, Interpreter,
Office of the Deputy Commissioner, Naga Hills.

KOHOTO SEMA, Interpreter.

LHOUVISIELIE ANGAMI, Interpreter,
Office of the Deputy Commissioner, Naga Hills.

NAMKIA BUING, 'Watch & Ward,' North Cachar Hills.

NIKHALHU ANGAMI, Interpreter,
Office of the Deputy Commissioner, Naga Hills.

PFUZIELHU ANGAMI, Headman of Jotsoma.

VILIEZHU RENGMA, Headman of Tseminyu Village, Kohima.

VIRIALIE ANGAMI, Cultivator and Artisan.

Zhuikhu SEMA, Interpreter,
Office of the Deputy Commissioner, Naga Hills.

AWARDS OF THE MILITARY CROSS

No. L.36. Jemadar PREMBAHADUR LAMA,
Naga Levies (Kohima Village).

APRIL/MAY/JUNE 1944. NAGA HILLS. Jemadar Prem Bahadur Lama commanded a Platoon of Naga Levies all through the campaign. His Platoon accompanied a Long Range Penetration Column. Throughout his conduct was exemplary, and he showed the greatest courage and a fine determination to overcome all difficulties. His leadership was an inspiration to his men. The work in scouting out forward of the column, carried out brilliantly by his Levies, resulted in the Column never once being ambushed or surprised. His work contributed in no small measure to the cutting of the Enemy Line of Communication, and the clearing of the Naga Hills. In addition, he has given over two years devoted service on the Line of Communication from KOHIMA to our forward outposts in the SOMRA TRACT. (TBNA)

Captain Ralengnao Khathing MBE, BA

19th Hyderabad Regiment attached to 'V' Force (Ukhrul Village)

For highly distinguished service and gallantry in action:

In June a force known as SANCOL was organised to harass the Japanese and report their movements in an area to the EAST of IMPHAL. Captain KHATHING was appointed as adviser to the commander SANCOL. SANCOL operated without Lines of Communication and lived entirely off the country. The period of the operations was 23 June '44 to 28 July '44. The operations were most successful. Japanese sources of supply were cut, their Line of Communication was most successfully harassed, and information of the greatest value was obtained. It is estimated that 150 Japanese were killed and 43 Jiff (INA) Prisoners of War were captured. The operations of SANCOL were a great embarrassment to the enemy 15th Division and assisted to a large extent in its final defeat.

As adviser to the commander Captain KHATHING was of the greatest assistance in the success of the operations. He is known and respected by the NAGA population from KOHIMA to HUMINE. He organised and controlled a most efficient system of obtaining information from villagers. He imbued them with the spirit to fight against the Japanese and to give the troops every assistance. He organised the collection of supplies for the column. Without him it would NOT have been possible for the column to live on the country and so carry out its task. Not only was Captain KHATHING tireless in his duties as adviser to the commander, but he also took part in several most successful ambushes. In these he showed leadership of a very high order and great personal bravery. During the period of the operations he gained the admiration and respect of all ranks of SANCOL, British and Gorkha, and proved himself to be a leader and commander of the highest order.

No. L.90. Jemadar ÜNILHU ANGAMI
Naga Levies (Khonoma Village)

*APRIL/MAY/JUNE 1944. KOHIMA. Throughout the cam-
paign Ünilhu Angami commanded a company of Naga Levies.
His conduct at all times was exemplary, and he showed the
greatest courage in contact with the enemy. His leadership was
of a very high order, and he inspired great confidence in his
men. He led five patrols which penetrated many miles behind
the enemy lines, and which came under heavy fire. When our
troops made their right hook to ARADURA, he raised three
thousand Naga tribesmen to act as porters, and he was responsible for providing local men as guides for the march. He
showed the greatest skill and initiative on this operation and
it was largely due to his efforts that complete surprise was
achieved. In addition, he has served for two years as headman
of the Naga Porter Corps, giving devoted service.*

No. L.7. Jemadar VISAI ANGAMI
Naga Levies (Chizami Village)

*APRIL/MAY/JUNE 1944. NAGA HILLS. Jemadar VISAI
ANGAMI commanded a Platoon of Naga Levies all through
the campaign. He showed leadership and courage of a very
high order. He volunteered for all patrols and was indefatig-
able. He patrolled many miles forward of our troops, through
country strongly held by the enemy, and enabled us to surprise
an enemy force of about 200. He did very valuable service in
encouraging the villagers in areas isolated by the Enemy, and
arranging for intelligence to be taken to the nearest troops. As
a result of his coolness under fire, the British Troops called him
'THE BRAVEST OF ALL THE SCOUTS.'*

AWARD OF THE INDIAN DISTINGUISHED SERVICE MEDAL

No. L.57 Havildar MEIBOTHA ANGAMI,
Naga Levies (Khezoma Village)

At PFUTSERO on 4th May 1944 and days following. Learning that the enemy was concentrating at the 24th mile on the KOHIMA-JESSAMI track near Pfutsero, Havildar Meibotha Angami set out alone from his report centre at KHEZOMA, and on reaching the enemy position he allowed himself to be captured. He well knew of recent atrocities on Nagas, and this was a very brave act. He worked for four days as a porter, then escaped. He thus pinpointed enemy food and ammunition dumps. He then did a patrol of 15 miles into Naga Levies HQ near Kohima. He confirmed our knowledge of dispositions in five villages. A very successful air strike resulted. During the enemy retreat, he located their concentration area near CHAKHABAMA, and enabled a second air strike to go in. His organisation of intelligence and leadership were of the highest order.

AWARDS OF THE MILITARY MEDAL

No. 356 Naik EMTISANG AO, 1st Assam Regiment
(Khenchang Village, Mokokchung)

Naik Emtisang Ao, having commanded a mortar section with considerable success in the JESSAMI action on 25 March 1944 to 1st April 1944, marched the 56 miles to KOHIMA through enemy lines, arriving there in time for the fighting. On the afternoon of 5 April 1944, he assisted in the firing of a 3-inch mortar from an exposed position on a hillside, engaging an enemy 75-mm gun at 800 yards. When ammunition in the position was exhausted, he assisted in carrying the mortar up a fire-swept hillside to a new position. Later in the evening, having organised ammunition carrying parties, he put down heavy fire in front of our last remaining position on GPT Ridge, broke up a Jap attack and enabled the position to be held for a further 12 hours, quite regardless of Jap counter-barrage. The following morning, returning to his mortar position at first light he was wounded. This Naik showed a capability in

handling his weapon, keen devotion to duty, and a calm disre-
gard of danger that was exemplary.

No. 555 Naik DILHU ANGAMI,
1st Assam Regiment (Khezhakenoma Village)

At KOHIMA on 15th April 44, this Naik led a small grenade
raid on a Japanese bunker position, which had a light machine
gun on a fixed line firing direct on Battle Headquarters. His
party had advanced to within 15 yards of the Jap bunker when
the light machine gun covering their advance had a stoppage
thus bringing his party under heavy Jap fire from two sides.
Undaunted the naik gallantly rushed the bunker shouting
'Charge, Charge!' using his CMT (short rifle) for giving cover-
ing fire. Inspired by his action and leadership, his four grena-
diers followed, completed their task and withdrew with 7 Jap
rifles, 2 grenades and a Warrant Officer's sword, under cover
of the light machine gun which by then had been got into ac-
tion again.

No. 2587 Sepoy DUONIO ANGAMI,
1st Assam Regiment (Kohima Village)

At KABWET on the 28th January 1945 No. 2587 Sepoy
DUNIO ANGAMI, when 'B' Company less one Platoon, 1st
Assam Regiment and 'A' Company 2nd Royal Berkshires in
attacking enemy strong point at Point 280 were pinned to
the ground approximately 30 yards from a number of bun-
kers, stalked forward alone and cleared two of them with gre-
nades. This allowed one Platoon of the Assam Regiment and
one Platoon of the 2nd Royal Berkshires to get to the flank
of the remaining enemy position. Shortly afterwards having
obtained more grenades No. 2587 Sepoy DUNIO ANGAMI
went forward again and on getting to within one yard of an-
other enemy bunker he rose to his knees and flung all his gre-
nades into the bunker. Whilst doing so his arm was smashed
by enemy fire from the bunker. Sepoy Dunio Angami's deter-
mination under very heavy enemy fire, his devotion to duty

and complete disregard of personal safety were an inspiration to all. His valour in tackling enemy bunkers alone was of the highest order and in the full traditions of the service.

No. L.60. Sepoy LOZELIE ANGAMI,
Naga Levies (Rekroma Village)

8th May 1944. REKROMA. Sepoy Lozelie Angami hid in the jungle near the DIHOM-REKROMA path. He waited until a single Jap came along, and sprang out and killed him with his dao (sword). A little later two Japs came, both armed; with a complete disregard for his own safety, he attacked them. He killed the first and the second fled, dropping his rifle. An enemy patrol came to investigate, and Sepoy Lozelie Angami threw one of the grenades he had captured into the middle of them killing at least a further one, and wounding several. He then returned through the jungle bringing the identifications documents, and weapons of his first two victims. A splendid example of courage and achievement.

No. L.230 Sepoy MALOO ANGAMI,
Naga Levies (Chedema Village)

CHEDEMA Area. 2nd May and days following. Accompanied by one other Levy (Zetseilie Angami) Sepoy Maloo Angami patrolled from Naga Levy HQ near KOHIMA through the enemy positions in CHEDEMA. He then watched the enemy traffic on the Jeep Track for 36 hours, and then pushed on to the CHAKHABAMA area, where he investigated the enemy HQ. The intelligence brought in allowed a highly successful air strike to go in. He patrolled this area consistently. The enemy were fully aware that these two men were working as scouts, and they were continually fired on. They were quite undeterred and they were successful on account of their superior jungle craft. They did valuable and devoted work for our troops.

No. L.206 Sepoy NIHOSHE ANGAMI,
Naga Levies (Nerhema Village)

When our troops approached Phekerkrima it was believed that the enemy had an ambush in the village. Sepoy Nihoshe Angami volunteered to enter the village alone, dressed as a villager and unarmed. He went forward at dusk, and searched the whole village, and reported it clear. It was a very brave act. He was very highly commended by the column he accompanied for his constant patrols, and his courage under fire. He served throughout the Naga Hills, Somra Tracts, and on to Imphal and his conduct was exemplary.

No. L.190. Sepoy PUNGOI ANGAMI,
Naga Levies (Purabami Village)

18th May 1944 at SAKRABAMI. Sepoy Pungoi Angami whilst patrolling forward, located an enemy patrol approaching our troops. An ambush was laid. Sepoy Pungoi Angami went out unarmed and dressed up as a villager. He went straight up to the enemy patrol leader, and by signs and the use of the word 'British' caused the patrol to change its direction, and he led it straight into the ambush. The (enemy) patrol was twelve strong, and only two escaped, seven being killed and three wounded. Throughout his courage was exemplary, and he entered the enemy camps to get intelligence fearlessly.

No. L.5. Sepoy SARE ANGAMI,
Naga Levies (Chizami Village)

Seeing one of our planes crash into the side of a mountain, Sepoy Sare took out a party of villagers and searched for the pilot. They located him alive but badly injured. They took him to Sepoy Sare's house, where Sare cared for him for nine days, completely disregarding the Japanese patrols searching for the pilot. The whole area was in enemy hands. Sepoy Sare then arranged and led a party of Levies who carried the wounded man three days' march through enemy territory to safety, handing him over to one of our columns. In addition to saving the life of this officer, Sepoy Sare took considerable intelligence to our columns, and entered enemy positions with a complete disregard for his own safety.

No. 32120 Lance Naik YANGRA SONGBA AO,
Assam Rifles attached to 'V' Force (Changki Village)

During the period under review, August 16th to November 15th, 1944, this Non-commissioned officer has performed his duty in an outstanding manner, being a perfect example to his men and leading them on many strenuous patrols and keeping up their morale in spite of the trials of the monsoon during an advance of 200 miles from Kohima to the Zibaw Taung dam. He has now served for many months with 'V' Force on the Chindwin during 3 monsoons.

No. 504 Sepoy (Lance Naik) YAMBHAMO LOTHA,
1st Assam Regiment (Bhuo Village, Wokha)

On the 29th July 1945 at AUNGGYANTHA, near TOUNGOO, BURMA, No. 504 Sepoy (Lance Naik) YAMBHAMO LOTHA was second in command of a Section forming part of a fighting patrol ordered to destroy any enemy found WEST of the SITTANG river in this area. The patrol was engaged by light machine gun fire from a position dug in on the river bank and the leading Section having been pinned down the remainder of the Platoon executed a flanking attack. In this attack, a three-man post was first encountered by YAMBHAMO's section, and was charged at the bayonet point. In this charge, the Section Commander and another man were wounded by grenades but Sepoy (Lance Naik) YAMBHAMO undeterred rushed ahead and killed the enemy in the post with a grenade and his sten gun. The enemy light machine gun then opened up on the section at about 40 yards range and mortally wounded the already hit Section Commander. YAMBHAMO in the face of this fire immediately charged across the open ground and firing from the hip killed the light machine gunner. His dash and skill undoubtedly saved his comrades from suffering a considerable number of casualties, and his courage and leadership in twice charging across open ground in the face of close range fire was an inspiration to all. This Non-commissioned officer has already been awarded an Immediate Mention in Despatches for gallantry in the face of the enemy in May.

No. L.146 Sepoy ZASHEI ANGAMI,
Naga Levies (Phekekedzumi Village)

5th May 1944. At PHEKEKEDZUMI. Sepoy Zashei Angami was serving with a Long Range Penetration Column. When they approached his native village, he volunteered to go on ahead, and find out the enemy dispositions. With a complete disregard for his own safety he made a very close reconnaissance single handed. He then returned and led our troops by a cleverly chosen covered line of approach into an advantageous position near the enemy. Complete surprise was achieved. In the attack Sepoy Zashei Angami's courage was exemplary. Thirty enemy were killed, ten wounded for practically no casualties. Throughout his scouting was of the greatest value, and he worked untiringly, and showed himself fearless.

No. L.87 Sepoy ZIECHAO ANGAMI (WHUORIE),
Naga Levies (Kohima Village)

20th April 1944 at KOHIMA. In order to secure intelligence urgently needed by our troops Sepoy Ziechao Angami went alone from JOTSOMA report centre across the ZUBZA River to MEREMA, where he daringly investigated enemy positions. He continued until driven off by machine gun fire. He then continued through Kohima Village and on to Jail Hill. He returned through the Bazaar area and down the ZUBZA River, bringing in the most valuable intelligence from the above areas. This Intelligence assisted greatly in the decision to move a Brigade into Kohima Village. On a second occasion, he brought intelligence from REKROMA through the enemy lines at great risk. He was absolutely unafraid of the enemy.

No. L.245 Sepoy ZETSEILIE ANGAMI,
Naga Levies (Chedema Village)

CHEDEMA Area. 2nd May and days following. Accompanied by one other Levy (Maloo Angami) Sepoy Zetseilie Angami patrolled from Naga Levy HQ near KOHIMA through the enemy positions in CHEDEMA. He then watched the enemy traffic on the Jeep Track for 36 hours, and then pushed on to the CHAKHABAMA area, where he investigated the enemy HQ. The intelligence brought in allowed a highly successful air strike to go in. He patrolled this area consistently. The enemy were fully aware that these two men were working as scouts, and they were continually fired on. They were quite undeterred and they were successful on account of their superior jungle craft. They did valuable and devoted work for our troops.

MENTIONS IN DESPATCHES

(MiD Emblem on Second World War Medals)

Jemadar MEGOSIESU SAVINO (No. L86) (Naga Levies)
No. L37 Havildar PHU HOTO SEMA (Naga Levies)
No. L8 Havildar RUDAI ANGAMI (Naga Levies)
No. L253 Havildar TOLOPU SEMA (Naga Levies)
No. L94 Havildar ZAPUTSOLIE ANGAMI (Naga Levies)
No. L158 Sepoy INAGHU ANGAMI (Naga Levies)
No. L145 Sepoy KHEHOYI SEMA (Naga Levies)
No. L287 Sepoy KUZUKHA ANGAMI (Naga Levies)

No. L68 Sepoy LHOUJOU ANGAMI (Naga Levies)
No. L69 Sepoy LHOUKUO ANGAMI (Naga Levies)
No. L83 Sepoy MELHUZU ANGAMI (Naga Levies)
No. L33 Sepoy PUKHATO SEMA (Naga Levies)
No. L203 Sepoy PUKHEHO MAO (Naga Levies)
No. L3 Sepoy THEPFUSI ANGAMI (Naga Levies)
No. L50 Sepoy TOKIHIE ANGAMI (Naga Levies)
No. L56 Sepoy VISIEZO ANGAMI (Naga Levies)
No. 27131 Rifleman AMOS AO, Assam Rifles
Mr KAWATO SEMA
No. 563 Lance Naik KEMVU ANGAMI, 1st Assam Regiment
Mr KRUHI ANGAMI
Mr LIBEMO LOTHA
Mr MHIASIZOLIE ANGAMI, Interpreter for Charles Pawsey
Captain Ralengnao Khathing MBE BA, 19th Hyderabad Regiment
attached to 'V' Force. (Ukhrul Village)
No. 635 Naik TEKASASHI AO, 1st Assam Regiment
Mr THEPFOORYA HARALU
No. 504 Sepoy (Lance Naik) YAMBHAMO LOTHA, 1st Assam
Regiment (Bhuo Village, Kohima)

YAMBHAMO'S CITATION:

*On 8th May 1945 at PEINNEBIN near TOUNGOO, BURMA
No. 504 Sepoy (Lance Naik) YAMBHAMO LOTHA was moving with the leading group when in command of the forward
section of No. 7 Platoon which was patrolling in the jungle
with orders to locate and destroy an enemy party reported in
the vicinity. The section by its silent approach completely surprised a party of 18 Japanese. On seeing them Sepoy (Lance
Naik) YAMBHAMO LOTHA personally crept with the light
machine gun to a flank position within 25 yards of the still unsuspecting enemy and opened fire, killing three. The remainder
took up positions in bunkers and returned his fire, whereupon
he moved further to their rear, and now some 200 yards from*

our nearest troops, continued to fire on this and another party,
thus acting as stop gun and preventing any attempt to out-
flank his Section until the remainder of the Platoon was in ac-
tion. By his good leadership in the approach and by his prompt
initiative and offensive action he enabled the patrol to inflict
several casualties on the enemy without loss to themselves. His
skill and dash in the face of an enemy superior in numbers was
an inspiration to the men under his command.

INDIAN POLICE MEDAL

No. 3 KHRULHEL ANGAMI
No. 26 MENGUZELIE ANGAMI

At least four other Nagas received the Indian Police Medal, but
their names are not known.

APPENDIX 3

NAGA GREAT WAR CASUALTIES 35TH LABOUR CORPS, FRANCE

Name	Rank	Service No	Cemetery	Next of Kin
Khuk Hetha	Labourer	974	La Chapel, 111. D 2	Zevni, Kingokhu
Khuzulho	Labourer	973	Neuve-Cha. Panel 39–41	
Koho Senuna Nagi	Mate		Mazargui V. B.1.	
Lhovekhe	Labourer	1683	La Chapel Indian 111.	s/o Kehisi
Lhozuo	Labourer	968	St. Sever P. V111. A. 17.	
Nachehe	Labourer	1248	St. Sever Indian, C. 6.	
Thazamo Lotha	Labourer		1493 Unicorn Indian Plot, North Corner. 2.	
Ye Khul	Labourer	1741	La Chapel 111. K. 2.	Haivikhe
Zukhehe	Labourer	972	La Chapel V.C.3.	Yikeshe

NAGA GREAT WAR CASUALTIES 36TH LABOUR CORPS, FRANCE

Name	Rank	Service No	Cemetery	Next of Kin
Etsowo	Labourer	1082	St. Sever, Indian C.2.	
KhoirKahmo	Labourer	1079	La Chapel C.3.	Phuntsurva
Raliwir	Labourer	1060	La Chapel IV. C.2.	Hatowa, Lotso
Zerenthang	Labourer	1786	La Chapel 1V. B. 2.	Monsathang

NAGA GREAT WAR CASUALTIES 37TH LABOUR CORPS, FRANCE

Name	Rank	Service No	Cemetery	Next of Kin
Pammat Kaleppa	Labourer	1908	La Chapel Indian VI.	Sakaehu, Yali
Yenko Alika	Labourer	1479	La Chapel V. C.5.	Chakchimung

NAGA GREAT WAR CASUALTIES 38TH LABOUR CORPS, FRANCE

Name	Rank	Service No	Cemetery	Next of Kin
Khukhei	Labourer	1855	La Chapel V.B.10	Kuchelho, Lizumi
Shekhu	Labourer	596	Ayette, II.A.17	
Yosukhe	Labourer	814	La Chapel IV.C.6	Hokhovi of Satakha

NAGA GREAT WAR CASUALTIES 21ST–38TH LABOUR CORPS, FRANCE

Name	Rank	Service No	Cemetery	Next of Kin
Luvutha	21st/38th unit	1631	St. Sever P. V111. B. 16.	Sakaehu, Yali

NAGA SOLDIER CASUALTIES OF THE SECOND WORLD WAR

Name	Age	Service	S. No	Cemetery	Next of kin
Indro Lotha	21	3rd Assam Rifles	32131	Rangoon Face 96	S/o Khombemo Lotha of Pangti
Khandao Lotha	24	3rd Assam Rifles	31923	"	S/o Zivengo Lotha
Sashio Lotha L/N	24	1st Assam Regt.	653	Rangoon Face 53	S/o Rena Lotha of Mekula
Mikhase Sema	21	3rd Assam Rifles	32135	Rangoon Face 96	S/o Khaise Sema of Nakhotomi

Yevito Sema	20	3rd Assam Rifles	32112	"	S/o Zetovi Sema of Muhumi
Duotsolie Angami	20	Sep. 1st Assam Regt	2987	Imphal, W.7.M.2.	S/o Theyelhu, Ciechama
Kruzetso Angami		Civilian War Dead	-	Kohima Village	
Pekuovi Angami	21	Sep. 1st Assam Regt	1695	Rangoon, Face 53	S/o Dewakhwe
Rohutsey Angami	20	"	550	"	S/o Vepohu
Saliezu Angami	21	"	533	Kohima, VII.B.1A	S/o Perhile and Bonuo
Solhulie Angami	20	"	572	Delhi/Karachi 193	S/o Mejio of Merema
Solhulie Angami	20	"	535	Rangoon, Face 53	S/o Tenyilhou of Kohima
Thesie Angami	25	"	566	"	S/o Dazo of Zame
Vinitso Angami	21	L/N 1st Assam Regt	534	"	Lhusietsu, Chesezuma
Tiatense Ao	20	N 1st Assam Regt	340	Taukkyan, 26.D.18	S/o Thamtin-chungshi
Tsulansang Lotha	25	Sep. ? Assam Regt	436	Rangoon, Face 53	S/o Pwathang of Longsa
Vihoshe Sema	20	"	3348	"	S/o Gozukha of Ephulumi
Wanchemo Lotha	21	"	3520	"	S/o Lumpurhomo of Longsa
Yankong M Ao	20	"	2255	"	S/o Mapunokdang, Chuchuyimbang
Ozeng Ao	20	Sep. 2nd Assam Rifles	27583	Rangoon, Face 96	S/o Jungbangme-ren, Marimikohu
Nongwom Raguinao	22	4th Assam Rifles	44526	"	s/o YarnaoRagu-inao, Ukhrul

APPENDIX 4

ORGANIZATION NAGA LEVIES AND HOME GUARD

No. 22104/SD1
Main HQ 11 Army Group SEA
14 Jul, '44

To: HQ Fourteenth Army
Reference your No. 437/165/G(SD) of 23 May, 44.

1. The formation of a corps of Naga Levies is approved.
2. They will be organized into platoons on the establishment attached at Appendix A. The number of pls to be raised in any one area will be left to the discretion of the Force Commander; but the total strength of the levies will not exceed 2,310 at any one time.
3. Levies will be issued with rifles and shot guns and receive pay at the following rates:
   Jemadars ₹60 per month
   Havildar ₹45 per month
   Naik ₹35 per month
   Sepoy ₹25 per month
4. Free rations will be admissible on the same scales as issued to columns with which they operate. A ration allowance of ₹8 per day may be issued in lieu of rations.
5. Naga Liaison officers may be authorized to accompany Special Force or other columns of bn level at the scale of one per

column. They will be paid ₹150 per month and rations or an allowance of ₹8 per day will be admissible.

6. Naga Home Guards may be appointed to work in their villages and for general tasks. Their pay will be ₹5 per month. Rations or in lieu will not be admissible.

7. A Force Column or Commander not below the rank of Lieut Colonel may appoint interpreters on the conditions set out in Appendix B.

8. Death Payment

   In the event of death of a Naga Levi, Home Guard, Liaison Officer, or interpreter as a result of direct contact with the enemy an immediate payment of ₹300 to dependants without prejudice to any future award by the Government of India. Cases of death from diseases to be very carefully considered and an award of up to maximum of ₹300 to be paid if circumstances show that death was directly attributable to service in interests of Govt.

9. Disablement – Naga Levies, Naga Home Guard

   Total disablement – ₹300 without prejudice to any future award.

   Partial disablement – ₹150 by the Government of India.

   Payments for disablement to be made only as a result of direct contact with the enemy or after consideration vide para 7 second sub para.

10. Rewards for services will be admissible on the scales given in Appendix C.

11. Payment of Naga Levies, Liaison Officers, Home Guards, Death and disablement payments and rewards under Appendix C will be made of on approved Imprest accounts.

Sd/-
Brig. GS
11 Army Group, SEA

REH/WG
Copy to: The War Office
           GHQ (1) CGS (10)   Army Groups

	Ops 2
H.Q. Supreme Allied Commander, SEA.	GSI (x)
	SD2
	SD3
O i/c No 3	A
Base Clearing House, Allahabad.	Q
	FA (2)
	D.P.I.C.

Chief Paymaster
British Troops, Meerut.
FCMA, Poona.

CONFIDENTIAL

Appendix 'A'

Provisional War Establishment Naga Levy Platoon
WE SEA No. 65/1/44
Effective Date 23 May '44

(1) Personnel	Jem	Hav	Nk	Sepoy	Total
Comd.	1	-	-	-	1
2nd in Comd.	-	1	-	-	1
Section Comd (Three Secs)	-	-	-	-	3
Sepoys	-	-	-	30	30
Grand Total					**35**
(2) Weapons					
Rifles or Shot Guns	-	-	-	-	35

File 22104
Serial X Ptl/64

Appendix 'B'

Terms of Service Dated 11th August 1942 for Interpreters Serving with the Military Forces

1. The following terms of service for interpreters employed with the military forces will apply until the issue at a later date comprehensive terms.
2. An interpreter will be engaged in the first instance, on probation for a period of three months.
3. An interpreter on probation may be discharged or may cease to serve, in either case upon the giving of three days' notice.
4. After three months, an interpreter will be entitled to one month's notice (or to one month's pay in lieu) before discharge, and he may cease to serve upon giving one month's notice of his intention to do so.
5. An interpreter may be dismissed by the officer who engaged him or by any superior authority at any time and without notice for misconduct proved to the satisfaction of that officer.
6. An interpreter who is dismissed or ceases to serve without having given due notice, will forfeit all pay and allowances that may be due to him.
7. There will only be one grade of interpreter. They will be paid ₹60 per month (or proportionately for part of a month) with free rations. This pay will be issued in arrears from Imprest.
8. An interpreter who falls sick as a result of duty is entitled to normal pay, unless sickness is caused wilfully or by his own imprudence.
9. The following rates of compensation will be paid to interpreters, and in the case of death to their dependants:
   Death   6 months pay
   Total disablement 6 months pay
   Ordinary injuries Full pay while in hospital
   In the case of permanent injury, other than total disablement, the compensatory allowance will be in proportion to the seriousness of the injury.
10. A gratuity of one month's pay for each year of service will be paid on expiry of war service.
11. An interpreter will not be required to take part in military operations in contact with the enemy.
12. The Commanding Officer of an interpreter will be the

Commanding Officer of the unit to which he is attached, or if he is attached to a formation, the officer appointed by the Commander of the formation to be his Commanding Officer.

Appendix 'C'

Rewards

(a) To be paid to Naga Levies, Naga Home Guard or any Naga who produces the following:

(i) Live Jap Officer	₹200
(ii) Live Jap O.R.	₹100
(iii) Dead Jap Officer	₹100
(iv) Dead Jap O.R.	₹50
(v) Live Hostile individual other than Jap	₹75
(vi) Dead Hostile individual other than Jap	₹25

(b) (To be paid from Imprest supported by a certificate from Imprest holder that he or an officer in his unit is satisfied that a Japanese has been killed by the Naga claiming the reward and that no other reward has been paid for the same incident or that the live body has been handed over to Provost, P.O.W. Cage or Intelligence.

APPENDIX 5

MEMORANDUM OF THE NAGA HILLS TO SIMON COMMISSION

January 10, 1929

Sir,

We the undersigned Nagas of the Naga Club at Kohima who are the only persons at present who can voice for our people have heard with great regret that our Hills were included within the Reformed Scheme of India without our knowledge, but as the administration of our Hills continued to be in the hands of the British Officers we did not consider it necessary to raise any protest in the past. Now we learn that you have come to India as representatives of the British Government to enquire into the working of the system of Government and the growth of the education and we beg to submit below our view with the prayer that our Hills may be withdrawn from the Reformed Scheme and placed outside the Reforms but directly under the British Government. We never asked for any reforms and we do not wish any reforms.

Before the British Government conquered our country in 1879–1880, we were living in a state of intermittent warfare with the Assamese of the Assam Valley to the North and West of our country and Manipuris in the South. They never conquered us nor were we subjected to their rule. On the other hand, we were always a terror to these people. Our country within the

Administered Area consists of more than eight tribes, quite differ-ent from one another with quite different languages which cannot be understood by each other, and there are more tribes outside the administered area which are not known at present. We have no unity among us and it is really the British Government that is holding us together now.

Our education at present is poor, the occupation of our Country by the British Government being so recent as 1880, we have had no chances or opportunity to improve in education and though we can boast of two or three graduates of an Indian University in our Country, we have not got one yet who is able to represent all our different tribes or master our languages, much less one to represent us in any Council or Province. Moreover, our popula-tion numbering 1,02,000 is very small in comparison with the population of the plains districts in the Province, and any repre-sentation that may be allotted to us in the Council will be negli-gible and will carry no weight whatsoever. Our language is quite different from those of the Plains and we have no social affinities with Hindus or Muslims. We are looked down upon by the one for our 'beef' and the other for our 'pork' and by both for our want in education which is not due to any fault of ours.

Our country is poor and it does not pay for its administrations. Therefore, if it is continued to be placed under the Reformed Scheme, we are afraid, that new and heavy taxes will have to be imposed on us and when we cannot pay them and all our land will have to be sold and in the long run, we shall have no share in the land of our birth and life will not be worth living then. Though our land at present is within the British Territory, Government has always recognized our private rights in it. But if we are forced to enter the Council of the majority all these rights may be ex-tinguished by an unsympathetic Council, the majority of whose number is sure to belong to the Plain Districts. We also much fear the introduction of foreign laws and customs to supersede our own customary laws which we now enjoy.

For the above reasons, we pray that the British Government will continue to safeguard our rights against all encroachment from other people who are more advanced than us by withdrawing our country from the Reformed Scheme and placing it directly under its own protection. If the British Government, however, wants to throw us away, we pray, that we should not be thrust to the mercy of the people who could never have conquered us, but to leave us alone to determine for ourselves as in ancient times. We claim to represent all those tribes to which we belong – Angamis, Kacha Nagas, Kukis, Semas, Lothas and Rengmas.

Yours Faithfully,

1. Nihu, Head Interpreter, Angami
2. Nisalie, Peshkar, Angami
3. Nisier, Master, Angami
4. Khosa, Doctor, Angami
5. Gepo, Interpreter, Kacha Naga
6. Vipunyü, Potdar, Angami
7. Goyiepra, Treasurer, Angami
8. Rüzhükhrie, Master, Angami
9. Dikhrie, Sub-overseer, Angami
10. Zapuzhülie, Master, Angami
11. Zepulie, Interpreter, Angami
12. Katsümo, Interpreter, Angami
13. Nuolhoukielie, Clerk, Angami,
14. Luzevi, Interpreter, Sema
15. Apamo, Iterpreter, Lotha
16. Resilo, Interpreter, Rengma
17. Lengjang, Interpreter, Kuki
18. Nikhriehu, Interpreter, Angami
19. Miakra-o, Chaprasi, Angami
20. Levi, Clerk, Kacha Naga

INDEX